Finding Courage to Speak

NORTHEASTERN UNIVERSITY PRESS *Boston*

FINDING COURAGE TO SPEAK

WOMEN'S SURVIVAL OF CHILD ABUSE

PAIGE ALISEN

Northeastern University Press

Library of Congress Cataloging-in-Publication Data

Alisen, Paige, 1963–
Finding courage to speak : women's survival of child abuse / Paige Alisen.
p. cm.
Includes bibliographical references (p.) and index.
ISBN 1-55553-581-X (cloth : alk. paper)
—ISBN 1-55553-580-1 (paperback : alk. paper)
1. Adult child abuse victims. 2. Women—Mental health. I. Title.
RC365.5.C65A43 2003
362.76′4--dc21 2003008316

Designed by Lou Robinson

Composed in Adobe Garamond by Coghill Composition Company in Richmond, Virginia. Printed and bound by Edwards Brothers, Inc., in Ann Arbor, Michigan. The paper is EB Natural, an acid-free sheet.

MANUFACTURED IN THE UNITED STATES OF AMERICA
07 06 05 04 03 5 4 3 2 1

To Kim and Peg

for making a difference

and to survivors everywhere

for finding the courage to speak

Contents

Preface *ix*

Acknowledgments *xvii*

1 Trauma, Violence, and Women's Mental Health *3*

2 Severe Child Abuse and Its Effects *17*

3 The Body Speaks: Trauma and Multiple Personality *50*

4 Women, Children, and Trauma: A Societal Perspective *83*

5 Supporting the Survivors *130*

6 Working Together to Ease the Suffering *171*

Postscript *189*

Appendix A: Resources on Traumatic Stress and Dissociation *191*

Appendix B: Applying for Social Security Disability *197*

Appendix C: Letter Requesting Change of Doctor *201*

Notes *203*

References *219*

Index *231*

Preface

Millions of children in the U.S. suffer with inhumane and terrorizing conditions in their everyday lives: maltreatment . . . molestation . . . physical abuse . . . poverty . . . neglect . . . trafficking of children . . . cult and ritualistic abuse . . . sexual assault . . . kidnapping . . . killings . . . prostitution . . . sibling abuse . . . child pornography . . . incest . . . domestic violence. Most of us can't even begin to fathom why so many children are abused in this country. Yet we are obliged as a collective society to understand these seemingly incomprehensible atrocities.

Most of us think of child abuse in individualized ways, that is, of child abuse happening in a dysfunctional home with a sick abuser. Rarely do we stop and think about the hundreds, if not thousands, of ways children are violated, degraded, and negatively influenced and harmed on a regular basis *without serious public recognition or outrage.* Here are a few examples:

1) The law supports adult battery against children. Legally, parents can hit and beat their children so long as it is "reasonable" for the child's welfare and safety. The same behavior committed against a stranger would be considered a felony crime.[1]
2) Gun violence is commonplace. Sixteen children are killed *every day* in the U.S. by gun violence; children with guns in their homes are three times more likely to be involved in a homicide and five times more likely to commit suicide.[2] One in five high school boys took a weapon to school at least once in 2000; 60 percent said they could get a gun if they wanted to—most often from their own homes.[3]
3) Teachers and principals have a legal right to hit, spank, and paddle students.[4] According to records, public school teachers struck about 1 percent of children in their classrooms; and minority youth are two and a half times more likely to be hit than white youth.[5] Both medical and mental health professionals have found that corporal punishment is traumatizing and inhumane.
4) Poverty and homelessness rates remain abominable. More than

twelve million children live in poverty,[6] and poverty rates for black and Hispanic families are three times as high as those for white families.[7] Most homeless youth have been abused physically or sexually (or both) by a family or household member.[8] By all medical and mental health standards, poverty and homelessness are traumatizing and place children at risk for long-term developmental, behavioral, and psychological problems.

5) Television violence continues to escalate. Millions of children each day are negatively affected by elaborate and alarming television violence passed off as entertainment. Violent and aggressive action figures, both inanimate and human, are idolized and imitated by millions of children, especially boys.

When we expand our perceptions of the many ways children are harmed, neglected, and abused, we can see similar patterns across many different institutions in society, such as the school system, religious institutions, the media, the medical establishment, and the government. Social and political institutions create and exacerbate conditions that make child abuse possible; institutions are culpable for abuse and the resulting problems that develop.

For over a decade friends have been telling me to write a book. At first the idea seemed ludicrous. But gradually, I began to realize how much I had to say about my life and about the lives of many others suffering from abuse. I experienced and witnessed horrible cruelty as a child—incest by several family members, suffocation, beatings, terrible violence, the maiming of cats, deprivation. I internalized the fear and terror, the submission and helplessness, believing my siblings and I were going to die. But I had never considered my survival to be anything more than sheer luck. What I have discovered through a long and arduous journey of healing are the extraordinary measures I took to survive.

Unbeknownst to anyone, as a toddler, I developed multiple alter personalities, a serious psychiatric disorder known as dissociative identity disorder, or DID. (In 1994 the psychiatric diagnostic label changed from multiple personality disorder to DID to reflect the condition more accurately.) Ninety-eight percent of the people who develop multiple alter personalities do so in order to handle the terror of severe child abuse. The disorder of multiple personalities is highly misunderstood and stigmatized. What is most important is that DID is the result of human cruelty. It is a serious psychiatric disorder that is, more than any other experience, caused by severe child abuse. In order to share my abuse history, I must also share my multiplicity, the term I use to describe the experience of living with multiple alter personalities. Developing DID saved my life, because without this extreme coping mechanism, most probably I would have gone insane or committed suicide. Not everyone survives such cruelty, and too many survivors of severe child abuse are suffering in isolation and living desperate and difficult lives. In this sense, I am one of the lucky ones. I write this book because I am obliged to do so, because not only did I survive, I am happy and well today. There is far too much at stake for me to remain silent.

I will always think my survival was partly due to luck. But I also possess certain skills that have helped me tremendously. One of the ways I learned to cope with severe child abuse is through education. School became a refuge, perhaps the only place where I felt safe. Fortunately, I was always good at school and it came easily to me. With the help of my mother, supportive friends, and financial aid, I pursued a college education. After three college degrees and many years' worth of schooling, I received a doctorate degree in political science with a minor in women studies. School became my way out.

It was during my studies for the Ph.D. that I had a mental breakdown and learned of my multiplicity. The process of coming to understand the extent of my mental fragmentation happened rather quickly. I had begun to have upsetting flashbacks, or the reliving of past traumas, which triggered serious symptoms of post-traumatic stress disorder (PTSD): frequent nightmares, intense anxiety, hypersensitivity to sounds, people, and certain movements, and an inability to concentrate. I was familiar with these symptoms, as ten years previously I had been in intensive therapy for child sexual abuse. So I did what was familiar: I sought out a therapist. But the flashbacks and PTSD continued to escalate. At the end of my third session with the therapist, I told her she should consider the possibility that I was multiple. It felt surreal to hear myself say this, as if someone else was talking for me. The therapist's response was simply, "OK."

In the following days, I began to get terribly confused and called a close friend one evening when I was very disoriented and panic-stricken. My head was pounding so hard, it felt like it was in a vise. I was so anxious that I wanted to throw myself out the window of my two-story apartment. I was out of my mind, desperate to make the noise in my head stop. Lisa was familiar with PTSD from her own experiences with abuse and was aware I had been having difficulties. She immediately tried to calm me down and get me focused in the present.

"Paige, look in your office. You have lots of books, your computer. You do lots of things in your office. Talk to me. What do you do in your office?"

Eventually a calm began to take hold. "I e-mail friends," uttered a strange, shy voice.

"What else do you do in your office?"

"Nothing," the voice said, uncertain of how to respond.

Lisa paused. "Of course you do other things . . . didn't you tell me you just wrote two papers and one is getting published?"

I began to watch myself float to the ceiling. I looked down at the computer, and a queer feeling washed over me. I realized someone helped me write those papers. The panic surged again, and something inside me changed instantaneously. I watched myself as a little girl spoke on the phone. "But I don't write papers," she said, giggling. I heard and watched this strange, giggling voice coming from my mouth.

Something snapped inside me. This wasn't *my* voice. And those aren't just *my* papers. In that instant, I knew exactly what was happening to me. It was like being in a car right before it crashes—everything freezes, suspends in time, you see the crash coming with amazing clarity but are too paralyzed to stop it. You watch, knowing that things will never be the same again. So in that split-second moment when things are about to shift forever, you even ask yourself if this could be happening. But as much as you want to deny it, the truth is too obviously clear: you are crashing and there is nothing you can do about it. The truth of my multiplicity was unmistakably clear: it wasn't just me who sends e-mails to friends or writes academic papers in my office. For the first time in my life, I realized I was multiple.

The very next morning I found myself at another close friend's house, and it was as if she knew something I didn't know. I remember going to the couch and grabbing her afghan, burying myself underneath it. "Whatever you need to do, you are safe here," Michelle said calmly. It was what we needed to hear. The floodgates opened, and I became completely incoherent, switching from one alter personality to the next, over and over again, without any control. Michelle stayed calm and immediately called my therapist, who got me admitted to a psychiatric unit of a local hospital. I wrote the following about a psychiatric consultation held that afternoon:

> – THE ROOM WAS SPINNING, lights flashing, screaming voices in my head. I couldn't stay focused and was drifting in and out of consciousness, pulled into pieces in every direction, out of control and not able to stop it. I was terrified. "You don't hear voices do you?" the psychiatrist asks a second time. Why does she keep asking that, does she think I'm crazy or something? Whatever I say will be wrong, misunderstood. She persists one last time, "Do you hear voices?" I try to laugh to show her how ridiculous her question is, but what comes out is a pathetic grunt. I finally answer, "Well, I don't hear stuff like radio waves or dead people talking or anything like that, if that's what you mean." I flip my hand in the air to show her how silly the question is. She ignores it and proceeds with the questions: "Do you hear voices *inside* your head?" I feel trapped . . . what did she mean by "voices"? Should I tell her about the conversations and screaming and how I can't make them stop? She's waiting. I'm fumbling. I finally cave. "Well, I don't really hear voices but there's conversations. You know, like when you walk into a loud room with a bunch of people talking. It's like that in my head and sometimes it hurts real badly." I've said too much and I can feel my head pounding, the noise getting louder. At least I didn't tell her about the screaming . . . she'd really think I was crazy then. I finally look up at her, "Is that what you mean?" Her eyes penetrate mine, "Yes, that's what I mean."

My self-diagnosis of multiple personalities was confirmed.

It was clear I would use all of my educational tools to understand my fragmented mind and what multiplicity had to do with it. I launched a full-scale research project about trauma, women's mental health, and multiple personality and commenced with my own writings. After receiving a journal as a birthday gift, I began journal writing when I was twenty-three years old. Although my writing was sporadic for many years, I knew it would become a perpetual force throughout my healing process. I found comfort in writing about my experiences with multiplicity and abuse, my encounters with the mental health system, changes in relationships with my friends and colleagues, and the ways I handled it all. Writing my narrative became a safe way for me to express myself; it gave me courage.

Through writing my own narrative, I began to see parallels between my life and those of other trauma survivors, people not just in the U.S., but all over the world.[9] In understanding multiplicity and its relationship to childhood trauma, I wanted to read everything: psychiatric literature, self-help books, books on spirituality and alternative forms of healing, and trauma stories themselves. I found survivors' testimonies to be quite compelling, and together with these other readings, they told a story of abuse that is much more profound and systematic than anything imaginable. It is predominately women who are diagnosed with trauma-related disorders and females who take the brunt of sexual assault, both within and outside the family. So I set out to investigate the connection between women's mental health and child abuse. As an activist and scholar, I knew my undertaking to learn about childhood trauma wasn't just about me and my life; it was a social obligation, and women's mental health was at stake.

A focus on women and girls in no way negates the male experience of abuse. Many boys are severely abused in childhood and struggle to heal from it. Perhaps this is most evidenced by the onslaught of men, especially, coming forward with their childhood experiences of clergy abuse in the Roman Catholic Church. While there are similarities among trauma victims, significant gender differences exist between female and male survivors.[10] Sexism in society impacts how children react to, cope with, and recover from abuse. Current studies continue to show gender differences in victimization rates, with females being the primary target. Therefore, studies on trauma, except for research on military veterans, tend to focus on females. Similarly, most abuse narratives tend to be written by women. For these reasons, I focus on the female experience. Research is desperately needed on many aspects of trauma and recovery. For now, I hope male survivors and their loved ones can benefit from this book and that they continue to speak out so all voices may be heard.

Portions of this book, particularly the personal testimonies of survivors, may be difficult for some readers to read, i.e., they may trigger past traumas and be potentially upsetting. For abuse survivors, especially, I recommend you take the reading very slowly. For some it may be important to skim or skip certain sections until you are ready. At times throughout my healing process, reading about survivor accounts of abuse would have been unimaginable. Even today I have a difficult time reading about ritualistic abuse. My head starts pounding, my skin gets cold and clammy, and I become nauseated; I have literal physical reactions to these readings. It is important to know your own limits and to be patient with yourself. If you are able, I fully recommend that survivors have a friend or therapist read the book at the same time. Sharing your reading experiences with someone safe and close to you can be very empowering. The more we open up about the shame and horror of abuse, the more we expand our collective knowledge and understanding of its devastating consequences.

The body of memoirs and personal narratives of child abuse survivors continues to grow. I selected over twenty different authors for inclusion in this book, most of whom are child abuse survivors, everyone diagnosed at some point in their lives with a serious mental disorder, including DID, post-traumatic stress disorder, eating disorders, depression, or a combination of these disorders. Together these authors provide a picture of the sadistic nature of abuse and how we, as a society, propagate it. Collectively, the writings also represent a vision of hope for a better world. The narratives, but for three exceptions, are published works and accessible in libraries and bookstores. My hope is that I have done them justice and that their collective spirits shine through.

I am breaking a deep family and social taboo by coming forward with this book. It is not my intention to hurt any of my family, as we all have been hurt enough. Out of respect for their privacy, I use pseudonyms in reference to family members, and I have done my best to conceal their identities. What I present here are my own recollections and childhood experiences. It is my personal truth alone.

As someone living with a serious psychiatric disorder, I struggled to come to terms with my own worthiness and why I even mattered as a person. It finally came to me one day that the courage we showed in childhood was our own, the very heart of who we were and are as a person. We were important not just because we were everyone's helper or protector, or because we knew how to keep family secrets. We were just a little person trying to survive—we mattered because we were. However isolated or terrified child abuse survivors might feel, what matters most is that they realize, deep down to their very core, how much they matter. The collective will to matter can be a very powerful force in the elimination of abuse and suffering. I firmly believe child abuse is a societal condition that can be eradicated if enough minds, resources, and committed people work together to stop it. My hope is that this book is utilized to empower individual lives and to educate and motivate those who are in key positions to advocate for and effect social change.

Annette Gilbertson, a survivor of horrific child abuse, asks:[11]

How do I speak
that which is
unspeakable
unmentionable
unacknowledged
unsubstantiated
uncorroborated
unseen
unheard
unworthy
unclean
unwomanly
unworldly?

We must find the courage to speak the unspeakable; too many lives are at stake for us to remain silent.

Acknowledgments

First and foremost, I would like to thank the many survivors of child abuse who shared their stories and lives with me over the past several years. I have learned a great deal from you about the capacity of the mind and human spirit to both endure and survive tremendous suffering and violence. I am truly inspired by your remarkable courage and your unfailing resolve to matter.

I would not have been able to write this book had it not been for beloved friends who provided love, support, and hope to me during excruciatingly difficult times. There was a period in my life I wanted to die, and came close to it a few times. But friends threw me lifelines for which I will always be grateful. My deepest thanks go to Peg Bortner, Michelle Comstock, Lisa Poupart, Viviana Abreu-Hernández, Jolan Hsieh, Diann Peart, Kathleen Ferraro, Berenice Carroll, Rachel Groner, Kirsten Lindquist, and Kim Sorini-Wilson. I am also very fortunate to have the friendships of Sarah J. and Skye; you have enriched my life immensely by being strong and loving young people.

My recovery and health would not have been possible without the exceptionally accomplished healers I have had the good fortune to work with: P. C. Moisan-Thomas, Dr. Meijuan Lu, Kathleen Todd, Donna Cannon, Michael Hoffmann, Susan Lysiak, and Dr. Walter Byrd.

I also want to thank my dear friends and respected colleagues for reading, editing, and commenting on early drafts of the manuscript. Your comments were enormously insightful, and I remain awed by your collective wisdom and compassion. I especially want to thank Lynda Seeley, for it is you I had in mind while writing this book.

This book would not be as it is without the commitment and support of my editors and the great people at Northeastern University Press. Much appreciation and thanks go especially to Elizabeth Swayze, who believed in this project from the very beginning.

The acknowledgments would not be complete without mention of the family who lives inside me. My most heartfelt thanks go to those inside who found the courage to speak and had a fierce determination to live.

I gratefully acknowledge the following authors, presses, and publications for their kind permission to reprint the works noted below.

Pages 394, 436, 437 from *The Courage to Heal,* third edition, revised and updated by Ellen Bass and Laura Davis. Copyright 1994 by Ellen Bass and Laura S. Davis Trust. Reprinted by permission of HarperCollins Publishers Inc. For additional rights/territory contact Charlotte Cecil Raymond, 32 Bradlee Road, Marblehead, Massachusetts 01945.

Pages 108–9, 158 from *I Never Told Anyone: Writings by Women Survivors of Child Sexual Abuse* by Ellen Bass. Copyright 1983 by Ellen Bass, Louise Thornton, Jude Brister, Grace Hammond, and Vicki Lamb. Reprinted by permission of HarperCollins Publishers Inc.

From *The Laid Daughter: A True Story* by Helen Bonner. Copyright 1995 by Helen Bonner. Used by permission of the author.

From *The Flock: Autobiography of a Multiple Personality* by Joan Frances Casey. Copyright 1991 by Joan Frances Casey. Published by Ballantine Books, a division of Random House, Inc.

From *Unspeakable Truths and Happy Endings: Human Cruelty and the New Trauma Therapy* by Rebecca Coffey. Copyright 1998 by The Sidran Press.

From *Multiple Personality Disorder from the Inside Out* by Barry M. Cohen, Esther Giller, and Lynn W. Copyright 1991 by The Sidran Press.

"How do I speak" printed with permission by Annette Gilbertson, published for the first time in this book.

Reprinted from James M. Glass, *Shattered Selves: Multiple Personality in a Postmodern World.* Copyright 1993 by Cornell University Press. Used by permission of the publisher, Cornell University Press.

From *The Minds of Billy Milligan* by Daniel Keyes. Copyright 1981 by Bantam Books, a division of Random House, Inc.

From *Becoming One: A Story of Triumph over Multiple Personality Disorder* by Sarah E. Olson. Copyright 1997 by Sarah E. Olson, published by Trilogy Books.

From *The Magic Daughter: A Memoir of Living with Multiple Per-*

sonality Disorder by Jane Phillips. Copyright 1995 by Jane Phillips, published by Penguin Books.

From "Breaking Silence, Telling Truths," by Lisa M. Poupart. 1997. Ph.D. dissertation, Arizona State University.

From "Commands of Silence" by Lisa M. Poupart. 2001. Published in *Society of Women Sociologists Network News,* vol. 18, no. 2.

"For Christine" and "Within and Without" printed with permission by Lynda Seeley, published for the first time in this book.

From *Because I Remember Terror, Father, I Remember You* by Sue William Silverman. Copyright 1996 by Sue William Silverman. Used by permission of the University of Georgia Press.

Page 17 from *The Stranger in the Mirror* by Marlene Steinberg and Maxine Schnall. Copyright 2000 by Marlene Steinberg. Reprinted by permission of HarperCollins Publishers Inc.

From *The Myth of Sanity* by Martha Stout. Copyright 2001 by Martha Stout. Used by permission of Viking Penguin, a division of Penguin Putnam Inc.

From *First Person Plural* by Cameron West. Copyright 1999 by Cameron West. Published by Hyperion.

Finding Courage to Speak

1 Trauma, Violence, and Women's Mental Health

> i hate feeling at the mercy of my own mind and body, trapped in all this freakishness. i do not understand how this could happen. was the abuse really *that* bad? i am terrified and confused, and deeply ashamed of what i've become. my old world has forever crumbled and i am left feeling brutally exposed with all these people living, breathing, and crawling around inside me. my mind has finally snapped from too many childhood years filled with violation and trauma.
>
> —Paige Alisen

In the fall of 1998 I voluntarily admitted myself into a psychiatric unit of a hospital. I had become completely incoherent and utterly confused about who or where I was. Nothing was familiar to me, not even my own hands, thoughts, or words. A team of doctors, two psychiatrists and a psychologist, diagnosed me with clinical depression, post-traumatic stress disorder (PTSD), and dissociative identity disorder (DID), or the experience of having multiple personalities. I have been hospitalized as the result of these conditions three times in two different psychiatric facilities. The genesis of these conditions is severe sexual, physical, ritualistic, and psychological abuse beginning at the age of three and ending in my teens:

— FORCED INTO SILENCE as i choked on the blood and semen, choked because i could not breathe from the massive flesh in my mouth. forced into silence because i could not tell another living soul about it. someone will die, someone will get hurt, no one will believe me anyway. no matter what i did it still kept happening. five years old and forced to suck on his dick, burning cold sores, neck aching, choking for air. my cold sores bled and cracked, scarring my lips forever. the condition of my lips doesn't just represent child abuse. my lips are a symbol of male power and dominance; they are a symbol of oppression. today my lips are an instrument of power. they reflect my own resistance and a determination to make my lips, my very body and soul, matter. these beautiful lips speak loudly and clearly for the millions of people who can't.

My story is the legacy of millions of people who have suffered at the hands of abusive caretakers. I share my experiences as a way to explain how and why it is so many adults continue to suffer years after the abuse has ended. There are countless compelling memoirs and personal writings by survivors of severe childhood trauma. Such stories are powerful and necessary because they demonstrate the lengths of human cruelty and the amazing capacity to cope in the face of it. By connecting the many testimonies of abuse survivors, including my own, I demonstrate how it is that our society shapes and fosters the conditions whereby child abuse can occur. Through understanding this process, we can begin to address more adequately the many ways to stop abusive and terrorizing conditions in the lives of millions of children and adults each year. Child abuse, and the resulting mental and physical health problems that develop, are a national public health crisis. Yet public and governmental attention about prevention, intervention, and treatment remains sorrowfully inadequate. I feel obliged to share my personal experiences so that others can become more informed, and outraged as well, about the devastating effects of child abuse. Such abuse is unspeakable, but it is imperative that these horrifying stories are spoken.

The State of Women's Mental Health

Women's health, and women's mental health specifically, is a combination of many factors and influences. Stress, economic factors, relationship issues, nutrition and exercise, and environmental factors (e.g., pollution and noise) all contribute to how mentally and physically healthy one is. A factor that almost guarantees a negative effect on anyone's mental health is repetitive and severe childhood abuse. Childhood abuse can be so severe and traumatic that children develop serious physical health problems, such as stunted growth of organs and bones, internal hemorrhaging, damaged reproductive organs, chronic pains, and developmental deficiencies, problems that can continue to haunt a person both mentally and physically in adulthood. Mental health problems are prevalent for child abuse survivors. Women, especially, spend millions, if not billions, of dollars each year on tranquilizers, mood stabilizers, antianxiety medications, and sleeping pills. Much of this medication taking is due to conditions from early childhood traumatization. The statistics on the condition of women's mental health are staggering:[1]

- Women and girls make up 85 percent to 95 percent of those with eating disorders, and millions are affected each year.
- Women are two to three times more likely than men to have anxiety disorders.
- Nearly twice as many women as men suffer from major depressive disorders, and it is estimated that twelve million women are affected each year.
- Women make up 75 percent of those diagnosed with borderline personality disorder.[2]
- Women make up 90 percent of those diagnosed with dissociative identity disorder.[3]

Collectively, millions of women are treated for psychiatric problems that can stem from childhood abuses and trauma. Of course, not everyone who develops these conditions has a history of abuse. However, research indicates it is a substantial cause.

There are, of course, mental disorders and illnesses where men are overrepresented, such as schizophrenia, attention deficit hyperactivity disorder, and autism.[4] Most of these illnesses are organic to the brain—that is, part of the brain composition. This is very different from environmentally based disorders, such as dissociative disorders and eating disorders, which are *caused by humans.* Acknowledging gender differences does not imply that boys who are abused do not also develop serious psychiatric disorders in adulthood. We know, for example, that 10 percent of those who develop multiple personalities are abused males.[5] What is important to understand is that as boys grow up, they become men in a society that is male dominated, whereas females continue to face sexism as they grow older. Both the causes and consequences of abuse can be markedly different depending on one's gender.

Abuse occurs in many types of relationships, i.e., in heterosexual and same-sex relationships, between and against elders, and between people who don't live together. There is something markedly distinct about abuses perpetrated against females in heterosexual relationships that differentiates this type of abuse from others. In other words, research demonstrates over and over again that violence against females is systematic and profound. Systematic means the abuse is intentionally and purposively directed at females; it happens because we are female. In chapter 4, I provide an in-depth discussion on this point. For now, understand that there are systematic ways in which females are treated and violated by virtue of the fact that they are female. For example, girls are vulnerable to sexual assault and are three to five times more likely than boys to be targets of sexual violence.[6] In the most extreme cases of sexual abuse, people develop severe trauma-related disorders in order to survive.[7] It is understandable, then, why females make up the majority of those who suffer from mental disorders caused by childhood traumatization: they are most often the victims of abuses that commonly lead to long-term problems. In analyzing abuse this way, we can better understand why so many adult women have psychological problems from extreme abuses experienced in childhood.

Throughout this book, I focus on two serious mental disorders based in traumatization: post-traumatic stress disorder and dissociative identity disorder. Most of us equate PTSD with military veterans, yet the primary cause for developing post-traumatic stress is childhood abuse, domestic violence, and rape (including spousal rape).[8] Seventy percent of the approximately 5.2 million people living with PTSD are women.[9] An estimated 1 percent of the general population, or 2.8 million people, live with multiple alter personalities.[10] PTSD and DID are related in that as many as 80 percent to 100 percent of the people diagnosed with DID have a secondary diagnosis of PTSD.[11] *Dissociative identity disorder, more than any other disorder, is caused almost exclusively by severe child abuse and human cruelty.* Ninety-eight percent of the documented cases of DID have histories of extreme child abuse.[12] Additionally, 5 percent to 20 percent of the patients residing in psychiatric hospitals are thought to have DID.[13] Studies in more than twenty countries around the world indicate a similar prevalence of DID in both clinical and nonclinical samples.[14] In other words, multiple personality is not just a condition occurring in the U.S. Multiplicity, or the experience of living with multiple alter personalities, is much more common than most of us realize. Mental health experts now consider dissociative identity disorder to be a very serious public health problem, yet it has failed to gain proper medical, public, and governmental attention.

Sitting with other women in a psychiatric hospital, I couldn't help but think of the many people suffering with severe trauma-related disorders. How many were unable to receive the kind of care I received? What happened to the people who didn't have adequate support or the resources to find help? And how in the world could a society allow this kind of abuse to happen in the first place? Dissociative identity disorder is the manifestation of human cruelty. It is a condition that could be virtually eliminated if not for the infliction of severe child abuse. By learning more about DID, we can understand better how and why it is children are so easily tortured and abused in silence.

What Is Dissociative Identity Disorder?

Under extreme traumatic conditions, many people learn to mentally dissociate as a way to escape the trauma. In other words, when people are unable to flee traumatic events physically, they escape mentally. Dissociation causes a person to disconnect mentally from the experience or feelings as if she weren't there. A dissociator can act as a spectator to her own beatings and rapes, watch from the ceiling, or meld into the walls, as if the abuse were happening to someone else. Such dissociative strategies can become extreme and happen not only during threatening situations but in nonthreatening conditions as well. While this coping strategy may have been beneficial and even lifesaving in childhood, severe dissociation can begin to impede adult life. Dissociative identity disorder is the most extreme form of dissociation and a serious psychiatric disorder whereby a person develops two or more separate and distinct personality states, also referred to as alters, alter personalities, or identities. Frequently absent from consciousness, alters can control a person's thoughts, feelings, and behaviors at different times and in different ways.[15]

The splitting off of consciousness to the point of developing separate alter personalities happens due to extreme and often brutal conditions. In chapter 3, I discuss more thoroughly how multiple alter personalities develop and are experienced. In the most basic sense, alters are created unconsciously out of terror and desperate survival. Sue William Silverman describes what it is like to lose consciousness while another personality takes over. For her it meant disappearing in a bubble of water while an alter personality, Dina, emerged.

> Concentrate on the bubbles of water. They make soft explosions as they crash against the surface, but then another rise rise rises out the roof of my head. But the room is still, yes. I am. My legs are paralyzed. My arms are useless. I am bloated with hot, heavy water, yet weightless, too: here, not here. I am opposites at the same time. And from the distance of my bubble my hazel eyes watch my daddy stick his finger inside Dina, telling her, whispering to her how much he loves her–me–us, loves her–me–us, with a love that is everlasting and true.[16]

Silverman feels her body yet simultaneously watches from a distance. She was able to create a bubble of safety for herself, but in doing so, another more able being was created. When people split off repeatedly to such extremes, separate identities can result.

The dissociative experience is different for each person, but the creation of new alters happens for similar reasons: the person is unable to handle an extremely terrifying event. Laurie was a survivor of horrific childhood abuse and hospitalized for multiple personalities. She recalls about her mother:

> Her anger terrified me. So what I did was set up in my mind a kind of perfect non-angry happy Laurie. I could meet my mother's expectations by not getting myself agitated or upset. It was an ingenious solution. I never told her when I felt bad; I never asked for any comfort. If I hid my feelings by literally forcing myself to believe I wasn't upset or angry, then I wouldn't bother my mother. Nor would I need her warmth, affection, care. I handled it alone, tearing out of myself the hurt and storing it up somewhere inside where it wouldn't affect me. I learned how to make myself invisible.[17]

Laurie's invisibility became so extreme that she developed an alter personality to deal with her mother's anger. The rest of her being worked its way deeper and deeper into unconsciousness to stay protected. For most of us, the separation of alters happens without our knowledge; it is completely unconscious.

People who develop alter personalities have had extreme, tortuous childhoods. Ninety-eight percent of the individuals diagnosed with DID have documented histories of "repetitive, overwhelming, and often life-threatening trauma at a sensitive developmental stage of childhood (usually before the age of 9)."[18] In other words, DID does not develop in a child because of a one-time upsetting event, however catastrophic it may be. The trauma is *repetitive.* Sixty-eight percent of those diagnosed with DID have histories of severe childhood incest.[19] The majority of people diagnosed with multiple personalities report being victims of father-daughter incest. An incest survivor myself, I wrote the following description fifteen years ago. It is a memory I have had since childhood.

> – IT WAS NIGHTTIME and I was sleeping in my crib. It was very dark in the bedroom and my father came to check if I had wet the bed. I woke up and remember feeling like he shouldn't be checking on me because I didn't wet the bed anymore. I kept my eyes closed

> and pretended I was asleep. He came to me, put his arm down over the crib, and put his hand, his fingers, in my diaper. I was dry, of course, but he left his hand there. I thought it would be really funny to pee on his hand. My diaper became warm and wet so I think I peed on him. The next thing I remember, the bedroom door opened, the light went on, and my mother and grandmother peeked their heads into the room. He moved his hand away quickly. "What are you doing with the lights off," my grandmother asks to no one in particular? All three began whispering about me. I was straining to see my mother through the bars in the crib. I remember wishing, praying, she'd come over to me. I will never, to the day I die, forget that stretch through the bars to see her, to want to be picked up by her. But she never picked me up. The lights went out, everyone left the room, and I was left alone.

What I know today is that an alter personality had already been created and came out during this incident. She dealt with this and many other abuses by a sort of wild humor, pushing situations to the extreme. She did the only thing she could do—pee on his hand.

Multiplicity is an extremely complex psychiatric disorder and is experienced in a wide continuum of ways. Those living with multiple alter personalities tend to be very intelligent, highly creative, adaptive, and capable people who might be skilled professionals, artists, and public servants holding very responsible jobs. Oftentimes those who interact regularly with such people are completely unaware of the multiplicity—they appear "normal." People can spend their lifetimes functioning satisfactorily or even well and never be treated for or diagnosed with DID. Others may have episodes in their lives when things seem to spin out of control to a degree in which one does not recognize herself. For some, the experience of living with multiple alter personalities can be quite severe and disabling, and people can be hospitalized for mental breakdowns, attempted suicide, and self-mutilation. The disorder is complex because we may seem extremely proficient and "together," yet simultaneously be severely pained and tormented. During my first hospitalization, I was a complete mess. I could vacillate from moment to moment from being completely lucid to having no coherency or logical thought. I was in a psych ward for a mental breakdown, yet I wrote an outline for my doctoral dissertation. During my third hospitalization, I outlined a proposal for this book. The experiences of those living with multiple personalities are wide-ranging. It is important for the reader to remember there is a wide continuum of reactions and responses for the person living with multiple personalities. Clearly, people who develop multiple alter personalities reflect the many contradictions of today's world: we are the remarkable survivors of brutal violence.

Why the Focus on Multiple Personality?

Dissociative identity disorder is a mental disorder that is, *more than any other,* based in childhood abuse. A focus on multiple personalities is essential because human cruelty and neglect force small children to become this way. Multiplicity continues to be falsely and negatively stereotyped. In 1973 the book *Sybil* was published, which documented one woman's lifelong and courageous journey living with multiple personalities and the continued torment of a brutal and violent childhood. The movie was released soon after. Although this was not the first movie portraying a multiple, it made a lasting impression on the public. Social stigmas regarding multiple personalities continue to prevail today. When someone is referred to as having multiple personalities or acting like Sybil, she is typically considered demonic, crazy, deranged, bewitched, pathological, or hysterical. The term *multiple personality* is even used to describe someone unable to make up her mind. Since my diagnosis, I have become increasingly aware of the barrage of television programs and movies that poorly reference Sybil, Sybil-like behavior, and multiple personality. When a television program attempts to actually make multiplicity a story line, most often it is grossly inaccurate and sensational, as in the cases of *Ally McBeal, 48 Hours,* and the ABC daytime soap operas *One Life to Live* and *General Hospital.* Unfortunately, such story lines fascinate people. Yet they have the effect of further stereotyping a serious psychiatric illness that is completely misunderstood. Talk show hosts, including Barbara Walters and Sally Jesse Rafael, have also contributed to negative stereotyping.[20] Mainstream television media are negligent when they portray outlandish and inaccurate depictions of multiple personality.

The only way multiplicity will be understood and treated as a national health problem is through proper information and education. Stereotyping and fear of this disorder are the results of a misinformed public. The following are some realities to consider about the experience of multiplicity:

1) Most experts agree that while some people have been able to fake multiplicity, such behavior would be extremely difficult to sustain over time.
2) People with multiple personalities aren't possessed or demonic, nor are they psychotic. Most of us seem "normal" to the outside world; we function in jobs, keep homes, and live our lives. We have survived *despite* the violence. We are people whose minds have formed in alternative ways to protect ourselves from childhood horrors. Stereotypes of demonic possession and being crazy have scared and misinformed too many people.
3) The majority of people who experience alter personalities are nonviolent toward others. As a group we aren't raging maniacs or masochists. Although a small portion of those with multiple personalities can be hostile or even violent, it has not been found to be any more so than the general population. What is more common is for people to self-mutilate or be suicidal; anger and hostility tend to be directed inwardly.
4) People who develop dissociative identity disorder represent a fraction of the number of people who live in abusive conditions. Many children who are abused do not develop such an extreme coping strategy. DID is an extreme response to extreme conditions. Nevertheless, it is unknown how many people live with undetected and undiagnosed multiple personalities.

Social stigmas can create barriers between the able-bodied and disabled, between those who are "well-adjusted" and those of us who aren't. Television media especially have played a significant role in the overall misinformation and stereotyping of multiple personality.

Another stereotype, although less common among the public, is that multiple personality is a condition created not so much by child abuse but by wayward physicians, susceptible and vulnerable patients, and social conditions and values of the time.[21] I do not provide a full discussion of this perspective, since so many others do, but I will say that to remain focused on this issue only detracts from the collective suffering of those victimized by abuse. Many memoirs and personal testimonies illustrate the extent of multiplicity in people's everyday lives well before any clinical diagnosis is made. Documented throughout this book, these mental conditions are the result of a culture that creates and allows for the suffering of females especially.[22] Scientific evidence, historical analysis, and psychobiological research abound as to the cause and consequences of multiplicity and severe childhood trauma.[23] I have read many divergent perspectives on this issue and firmly believe, as do most experts, that people (i.e., women) aren't hysterical and making it up. Physician-created DID is very rare, especially in the course of regular mental health treatment. While certain people are more susceptible to hypnosis and the power of suggestion, such susceptibility, especially in the case of a serious psychiatric disorder, would be difficult to sustain over time. Similarly, exploitation and ignorance by physicians and mental health providers obviously occurs, as it does in any institution. All of these critiques, however, do not explain adequately the preponderance of multiplicity in this society or other societies.

The experience of multiplicity remains extremely complex and misunderstood. Jane Phillips captures this complexity in the following passage:

> My selves contained my fierce desire to live, a desire too dangerous to display in the face of a brother so tormented, so jealous, and so wounded he wanted to see me dead. My selves hid the secrets of incest and of other cruelties that, all these years later, still take my breath away. My selves wept and sorrowed; they plotted wild, improbable scenarios of revenge. But they also kept safe my dreams, formed a tight protective circle around my soul, and acquired talents and traits that I would later smuggle, unbeknownst to my family and indeed to myself, out of the family circle.[24]

The human mind is truly amazing; incredible lengths can be taken to protect our mental integrity in the face of absolute human cruelty.

People who struggle with the experience of multiplicity can be severely isolated and in need of a great deal of help. Unfortunately, few realize the daily existence of someone suffering from multiplicity. People with DID can be medicated for such problems as depression, sleep disturbances, severe anxiety, mood disorders, and severe migraines. A number of those diagnosed with DID have such physical problems as autoimmune diseases, gynecological problems, eating disorders, and stomach and colon problems. Because of the numerous symptoms and medical conditions related to the disorder, pills can consume our lives:

> – I MEASURE TIME by my meds. . . . the hours, the days, the weeks. time floats slowly past, day-by-day, week-by-week. i'm not sure where time goes, but it does. and every Sunday morning i refill my weekly pillbox. pink pills, white pills, pills of all shapes and sizes, morning, afternoon, and evening pills. each day i leave the morning pillbox lid open so i remember what day of the week it is, what time of the day it is. I only have three appointments each week that i need to know the exact day and time: two therapy sessions and laundry because it's only 75 cents between 11 and 3 at the suds and duds laundromat down the street. once in awhile i might have an appointment, a call with insurance people or to see my psychiatrist who doles out more meds. so i write these other times down on a big calendar taped to my fridge. otherwise i forget. because time right now is one big blur, measured by my meds. actual hours are meaningless. so i go to the pillbox and see what's left for the day. it must be time to take another pill.

Medications can be a significant part of daily life for anyone living with a psychiatric disability. For those dealing with conditions resulting from childhood trauma, pill taking can reflect a myriad of both psychological and physical problems. There can be immeasurable pain for someone living with a fragmented and confused mind. Fortunately, DID is highly treatable, but people can spend years in the mental health system before they receive proper treatment and care. Examining this isolation and the debilitating aspects of DID can help us to understand better others who suffer from severe mental health problems.

A focus on multiple personalities is also desirable, since there are few resources and books that connect personal life struggles of child abuse with society's culpability for and response to violence, trauma, and women's mental health. A great deal can be learned from people who have survived extreme trauma and human cruelty. Most important, trauma survivors are among the most courageous and truly inspiring people. As Martha Stout writes so encouragingly:

> The survivors I see in my practice have known undistilled fear, have seen how nakedly terrifying life can be, and in many cases have seen how starkly ugly their fellow humans can be. Listening to their stories, no one at all could be surprised that they consider the possibility of not going on. In a struggle with the power of their past experiences, even the biological imperative to survive is puny.
>
> No. Their choosing to die would not be surprising. What is so extraordinary about these people is that they choose to live—not just to not die, not just to survive, but to live. . . .
>
> For I have become convinced that these courageous people, in winning their struggles, must learn things about genuine living, and about genuine sanity, that the rest of us have never even imagined.[25]

Trauma survivors are the result of a society that allows children and adults to be treated cruelly. But they also represent the extraordinarily complex ways human beings learn to survive and cope. A framework is needed to help people make sense of their own personal nightmares in relationship to the collective torment of others. Social conditions make it so abuse is tolerated. When abuse is permitted on such a large and vile scale, conditions such as multiplicity exist. We fulfill our social obligation to end abuse by learning how and why it is that such extreme coping strategies develop in children who are systematically and indiscriminately abused.

A focus on multiple personalities is beneficial for other significant reasons. People experiencing multiplicity are in a unique position to explain the thought processes, behavior, and attitudes of children. We have children inside us who find ways to live and speak in the world. In my own life, friends now ask me questions about their own kids. They understand that I am not a child psychologist or expert on child development, but that I have an uncanny way of recognizing the experiences of children. In an instant I am that age and can speak to the issue at hand. I have a friend who, during her healing process with multiplicity, began to volunteer with the Girl Scouts. She found a wonderful troop leader who needed help. My friend knew how to play with these girls, but she also knew how to talk with them about their lives. I want people who are ashamed about their child personalities to realize the kind of contributions they can make to others. Many survivors have retained a unique ability to relate to young people. People living with multiplicity have an incredible resource base to help children and adults in distress learn how to protect their children better. Collectively, we have an enormous contribution to make to the well-being of both children and adults.

Human cruelty and child abuse, specifically, is a reflection of our whole society. Child abuse is not simply a gruesome personal problem needing individual interventions and remedies. And it's not just about sick, dysfunctional families nor deranged pedophiles who need to be incarcerated. Abuse happens because of attitudes and practices in society that allow for the mass violation of millions of people on a regular basis. Child abuse, and the psychological and physical problems it generates, is a national epidemic with catastrophic results. Public testimony of trauma survivors can teach people about the real-life causes and consequences of severe child abuse. I want helping professionals and the public to become alarmed by the information they read in this book—the complete and utter helplessness of a six-year-old beaten, suffocated, and raped by her father, the reliving of childhood terrors day after day, the disabling and terrifying fragmentation of the mind, and the long-term scars and deformities that remain with us in adulthood. Specific individual and collective actions can be taken to stop this madness. And it starts with knowledge and an open heart.

2 Severe Child Abuse and Its Effects

> I'll knock some sense into you. *Crack.* Eyes rolling around in my head, side to side, as he jerks my hair in between strikes. Don't you ever talk. Not once. Not ever. Keep your stupid mouth shut unless I'm sticking my dick into it. *Crack.* Hitting me in the same spot repeatedly, over and over until I am no longer conscious of the pain. Nobody will listen to you. Liar. Fucking liar. Stupid drone. Talk one time and I will kill you, or better you kill yourself and be spared the torture I will inflict. Made myself clear? Now open up your mouth and take this.
>
> —Lisa Poupart, "Breaking Commands of Silence"

The consequences of severe child abuse and incest are enormously profound, from horrifying personal experiences to the social and economic costs of dealing with it. Child abuse is a national public health crisis, an epidemic causing monumental suffering to survivors, their families, and communities. Child abuse is responsible for people having poor mental health to the extent they develop, and sustain into adulthood, serious, long-term mental and physical disorders. Child abuse isn't just about individual experiences happening in a few dysfunctional homes. It's not just about sick pedophiles or strangers seducing young children. Child abuse is *systematic*, that is, the abuse happens repeatedly to the extent that children are violated and tortured all over the country in a similar manner by similar people. Careful investigation reveals that there are patterns in the lives of children who are abused:

1) Child abuse occurs most often in homes with parents and relatives who have been abused physically, emotionally, and/or sexually themselves.
2) Alcoholism is frequently present in the homes where child abuse occurs.
3) Girls are most often the victims of sexual abuse and incest.
4) Secrecy, denial, shame, and guilt keep children from telling grown-ups about the abuse.
5) Family privacy and assumptions that abuse is not occurring keep people within and outside the family from voicing concerns or even noticing abusive conditions.

Many people have spent their lifetimes trying to figure out how to understand, prevent, and treat child abuse. My belief is that child abuse is prevalent and far-reaching because of societal conditions that allow for, and even encourage, the belittlement and degradation of children and the subjugation of children to adult needs, desires, and power. These conditions make it possible for a child to develop serious psychiatric, medical, and physical problems that continue in adulthood. Child abuse, and the psychological problems that result, are a collective problem needing social and political remedies.

In this chapter, I provide a working definition of child abuse and discuss the many ways in which children are violated. I offer a view of child abuse perpetrators to help the reader begin to understand why child abuse is so insidious. I explain the many ways children experience and react to trauma, both mentally and physically. Children remain silent in their suffering for a myriad of reasons. I provide some insights into the often conflicting emotions violated children feel: shame, guilt, loyalty, love, hate. Despite their silence, children also find courageous ways to speak. What is most evident is that children are speaking in many creative ways, but adults need to learn how to listen.

What Is Child Abuse?

The federal government, in the Child Abuse Prevention and Treatment Act of 1974, defines child abuse as "the physical and mental injury, sexual abuse, negligent treatment, or maltreatment of a child under the age of 18 by a person who is responsible for the child's welfare under circumstances which indicate that the child's health or welfare is harmed or threatened."[1] Each state has its own tailored definition of child abuse, as well as differing, and sometimes contradictory, punishments for child abuse offenses. Federal and state definitions and laws regarding child abuse tend to focus on parents and guardians, reflected in national statistics. Current statistics on child abuse are staggering:[2]

1) More than *three children die every day* in this country from abuse and neglect; an estimated 1,200 children died in 2000, most of whom were younger than six years old.
2) In 1998 approximately *three million* children (based on two million reports) were reported to state child protective service agencies for alleged child maltreatment; approximately one million children were found to have been maltreated.
3) The youngest children suffer the most severe abuse, and almost 40 percent of the confirmed cases of child maltreatment *involved children five years of age or younger.*
4) Girls are disproportionately the targets of abuse and violence. Girls accounted for almost 70 percent of the serious violent victimizations in 1998, e.g., rapes and assaults.
5) An estimated *seventy million children* will be violated by sexual trauma before age eighteen.

These statistics are deeply disturbing, particularly since most experts agree that government figures on child abuse and sexual violence are seriously underestimated.[3] Laws do not protect children adequately from the abusive and terrorizing conditions in their lives.[4]

Child abuse is about power, dominance, and authority. It is about someone being able to control, manipulate, threaten, and/or intimidate another person. In other words, child abuse isn't just about adults being older or bigger and telling kids what to do. This is adults and older youth mistreating and violating young people *because* they are young. It means that when adults are doing horrible things to kids, the kids aren't in a position to stop it or tell anyone about it. Frequently, abused children are led to believe the abuse was their fault; shame and the belief in their own badness keeps them silent. Many abused children, even if they want to tell someone, think that no one will believe them anyway. Fear of breaking secrets or of negative repercussions if they tell also keeps children silent. If the perpetrator is a parent or loved one, the child most likely will be afraid to tell anyone. And if the abuser is a respected member of the community, such as a priest, teacher, or day care worker, then the child is almost guaranteed to remain silent. Unfortunately, it is common for children not to be believed or even listened to. Kids lack the social and political power to stop abusive conditions.

Whether the abuse is happening to a child directly, or she is forced to watch it, there is a profound sense of powerlessness and vulnerability. Despite all the abuses I experienced firsthand, what was most frightening to me growing up was witnessing what could happen when adults lost control. Charlie, my oldest brother, got the brunt of the adult cruelty in our house. My father would suddenly snap, pick him up by the ears, and throw him against the wall. Charlie was always being hit, smacked upside the head, and without warning. A nasty divorce, economic pressures, and fear of being left alone to raise five children led my mother to invite her friend, Maxine, to live with us for several years. One maniac was replaced by another. Maxine was physically aggressive, emotionally unstable, and particularly cruel toward my brothers. My oldest brother, Charlie, was a thorn in her side because he, even as a small child, tried to stand up to her. She would beat him up, push him around, and always belittle and yell at him. I remember one time especially when I thought Maxine would kill Charlie:

> — CHARLIE AND LOIS (my oldest sister) were yelling at each other; they were always arguing with each other but this time they were pushing each other around. To resolve the argument, Maxine told both of them to go outside in the backyard and "fight each other fair." She gave each of them a rake. All five kids were home

> that day and we stared at each other in alarm. She made my little sister, other brother, and me watch while she yelled in encouragement at Charlie and Lois to beat each other with rakes. Charlie finally knocked Lois to the ground. He was about to pulverize her with the rake when Maxine started screaming and tore after him, "WHAT THE FUCK ARE YOU DOING? You little fucker, you could have killed her!" She was beyond furious. She grabbed one of the rakes, pushed Charlie to the ground, and I thought for sure she was going to smash him with it. As we stood there helplessly, we had no doubt that she was going to kill him.

The incident ended by Maxine assisting Lois into the house, telling her how tough she was, and letting us all know what a pathetic and disobedient creature she thought Charlie was. The worst was watching, never knowing how far things would go, always thinking my father or Maxine would take it one step further. Their behavior was erratic and extremely cruel, with each child waiting for the next blow-out.

Parents and caretakers regularly assert power and dominance, and use extreme disciplinary measures, over their children. Such abuses, however violent or cruel, remain private family matters, rarely getting recognition from neighbors, teachers, religious leaders, or the community. As the core social unit, parents and caretakers are given much, and arguably absolute, authority and license in child rearing. Child abuse also happens because we live in a society that tolerates a high level of violence in everyday life: sports violence, violence on television, movie violence, and corporal punishment in schools. Child abuse also reflects the negligence of those in authority who refuse to acknowledge its prevalence or take a stand against it, such as government officials, church leaders, and even mainstream media. Numerous examples illustrate the extent to which our laws and social policies regularly deny children and youth a voice, human rights, or even basic protections against harm.[5] And we fail children by not enforcing laws designed to protect them. Still, most of us cannot even begin to fathom how and why it is so many people can be so unabashedly cruel to little kids.

Who Are the Abusers?

Abuse is embedded in the structure of our society. On an individual level, this means in certain situations some people are brutal and abusive, while others are vulnerable and victimized. This perspective keeps the focus on individual actors. For example, a stereotypical view of a pedophile is an ugly, hairy, demented man in an orange prison suit. Not only are such depictions largely inaccurate, they also enable us to cast blame on individual actors rather than on a society that helps create and sustain abusive conditions. By blaming a handful of people and stigmatizing them as malicious, we fail to acknowledge the depths and complexity of abuse. Perpetrators can be simultaneously cruel, indifferent, and loving. A father might beat his son with a whip yet still have love for him. In his professional life, he may be a teacher or policeman and help many other families in his job. A priest might be a pedophile yet donate much of his time to the poor. In this sense, stereotypes of men in orange prison suits fail us. Here are some important facts to consider about the reality of child abuse perpetrators:[6]

1) *Eighty percent to 90 percent of all crimes against children are committed by someone the child knows.* While it may be important to teach children about not talking to strangers, the fact is that abuse happens with people the child knows, most often a birth parent, caretaker, or relative.
2) *Abusers are ordinary people.* Most of us find relief when we imagine a convicted child molester as a hairy, ugly man in an orange prison suit wearing shackles. But most child abusers are ordinary looking people from all classes and races. Abusers might even be known by friends, business colleagues, and neighbors as generous, caring, dependable, and hardworking.
3) *Not all child abusers are physically violent.* There are degrees of violence in abusive situations. For example, acts of abuse can be intimate or harsh, arousing or terrifying, yet not involve physical assault. There are also degrees of violence and inconsistency in behavior between the abuser and his victim. However, a child sexually abused by her birth parent is more likely to sustain serious physical injury than a child abused by someone else.
4) *Most people who abuse children were abused themselves in childhood.*

The cycle of violence, particularly for males, has been well established. Males who are violent toward others typically were subject to physical violence in childhood.

5) *Not all child abusers are men and not all victims are female.* Although male caretakers are more likely to physically and sexually abuse their children than females, females, including parents and other caretakers, also commit terrible violations against children. Still, males commit 90 percent of sexual abuse offenses against girls *and* boys.
6) *Not all crimes are committed by adults.* Older youth commit about one-third of the reported sexual abuse offenses against children.

So when you picture a child abuser in your mind, remember that this person is most probably ordinary looking. In all likelihood, you personally know, though may not be aware of, a child abuser, perhaps someone you work with or in your own family. Abuse is about power over others.

During my course of healing, I was provided an opportunity to *feel* the power that an abuser holds. My cat, Frieda, woke me up several times one night—"meow . . . meow . . . MEOW!" The final blow was when she pounced on my stomach. For anyone dealing with post-traumatic stress disorder, such sounds and surprises are unbearably shocking and feel like electric voltage shooting through your veins. I heard myself screaming at her, "I could kill you if I wanted to!" In an instant I was thrown back in time to a scene with my oldest brother. Just like Charlie used to say, "I could kill you if I wanted to . . . snap your neck, yahhh, just like that!" He'd grab my neck and choke me, letting me know that he really *could* kill me. I saw white too many times to know he wasn't fooling around. So when I envisioned myself doing to my cat what Charlie did to me years ago, I was overwhelmed. I've been mad before, enraged even, but I don't think as an adult I'd ever had such intense and vivid thoughts of actually killing or seriously maiming another being. Frieda represented complete vulnerability and the ability for me to attain sheer, unbridled power over her. The rage against Frieda, and all the people in my childhood who terrorized me incessantly, completely overwhelmed me. In the far recesses of my mind, as the Frieda drama was playing out, I knew my rage against her was much more than being angry at a little cat.

The next morning I had a profound realization: I understood the power my brother was feeling being that much stronger and bigger than me. He needed so badly to release his rage and to feel more powerful than someone, anyone. I knew I could kill my cat, and the idea itself, for a moment, was intoxicating. I held such power, and the reality of Frieda's life or death was within my control. It makes sense that when you've been brutalized for years and years and your life is miserable, you may very well hurt those with less power, those more vulnerable than you. Young kids and pets are on the bottom of a very high pecking order, and they are easy targets. Fortunately, I had the wherewithal not to hurt my cat. But I understood in a very concrete and powerful way how much better it might feel, however temporary, to hurt another being. Children who have experienced prolonged abuse rarely have the sophistication and maturity to work through rage appropriately. It's no wonder sibling and pet abuse is so common: kids are enacting what's happening in their lives.[7] Of course, not all sibling and pet abuse is attributed to victimization through child abuse, nor do all victims of abuse become perpetrators themselves.[8] The most important point is that child abuse is about power and being able to control and dominate another being.

While the majority of the physical and sexual abuse against children happens within the family, there remain neighbors, teachers, priests and ministers, coaches, and store clerks who molest and assault children. In general, perpetrators prey on vulnerable kids. Young people who have been neglected or abused in their homes often become targets of abuse in other situations. While I consider the abuses that occurred in my family to be much more severe and detrimental than abuses that occurred outside the home, the sexual violations by non-family members have left a lasting impact. I began working when I was eleven years old and was sexually harassed and violated by three different managers before the age of fifteen. I was fondled, lured into rooms, and touched incessantly. I was prey to each of them.

– THE MANAGER OF THE MOTEL would pinch our nipples and laugh. they were so little too, like he found that cute or something. one time he made us lift our shirt so he could see them. we were small for our age—thank goodness cuz who knows what else he would have done. he would always touch us and stuff. touch our

> bottom and put his hands on us. we just thought that's what all bosses did. we didn't know better. then we started working at the fast food place. one manager would touch us too, feel our bottom way underneath every time we walked by. and sometimes he would touch under our top too like when we were near the french fries so other people couldn't see. he always took his break when we did and would make us go down into the workroom where nobody else would be. he turned off the lights one time and scared us real bad. i didn't like working the nights he was there. he was only a few years older than me but he seemed lots older. we didn't know that people aren't supposed to touch you like that.

It never even occurred to me to tell anyone about these episodes because I thought they were normal; I figured all young girls could expect such behavior. And even though I didn't like it and was scared at times, I assumed this is what all girls should expect. Perpetrators prey on kids who are dependent, helpless, distressed, and frightened already. It was only in college that I realized these experiences were wrong. I had learned as a young child that my body was the property of others, particularly males, and I took it for granted that this was how things were. Many children from abusive homes never learn what it means to have individual autonomy or personal rights over their bodies. As difficult as it may be to understand, I literally did not know these things at work were terribly wrong.

Of course, children from neglectful and abusive homes turn to adults and older youth who provide attention. Like many other abuse survivors, I was raised in an environment where my body was not my own. From gazing and touching to fondling and explicit sexual acts, my body was the possession of just about everyone around me. I lacked any understanding of personal boundaries, and I assumed this is how it was for all girls. Children who grow up in abusive and highly dysfunctional homes become easy prey for adults and older youth. Sexism makes girls especially vulnerable, and they can be readily victimized by multiple people in a variety of contexts. Abuse is systematic in that for many, there is no end to it; the cycle keeps perpetuating.

The cycle of abuse is widely understood: when children are abused, it increases the likelihood they will be abusive or complicitous with, and victimized by, abuse in adulthood. This does not mean that everyone from abusive homes will become perpetrators or victims in adulthood, nor that people who come from nonabusive homes won't become abusive themselves. We know, however, that most parents who abuse children were abused themselves in childhood. Maxine stabbed her stepfather with a knife while he was raping her; my father's parents most undoubtedly physically and sexually abused my father; my grandmother neglected my mother and may have abused her. While this by no means excuses abusive behavior, it helps us understand better the complexity and cyclical nature of abuse. The cycle of abuse is as persistent in our lives as violence itself.

Types of Abuse

Certain types of child abuse place children at an increased risk for prolonged psychological, developmental, and behavioral problems in later life. For example, histories of physical abuse, sexual abuse and incest, and sadistic ritual abuse are frequently present in the people diagnosed with dissociative identity disorder. Leading experts in the area of trauma and dissociation have found that between 89 percent and 96 percent of the people diagnosed with dissociative identity disorder had histories of repetitive and severe physical, emotional, and sexual abuse in childhood.[9] Psychiatrist Frank Putnam, an expert in the area of multiple personality, points out there are marked differences between the trauma experienced among patients with multiple personalities and other sexual abuse victims, including experiences of "extreme sadism," bondage, and sexual torture.[10] What appears common for people living with multiplicity is the sadistic nature of the abuses they have suffered.

In the following pages, I illustrate three of the most devastating forms of abuse against children that can cause extensive harm well into adulthood: (1) physical abuse, (2) child sexual abuse and incest, and (3) sadistic ritual abuse. Keep in mind that it is common for people to have suffered more than one type of childhood abuse, especially those who develop serious trauma-related psychiatric conditions such as dissociative identity disorder or post-traumatic stress disorder. Also, there is a continuum of severity, intensity, frequency, and duration with each type of abuse experienced. Although these three types of abuses have many commonalities, each has its own definition and distinct characteristics.

Physical Abuse

Child physical abuse is nonaccidental physical injury to a child resulting from caretaker acts, including such things as shaking, slapping, punching, beating, kicking, biting, and burning.[11] Based on reports from state child protective service (CPS) agencies, of the one million children found to have been maltreated in 1998, 24 percent of the victims suffered physical abuse.[12] Physical abuse can vary in intensity, severity, and frequency, and not all physical violence is traumatic. However, repetitive and severe physical abuse is more likely to be psychologically, physically, and emotionally damaging.[13] Particularly for children in their early years, physical abuse can cause developmental and sustained physiological problems as well.

The physical injury I sustained in my home was minimal compared with what happened to my brothers. What I did experience, I continue, even today, to minimize: suffocation with pillows, smacks upside the head, being strong-armed and choked at the neck, a few spankings with a belt. Most likely someone broke my collarbone, or at least tore much of the tendons in my shoulder, which continues to bother me today. Physical abuse can become extreme. There are children held at gunpoint and kids brutally beaten with hangers, hammers, fire pokers, and chairs. They are thrown against the wall and thrown out windows. They are left in dark, empty closets bleeding from their wounds. It is amazing anyone can recover from such cruelty.

What leaves a lasting impression on children, as well, is the violence they must witness. Studies now show that witnessing domestic violence, including wife battery, sibling and elder abuse, and pet assaults and killings, has a profound and traumatizing effect on children.[14] Witnessing violence can negatively impact a child's emotional, social, and cognitive development, and profoundly damage a child's ability to trust. In families where one parent is also being harmed, such as in the case of wife battery, the victim becomes less available to meet the emotional and physical needs of her children. Witnessing domestic violence as a child extends well beyond the violent acts themselves. Physical violence has become a significant part of scores of children's everyday lives.

Physical abuse can become extreme and sadistic, just like every other sort of abuse. Lynne Finney, attorney and psychotherapist, was beaten, tortured, and raped repeatedly by her father from the time she was four years old. She had such instruments as a fire poker, chisel, and a letter opener inserted into her vagina. Finney tells about an incident when she tried to run away from her father: "My running and screaming inflamed him into a fury, and he caught me and began to pound me with his fists. The blows continued and continued. They only stopped when he violently raped me and then he started to beat me again."[15] Millions of children suffer from such cruelty on a regular basis, and in some cases, it is fatal. Every day three children die as the result of child abuse in the home.[16] When physical abuse is accompanied by sexual abuse, especially in the case of biological parents, the results are frequently catastrophic.[17]

Child Sexual Abuse and Incest

Many children are exposed to sexual violence and abuse on a regular basis: graphic representations of sexual violence in the media, sexual harassment at school, and sexual intimidation on the streets. Such advances can escalate quickly. Child sexual abuse occurs when adults or older youth, and in some cases physically stronger youth, are able to lure a child into sexual acts and relationships because of their dominant position as an older or bigger person.[18] Child sexual abuse is not dependent on the victim's willingness or unwillingness to engage in such acts. In other words, it does not matter that an eight-year-old "agrees" to masturbate her uncle since she, as the child, lacks power in a situation where she is dominated. Child sexual abuse takes many forms, including child pornography, child prostitution, pedophilia (the sexual fixation on children), trafficking in children, extrafamilial sexual abuse (sexual relations between nonfamily members), and incest (sexual relations between two or more blood relatives). Like all abuses, child sexual abuse can differ significantly in seriousness, frequency, degree of violence, number of perpetrators, and the relationship between the child and adult. In a national study, over 75 percent of all abuses were committed by family and others known to the child.[19] Stepfather abuse also accounts for large numbers of girls, especially, sexually violated in their homes.[20]

When children are sexually abused by neighbors, friends' parents, teachers, doctors, priests, and ministers, the effects can be traumatic because in most cases, the child has a close relationship with the perpetrator. Traumatic stress researchers agree that the closer a child is to the perpetrator, the more traumatizing it can be for her. This is why incest is considered one of the most traumatizing forms of abuse.[21]

Incest represents a profound violation of trust and a betrayal by adults and older family members who claim to love you. The internal conflict that ensues for victims of incest can be tormenting. I walked on eggshells for most of my childhood, doing everything possible to be pleasant and inconspicious. Even though deep down I realized things weren't right in my home, I would have never admitted, to myself or anyone else, that I lived in an abusive home. The violence, humiliations, and intimidations were swept under my emotional rug. It was the only way I could deal with a father and caretaker who were violent and cruel, and a mother who chose not to notice. It is almost impossible for an adult, let alone a youngster, to make sense of the conflicted and crazy relationships within an incestuous and abusive family.

Incest varies significantly on time of onset, duration, frequency, and severity. However, most incest begins when the child is very young and too immature and powerless to stop the acts. The average duration of incest is four years, but in the most extreme cases, it can last through a youth's teens or even longer.[22] Incest typically happens in secrecy, oftentimes with threats of violence against the child or others close to her if she discloses the abuse. Lisa Poupart explains what happened when she tried to let someone know about her father's abuse:

> Seven years old. I feel the cold metal bars. Arms tied behind my back to a chair. The pink and white nylon rope my mother bought to exercise with cuts into my tiny wrists as I am tortured in the dining room. My birth father and I are the only ones home, as is always the case when incidents such as these occur. A few days or weeks earlier, I had tried to tell of his crimes against me. He was made aware of my attempt to speak and

delivered a lasting command of silence with a wooden stick, painted yellow, and sawed into sections. What once was a broom handle my mother pushed around sweeping his floors, an instrument of her oppression, inherited as mine. Struck on the head fifteen times, maybe more, maybe less. Stopping only as blood dripped from my ears; the ultimate arousal for his ejaculation.[23]

When incest involves a biological parent, it increases the likelihood the child will sustain significant physical injuries as well.[24] Relationships in an incestuous family are unstable and can change unexpectedly and rapidly. It is this unpredictability that leaves the child feeling confused, isolated, and always fearful of when the next terror will strike. Kids develop what expert Judith Herman calls a "frozen watchfulness."[25]

In many cases of incest, the child learns to find safety in the far recesses of her mind. Dissociative strategies can become so severe that children develop multiple alter personalities. Over two-thirds of the people diagnosed with DID were victims of childhood incest.[26] Sue William Silverman experienced years of agonizing abuse with her father, abuse that started when she was a toddler:

He asks me to raise an arm. He washes my underarm, my neck, my chest. I smile up at him, the soapy water warm and slick across my skin. He moves the soap down my chest and across my stomach. He tickles my belly button and I giggle, before he moves the soap down farther, farther. It is between my legs. Gently, he edges my legs apart. The soap slips from his hand, and it is the soap I watch now, bobbing to the surface. He touches me there with a finger, in a place I can't name. In a place I have no name for, for no word exists. I will never let myself know the word, except it is a place, simply "down there." My giggle stops. His breath is so heavy it seems to ripple the water into the thinnest of waves. His fingers massage it. And it feels good, yes. I discover pleasure before I discover its shame, discover that the definition for pleasure is the definition of the word, "shame."[27]

The majority of the people diagnosed with multiple personality report being victims of father-daughter incest.

Sadistic Ritual Abuse

A friend of mine, herself living with multiple personalities, said to me recently that she can't relate to the many books and memoirs about multiplicity and child abuse. "Most of them don't say anything about ritual abuse," Lynn complains, "and when they do they don't say nearly enough." A primary reason why little is said about ritual abuse is because people who have experienced it directly, such as myself, or others who have learned of it secondhand, such as doctors, therapists, and social service providers, do not want to lose their credibility by supporting outlandish stories of abuse. Even leading psychiatrists and psychologists are hesitant to take one position or another about the prevalence or validity of cult, satanic, and ritual abuse. Yet investigative and academic research, along with personal accounts of survivors, is testimony to the practice of ritualistic and satanic abuse. Many of those who actually survive such atrocities remain tormented and terrified, fearful to utter even a word about their experiences. There are cases upon cases where ritual and cult-related abuses occur, but journalists, the police, medical professionals, and child protective services typically downplay or ignore the ritualistic or satanic aspects of the case.[28] For those unfamiliar with the research in this area, or others who remain doubtful, it is important to *at least* consider the possibility that ritualistic types of abuse exist. We owe the survivors currently suffering this much, but more important, we must protect the many potential victims.

Ritualistic abuse can be one of the most blatantly insidious and sadistic of all violations against children.[29] Voodoo and witchcraft, dungeons, satan, and outlandish cults and symbols are frequently imagined when the phrase "ritual abuse" is spoken. Such practices, in fact, exist; ritualistic abuse can be extremely cruel and bizarre. More common, however, are those sadistic ritualized abuses committed in neighborhood centers and rectories. Just like other abuses, ritual abuse varies by severity, frequency, intensity, and form. It is important to understand that not all ritualistic abuse involves cults or satanism. Sadistic ritual abuse can be distinguished from other types of child abuse in the following ways:

1) The use of ritual indoctrination where leaders or perpetrators often rely on the supernatural or paranormal. The abuse is typically

grounded in beliefs involving spiritual, philosophical, or religious ideologies; people are manipulated by and with these beliefs.

2) The use of mind control techniques designed to break the will of victims, whereby victims experience a profound sense of terror and helplessness about what is being done to them.
3) The methodical, organized practice and sadistic nature of the abuse. Ritualistic abuse tends to be very organized and planned with purposeful, malicious intent.

It is the particular nature of ritual abuse that sets it apart from other types of abuses.

Many ritual abuse survivors remember similar things.[30] For example, leaders are often clothed, hooded, or masked in ceremonial attire. Many remember being confined in cages or having their arms and legs chained or tied. Crosses, candles, and other symbols might be used. Most often people describe situations occurring in the dark, either during the night or in buildings, such as cemeteries or mortuaries, shrouded in darkness with death being a predominant theme. Animals, and in some cases small children or babies, might be sacrificed or tortured. Children might be forced to watch these sacrifices and in some cases be forced to participate. Violent sexual abuse is often a focus and may be ceremonial. Various mind-controlling techniques are utilized to keep children and adults compliant, such as the use of hallucinogenic and other mind-altering drugs, food and water deprivation for several hours at a time, severe punishment if the child falls asleep or wets herself, or in more sophisticated cults, hypnosis and mind programming. Children might be forced to chant such things as, "Silence, silence, silence" or "If I tell, someone will die." Nora, a patient at Sheppard-Pratt Hospital, explains how ritual abuse and cult programming can remain with you for a lifetime:

> Cults use children to perform rituals; they cut each other up, but the real deadly stuff is done by adults to children. That is the real tragedy; and these rituals, those places. . . . I travel there in my head before these satanic holidays. . . . Why do I go there? . . . I don't know; I think maybe it's because I've been programmed . . . who knows? . . . But I'm there . . . by the stone, with the knives in my hand, with hooks being put up me . . . it's too

> horrible . . . I can't stand it . . . I see it now . . . keep away from me! . . . Please, no! . . . No, don't, don't! . . . Please don't![31]

Children are forced to witness and participate in horrifying, sadistic practices.

The tactics used in ritual ceremonies are meant to terrorize the people present, and it works. People who survive such brutality are convinced the leaders can read their minds and know their every movement. The leaders or perpetrators tell you so. After long, tortuous sessions, you believe them. When I was four years old, I became part of ritualistic practices that were instigated by two or three adults in my neighborhood. Several neighborhood children, including myself and two siblings, were shut in a basement and forced to watch neighborhood cats be beaten and maimed. Some of us were forced to participate. We were not allowed to talk, cry, or even move. We were told that if we told anyone about it, a cat, or one of our friends, would be harmed or killed. They demanded complete submission and convinced us they could read our minds. During one incident we were told that someone in the group "talked." Talking meant that either someone told or she was simply thinking of telling. I remember looking around, fearful it was me; "Was it my bad thoughts making this happen?" My memories of these incidents became severely fragmented. However, as a young child I became convinced there were spies in public places, people I wouldn't recognize, who would follow me to know my every thought and movement. This fear stayed with me until only recently. All of us present were terrified into complete silence and submission.

Despite what the general public may think, ritual abuse survivors often report continuous memories, i.e., memories the individual has always had of the abusive incidents, including certain sensations, visual pictures, or ceremonial chants. Although I did not remember the actual abuse, the sensation of being watched and terrorized was with me for years.[32] It was only in college when I learned that not everyone thinks people can read their minds. I also remember a cat being smashed flat in the backyard with no viable explanation and how our family cats always "disappeared." Other people have memories of chants or prayers, or are fixated on certain occult symbols or death. Frequently people develop adverse reactions during occult and Christian holidays. In the most extreme cases, people have recurring physical reactions, including "inexplicable pain, bruises, the spontaneous appearance of a rash in the form of an upside-down cross, three 6's, or any number of satanic symbols that may have been lightly traced into a survivor's body."[33]

Because victims of ritualistic abuse can be drugged, terrified, and deprived of food and water for long periods of time, memories of the abusive incidents are frequently scattered. In many cases, people have complete amnesia of the abuse. Typically, memories return when more attention is given to the abuse, and support and understanding is provided to the survivor. In my case, I started having terrorizing flashbacks of bloody cats, a cold, dark room, and a table where horrible things were taking place. I was in therapy at the time but refused to talk to my therapist about any of it. I did not want to be influenced by what my therapist did or said. I slowly began writing down what I remembered as soon as the flashbacks passed. Like many others, I knew I had experienced ritualistic abuse before I said a word to anyone about it. Unlike popular opinion about ritualistic abuse, most of us recognize the seriousness of our abuse experiences before we make it known to others.

As horrifying as what my brothers and I went through, ritual and satanic abuse can be extremely violent and sadistic. For sixteen years, James Glass conducted extensive research at Sheppard-Pratt Hospital, a large medical and psychiatric hospital in Maryland. He witnessed the horror of patients suffering as a result of satanic ritual abuse and cult programming:

> I was shocked by the stories I heard; I could not fathom the damage women imposed on their bodies as the result of so-called cult programming: massive injuries to heads, wrists, arms—physical self-torment and abuse written as disfigured texts and stigmata on the body. What is one to make of huge blood clots on the side of the face caused by banging the head against marble fireplaces; or gashes in the flesh, grim reminders of aborted suicide attempts; or screams coming from a patient who insists that she be trundled up in restraints in order to keep her from killing herself on the anniversary of a satanic holiday; or stories of ba-

bies' blood being drunk, or of limbs severed at nightly rituals that happened twenty years previously?[34]

This is one of hundreds of published and documented stories of sadistic ritual abuse, and there are thousands of stories by unnamed, forgotten people left unheard.

I do not know how any of the ritualistic abuse started in my life, nor even when it ended. But the result was an extreme psychological splitting where I became numb and partly amnesiac of what took place. Understandably, most children who survive such atrocities develop severe trauma-related disorders, including the development of multiple alter personalities. Whatever form it takes, severe physical, sexual, and ritualistic abuse is traumatizing and profoundly disturbing. Children react to these conditions in a myriad of ways.[35]

How Children Experience Trauma

Children cope with traumatic events to the extent they are socialized and taught to do so. Youngsters become equipped to deal adequately with traumatic stress by example from adults, particularly caretakers, but teachers, neighbors, and religious leaders as well. When the traumatic stress originates in the home, as is the case in much child abuse, children have difficulty integrating the violence and neglect, since there is nobody "safe" to mitigate the event. One result is children who learn to distrust adults and other authority figures or who form unhealthy attachments to anyone providing attention or care.

There is a range of reactions to trauma, from bad memories and worries to the development of severe psychiatric disorders: clinical depression, somatization disorder, borderline personality disorder, anxiety disorders, eating disorders, sleep disorders, and dissociative disorders. Of course, not all people who live with these disorders are victims of severe childhood abuse, nor do all survivors of child abuse develop serious medical and psychiatric disorders.[36] Nevertheless, many of these illnesses and disorders originate from childhood trauma. Psychological and medical problems can begin immediately after the trauma, months or even years later.

Certain reactions to trauma are common for children regardless of age: excessive worrying, nightmares, crying, and loss of trust in adults.[37] Children might become inappropriately aggressive toward others or, conversely, become clingy and more dependent. Traumatized children frequently exhibit physical symptoms, such as chronic stomachaches or headaches; others might develop new allergies or become prone to accidents. Medications may become ineffective in treating these new afflictions, since the cause is traumatization.

Other traumatic reactions are more age-based. The National Institute of Mental Health has funded studies that look at childhood reactions to trauma.[38] Children age five years or less are the most affected by the parents' reactions to the traumatic event. So when the trauma is family induced, the child is often left feeling extremely confused. Typical reactions to traumatization for children this age include separation anxiety, i.e., the fear of being separated from caretakers, increased crying and whimpering, and excessive clinging. Toddlers might throw more tantrums or, conversely, become completely frozen. Facial expressions frequently appear frightened or blank. Young children also tend to exhibit regressive behaviors, such as sucking their thumbs or bedwetting, behaviors they had previously outgrown.

Children age six to eleven years who have been traumatized also exhibit regressive behaviors; they may become more withdrawn or disruptive or act out inappropriately. They may have frequent nightmares and problems sleeping. Outbursts are common, such as acting out or fighting in school. Physical problems can also develop, such as stomach problems, chronic headaches, and irritability.

Traumatized adolescents, youths twelve to seventeen years of age, exhibit responses similar to adults, including flashbacks, nightmares, and night sweats. Depression is common, as well as antisocial behavior. Many youth cope by numbing themselves out or avoiding anything that reminds them of the traumatic incident. Teens may turn to alcohol and other drugs as a means of escape. This is the age when youth may feel guilty for surviving or even causing the traumatic event; they may want revenge or be attracted to situations where they can rage.

Children of all ages often deal with trauma, or the threat of trauma, by attempting to be inconspicuous. Some take to hiding, finding safety in closets or behind and under furniture. Judith Herman, a leading medical expert on traumatic stress, explains in *Trauma and Recovery* that some children attempt to become inconspicuous in the hopes of not drawing attention to themselves. One of my siblings would sit huddled against the wall and sit behind furniture as a way to become invisible. I remember hiding under my mother's bed and burying myself under blankets in my closet for long periods of time in the hopes no one would find me. Children develop all sorts of strategies to find safety in abusive homes. The paradox is that as much as a little child can feel safe in a closet, she is constantly vigilant of her surroundings; there is no real safety because she is constantly fearful the perpetrator will strike. This produces a state of "frozen watchfulness," a characteristic Herman has found in many abused children. These techniques, such as crouching in a ball or running away, are utilized not only to cope with the trauma of abuse, but in some cases as strategies to minimize abusive conditions. But rarely are these strategies effective in the long term. For the most part, children are unable to fend off adults or older youth who are motivated to hurt, belittle, exploit, or abuse them.

Perhaps the most insidious of the responses to childhood traumatization is the profound psychological and emotional splitting that occurs, particularly for those abused by caretakers and other loved ones. Children must somehow justify, rationalize, or minimize abusive conditions while simultaneously maintaining the relationships of the abusers. "The myth of my childhood was borne in the notion that our family was so completely normal," writes Sarah Olson.[39] We might romanticize or idealize our relationships with our abusers, calling our situation "normal" in order to justify its craziness. But as survivors get older, it becomes next to impossible to sustain these beliefs in light of the vast information that tells otherwise. The newfound understanding of our lives can be shocking to say the least.

Up until the age of twenty-five, I had this ridiculously idealized belief of my family. I would have told you then that I was a happy child in a happy, loving household. That belief was far from anything accurate, yet it is what I held on to in order to make sense of all the incest and abuse. It was college friends who began to point out how awful and abusive things had been. I could no longer deny my childhood experiences. But the absolute belief in the goodness of my family, the normality of my experience, was what helped me get through a horrendously ugly and painful childhood.

Understandably, child abuse can result in long-term emotional problems. Children frequently internalize the mixed messages of love/hate by blaming themselves for the abuse. Lisa Poupart explains:

> If I believed my caretakers were at fault, then there was no difference between being abused and being dead. If it was my father's choice to rape and beat me, then he could choose to starve me, lock me out in the winter, or actually pull the trigger (of a gun). That realization would have been too much to accept.[40]

Blaming her abusive father, or even her unprotective mother, was not an option for Poupart because as a child she was fully dependent on her parents for survival. Abused children frequently blame and shame themselves because it is beyond their capacity as young people to understand how a supposedly loving caretaker could inflict such cruelty. Especially as a young child, it is more logical, and often times safer and easier, to blame yourself for being bad or unworthy than to blame your parents for being abusive or neglectful.

Sexually abused by my father, I was made to believe it was I who made my abusers want me. I think about when my father told me on a visit (my parents were divorced at the time) that I'd make a great model because I "had a model's body." I was going on thirteen with the body of an eight-year-old. But I remember strutting in the motel room in front of my father and brothers, lifting my shirt to show a little skin, pretending to be a sexy model. Of course I thought the abuse was my fault. I was made to feel like my body was irresistible:

> – IT WAS HOW I WALKED, how i moved, how i smiled and tilted my head. in my innocence and naivete i tantalized them, titillated them. i was the bewitched girl/woman. in having this power i also took on all the guilt. it was my fault, you see, for causing them to molest me, rape me, sodomize and suffocate me. but in taking on this guilt, i took on a semblance of control in a situation that was quite out-of-control. i think of myself in this household as standing next to a revolving door. whoever entered my space, i did what they wanted, how and when they wanted it. i learned to be inside their minds and bodies. i became an expert at reading people and i felt tremendous power in this.

The power I felt was terribly shameful for me, as if the abuse was solely my fault. These feelings continued well into adulthood when I could finally see the situation for what it was: the total exploitation of a young girl.

We take on the guilt and shame of abuse partly because it gives us a perverse feeling of control in a situation that is quite out of control. This is why many survivors become adamant, even well into adulthood, that the abuse was and is their fault despite well-intentioned friends, therapists, and experts who say otherwise. The survivor utilizes intricate psychological mechanisms to deal with this sense of badness, from self-deprecation to complete denial of the abuse. Such coping strategies can lead to severe psychological fragmentation and a disorientation of one's identity.

As the survivor's own sense of self becomes more intricately fragmented, so too are her relationships with others. Her ability to trust is damaged, and for many the damage remains permanent in adulthood. When we believe our bodies are the property or right of others, this can impair our ability to develop and maintain healthy relationships. Idealizing bad relationships may become a way of life, and developing a sense of boundaries with others can be seriously compromised. Learning to have healthy relationships with appropriate boundaries can be a lifelong task for the survivor of heinous abuse. Given this, it is not surprising that victims of childhood abuse more readily grow up to be victims, and sometimes perpetrators, in adulthood. Psychologically, emotionally, and spiritually we never learned otherwise.

Researchers do not fully understand why certain children are prone to traumatic stress. Some argue it is due to genetics, a biological predisposition in some children to dissociation, or an individual's personality. But certain features are well acknowledged by the experts:

- Adolescents who have experienced child abuse in the past are prone to greater traumatic stress reactions and poor mental health in the future.
- Kids who lack family and other emotional support during a traumatic event have a lesser chance of recovery than kids who have strong family support.
- Children will find maladaptive ways to cope when no other healthy or productive ways are available to them.

These factors can help us to understand why children in abusive home environments struggle with poor mental health in later life.

Ultimately, many children from abusive homes become severely traumatized and develop intricate psychological mechanisms to cope. Depending on the child's age, she might create vivid fantasy worlds or invisible play friends as an escape. Some youngsters learn to dissociate from the abusive experience, whereby they might float to the ceiling or create an invisible barrier between themselves and the perpetrators while the abuse is occurring. Gayle R. writes in "6 Years Old":[41]

You stood
  and
I crouched

You beat
  and
I fled

Inside where
  the terror was trapped
  as I watched you take

My little girl's body
  and squeeze and shake and beat it
  to your heart's desire

While I stood far inside
  and screamed to the corners
  of my soul

To stop this madness.
  But you are my mother
   And things did not change.

Alter personalities are created in order to protect the psychological integrity of the person. The events are too much psychologically or physically (or both) for the person to endure, so she "splits off" as the traumatic experience occurs. Dissociation becomes a necessary form of psychological coping in the midst of such terror. Mentally escaping from these conditions becomes a viable alternative to suicide, death, or insanity.

Why Children Remain Silent

One of the most perplexing aspects of extreme child abuse is why a child remains silent in her personal terror. There are many complex and multifaceted reasons why children keep silent about their victimization. In my life alone, the reasons were numerous:

> – MAXINE CALLED US into the bedroom, a dark room at the front of the house. it was daytime and she was being abnormally friendly. a record was playing and she asked me and my little sister, Helen, to start playing the tambourine and dance to the music. Helen was afraid, but we started dancing and she picked up the tambourine. then Maxine had us dance closer together, and asked us to start touching each other's hair, had us start taking off our clothes and get close to each other.
> – i must have floated away, because all i remember is coming back into the room and looking into Helen's petrified eyes. she had a look of betrayal in her eyes . . . directed at me. i seemed to be having too much fun and this hurt her deeply. i started laughing real hard and fell to the floor holding my sides like everything was funny. Maxine was pissed-off because it meant the kiddy-porn show was over. she looked at Helen and me, and started laughing like an evil witch—a deep, haunting laugh to humiliate and scare us. it worked.

In retrospect I now know that an alter personality took over to deal with this terrifying situation. She responded by getting lost in her own dancing. At some point the situation became too shocking for even her, and I believe another alter took over at that point and figured out a way to make it stop. She fell to the floor laughing uncontrollably, just as she had done when she was four years old when a cat was being mutilated. Maxine made it clear that nothing happened that day. I knew never to speak of that incident because our very lives depended on my silence. If I told, I knew things could get exponentially worse and her cruelty toward everyone would only escalate. When I finally remembered this incident in its totality, I was so ashamed of my behavior. I felt like I had completely betrayed my little sister. She meant everything to me, and I terrified and hurt her deeply. I saw it in her eyes and it is a look I will probably always remember. Denial and shame are very powerful forces that keep abused children silent.

Children are shamed, terrorized, and made to feel guilty about abuses they have experienced. Perhaps the most obvious reason kids remain silent is that they are completely dependent on adults for most of their basic needs. To speak ill of an adult, especially a parent, caretaker, or relative, makes the child more vulnerable than she already is. To speak out is an act of betrayal, toward the self for not being brave or strong enough, and toward the perpetrator for allowing his or her weaknesses to be known.

When the abuse becomes part of the child's imagination, through lies, threats, and constant submission, anything becomes possible.[42] Even when there are no direct threats of harm or violence, there is often an implied sense that something catastrophic will happen if one tells. Frequently young children are convinced that the perpetrator has "supernatural powers" or can read their minds.[43] Of course, many children are led to believe that the abuse is their fault because the adults or older youth causing the harm say so. The result is that children are silenced even further. Sarah Olson writes of her own suffering at the hands of Ron, a friend of her mother's: "Someone should have questioned what was happening. No one asked why two little girls were acting out in such strange behaviors. Ron could say with complete confidence, 'You see, little girl? Nobody cares.'"[44] It is all too common, and terribly effective, for perpetrators to remind children that they will not be believed if they tell. Most children, regardless of age, are apprehensive to disclose any abuse due to fear of being disbelieved or, worse yet, being punished further. In the case of sexual abuse, youth may be shamed into not telling because they realize the social taboo of having sexual relations with a relative, even if the sexual activity is unwanted or despised.

Victims do not remain submissive and fearful from threats alone.

Especially in the case of domestic abuse, after an assault the abusive person might beg for forgiveness, plead undying love and support, or convince the victim it will never happen again.[45] In the case of child abuse, perpetrators might increase affections or provide other means to show the child how much they care. Maxine wasn't always aggressive and cruel. She would buy us chocolate-covered donuts and hot chocolate and let us come to work with her. Helen and I would play "secretary" with the office phones and have lots of fun. Maxine took care of us when my mother wasn't around and even rushed me to the hospital one time when my finger was broken. My oldest brother, too, wasn't always violent and aggressive. Nor were all the sexual advances he made against me harsh or violent. There were times he would give me hugs and listen to me and be nice to me . . . but just as quickly, he could take advantage of me sexually. There was an enormous cost to the attention he gave me. But the more desperate I became for genuine affection and love, the more willing, and perhaps more oblivious, I was to pay the cost. My brother learned this manipulative behavior from the adults around him, including Maxine and my father.

There remain, of course, far too many children who are silenced by actual threats of harm or death. Maxine caught Charlie molesting me and threatened to kill him if he ever did it again:

> – HE'S ON TOP OF ME. my knees are pinned down like a frog so my legs are spread apart. the linoleum tile is very cold and my legs and hips are hurting. this has happened before so i try to lay still. all of a sudden Maxine is in the doorway. she's screaming, furious at my brother. i'm not sure what i'm supposed to do. i'm afraid to look up, but i peek and see her face turning beet red. she's gonna kill him! she stares in the most menacing way possible, "if I ever see this again, I'll kill you!" i was only four years old and i believed her.

The abuse with my brother eventually started again, and I knew, for his sake, I would never tell. For a youngster, the possibility of a loved one getting harmed, even if the loved one is another perpetrator, makes it so there is no real option to tell, within or outside the family.

Loyalty toward the family, even other "respected" people outside the family, is taken for granted and often goes unquestioned.

Loyalty works to keep kids silent. No matter how crazy things can get, there's a perverse belief that the family is worth dying for and certainly worth your silence. Some of us take this literally, escaping abuse by suicide. Others just dig deeper within themselves, dissociating further and further to prove their undying loyalty. This loyalty creates a seemingly unbreakable bond of love-hate between the child and her abusers. Perpetrator bonds, coupled with an overwhelming sense of wanting bad things to be over, give perpetrators an enormous amount of power over their victims.

Trauma that is repetitive or constant can bond perpetrators and victims in very complex and twisted ways. Referred to as trauma-bonding, or traumatic bonding, the more a victim is terrorized, the more she becomes fully dependent on her abuser for comfort and protection.[46] Such relationships can be particularly acute when the acts are between family members. There was an unspoken pact in my family about the meaning of family, loyalty, and self-worth:

> – I PROTECTED MY SIBLINGS and mother because they were family. i did it out of solidarity, as a means of being accepted as an essential part of the family. it guaranteed me membership in the group, or at least i thought it did. i felt part of this family because of what i did for them. without the protection and love i gave to them, i wouldn't have been one of them. my fears of invisibility and disregard would have been realized. by helping and giving, i was part of the group. that was the unspoken pact. but the family was a facade, the unspoken pact a lie. i will always remain an outsider to my own family.

Loyalty toward family, or even a church or school, can be stronger than love itself. Trauma can bond people together despite and because of its insidiousness and revulsion. These bonds can have the effect of increasing the secrecy, silence, and shame of abuse.

Personal shame becomes a fundamental reason why people remain silent about child abuse, particularly in the case of sexual abuse and incest.[47] It is common for sexual abuse survivors to feel both dirty and responsible for causing the abuse. I felt ashamed of myself for strutting sexy in front of my father and brothers. For years I felt ashamed for liking my brother's attentions; it wasn't entirely bad, and at times it was even pleasurable and comforting. I have a close friend who had orgasms when her dad sexually abused her. One of the effects of this shame for her has been an inability to orgasm as an adult. The body responds to physical stimulation despite how we might feel emotionally or physically about the situation. Orgasm is a natural response to physical stimulation, however violent or brutal it may be. This is why it is not uncommon for victims to have orgasms during a rape or molestation. As much as we might know something intellectually, any sort of physical arousal during a sexual assault or molestation can make a victim of abuse feel very ashamed for what she interprets as "enjoying it." We feel shame for deriving pleasure, whether it be emotional or physical, in an exploitive situation, and females especially react by feeling wicked, sinful, and bad.[48] We internalize this badness as personal shame, making it all the more difficult to tell anyone about it. There have been times when I have literally felt strangled by my shame. It has choked me and smothered me in a way that anger, rage, grief, and revulsion have not:

> – I CANNOT BEAR THIS UGLINESS. i know people see it. so dirty and ugly, a filth fixed permanently on and in my skin. don't touch me. don't look at me. i am not here. shamed into nothingness, i crawl inside a cocoon, escaping deeper and deeper within myself. if i could keep wrapping, keep spinning the web of the cocoon, i could stay gone forever. no one will see me. no one will ever know. the dirt will be hidden. forever lost, forever alone.

Shame is definitive: the more we are shamed, the more we are silenced. As a group, children lack the political, social, and economic power to counteract, let alone stop, abusive and terrorizing conditions, conditions that occur predominately in the home.

Ways Children Speak

Despite the many reasons to remain silent, abused children continue to find ways to speak.[49] When child abuse allegations are made against family, both the personal and societal reaction typically is the immediate dismissal of the claims. Yet children rarely invent false allegations of child sexual abuse, and as many as 95 percent of the allegations of child sexual abuse are confirmed.[50] Despite perpetrators telling kids they won't be believed, along with the many other reasons children fear disclosure, children still come forward with their experiences of abuse. One of the most well-known cases of kids coming forward with sexual abuse happened in 1983 with parents and children from the McMartin preschool. Despite all the evidence that showed children being violated, tortured, and abused, most of the charges were dropped against the McMartin family.[51] To this day what most people remember about this case is the "falsely accused" McMartin family. Most of us fail to remember or even consider what the children went through, including the many ways they were traumatized by the investigation and trial itself. Children are seldom believed even when they do tell. Sarah Olson writes in her memoir:

> Some original materials presented here are graphic and ugly. Child abuse is not pretty, and any effort to make nice with it is an even greater obscenity. I want these images to create such indelible outrage that no one will hesitate to report incidents of suspected child abuse. I want the limits of a three-year old's resources and vocabulary recognized, in the hope that the next child automatically earns the benefit of any doubt.[52]

While some children come forward with stories of abuse, most children don't. If you're like many adults and are waiting for a child to tell you verbally about a specific incident, you could be waiting a long time, maybe even years.

Even when a child is unable to talk about abuse, there are distinct ways children speak about abusive and terrorizing events. They may not tell by words, but they tell by their *behavior*. An abused toddler or youngster might not want to be near a particular person, or they may not want to hug or talk with someone. They may be afraid in a situation that seems harmless to you. Perhaps someone older wants to quit an organization they used to love. They may be having recurring nightmares, wetting the bed, or getting sick regularly when they never used to. Some kids might start stealing or lying, skipping school, or becoming belligerent and antisocial. Abused children might develop asthma, allergies, or eating disorders. Most of us who have been victims of childhood abuse can think of numerous ways we let others know what was going on without ever speaking the words, "Dad molested me." Children find creative and courageous ways to let us know they are being hurt. Although young children lack developmentally the vocabulary and writing skills to describe child abuse, they still speak through physical symptoms, utterings, and drawings. Most kids let us know when they are being traumatized, but it is our ignorance, inability to understand, and unwillingness to really listen that keep children in abusive situations.

I think about my own family and the many different ways my siblings and I exhibited signs of child abuse. I developed severe asthma and allergies and was always sick—bronchitis, tonsillitis, strep throat, and colds. I had chronic headaches that medication would not help. I would forget things all the time. I used to hang on to kitties, hold them tight as if someone were going to harm them. My youngest sister, Helen, was a bedwetter, developed arthritis at an early age, and had bulimia for many years. As a youngster she would throw tantrums regularly and hit her head frantically against the wall. She'd bite me and scratch me all the time. Ben, just eleven months older than me, hated to have his picture taken or be forced to smile; he did everything he could to be inconspicuous, and pictures made that impossible. He'd crouch in corners, never look at anyone in the eyes. He was a sleepwalker and had bad dreams. He developed ulcers and had chronic stomach problems. My oldest brother, Charlie, was the most overt in his reactions. He became aggressive and hostile toward everyone; he'd hit us and terrorize us. He ran away a lot. He was diagnosed with attention deficit disorder and put on Ritalin, a medication to help hyperactivity. He skipped school and always acted out in the classroom. As a teenager he became a heavy drug user, a "delinquent," and eventually landed in prison. Lois is the oldest sibling and, for a few years after my parents' divorce, she helped raise us. Being four years younger, I don't remember her having many somatic complaints or behavioral problems. She had painfully debilitating menstruations though. By the time Lois was in high shool, when she wasn't holed up in her bedroom reading books or caring for us, she had found every legitimate way to escape the house: Girl Scouts, volleyball, church group, overnights with friends. The collective responses of my siblings and me are incredible.

I think about all my relatives and caretakers, teachers, scout leaders, friends' parents, and other adults who had access to my life. It's unfathomable to me that no one noticed the abuse, and if they did notice, they did not intervene. I would be shocked to learn if anyone within or outside the family attempted to intervene. And if they somehow tried to, they certainly weren't effective. *People have to be in the right frame of mind and have the ability and willingness to listen to really notice child abuse.* I want everyone to know that the eradication of child abuse can only happen when we, individually and collectively, become personally responsible for *all* children. But individual behavior is simply not enough; it is only a start.

There are many reasons why children cannot describe and explain the abuses they have experienced. While children may be terrified to speak, they desperately want the abusive conditions to end. So when a child does talk through utterings, acting out behaviors, or chronic physical pains, she needs people to be aware enough to pay attention. Perhaps the most convincing way children speak is through their bodies. Sylvia in "Within and Without" captures the delicate and seemingly unrecognizable fragmentation that can occur in the body and mind because of severe trauma:[53]

One body
cannot contain the dream girls

wobbly wooden dolls
within dolls

We echo ancient grievances
dissolve

then reappear
each one untouchable

nerve curlers
without bones or mother blood

Polish the surface
we remain indelible

the inevitability of morning
the persistence of night

By understanding the many ways our bodies are unable to deny ugly truths, we can begin to listen more closely to the children in our lives.

3 The Body Speaks

Trauma and Multiple Personality

> my body talks. it speaks loudly of all the abuse—the scars and deformities, my discolored lips, scar tissue in my vagina, arthritis in my hips and knees, all the dryness in my eyes and mouth, stomach problems, pains in my side and back, an abnormal brain wave. . . . the abuse is real, was real, a part of my everyday existence. i continue to relive bodily what my mind can't handle—years and years of sexual abuse and terrorization.
>
> —Paige Alisen

People who have been severely traumatized in childhood can bear the emotional, physical, and psychological scars for a lifetime. Abuse can be so severe that children develop elaborately intricate dissociative strategies in order to cope. The development of multiple personalities, officially called dissociative identity disorder, is one such strategy. People who develop DID do so primarily because of extreme and repetitive abuse experienced in childhood. Dissociative identity disorder represents one of the worst aspects of this culture: the deplorable amount of violence and abuse directed at children, especially girls. At the same time, people who develop multiple personalities demonstrate how incredibly adaptive individuals can be under extreme trauma and deprivation. Bodies become repositories of all the positive and negative aspects of our lives. For those who have suffered horrific cruelty, negative and hurtful stimuli can affect our bodies more intensely and deeply than positive forces of love and compassion. Bodies are mutilated in the name of love; they are betrayed, beaten, and stolen. While we may repress, forget, or deny the awful conditions of our childhood, the physical body remembers all of it. The body becomes a toxic waste yard for all the bad that has been dumped on, in, and around it. Toxins can be much more difficult to release from our bodies than love is to enter our hearts.

In this chapter I illustrate the most significant ways traumatic stress impacts the body. One of the most profound effects of traumatic stress, particularly for those living with multiple personalities, is amnesia and loss of time. I examine the ways memory is affected by trauma and discuss the phenomenon of memory recovery and how and why it happens. I bring together contemporary scientific research on trauma, memory, and the body with personal narratives of survivors of horrid childhood abuse. Dissociative identity disorder is not just a psychiatric problem—it is experienced physically, biologically, and spiritually as well. People diagnosed with DID often have a secondary diagnosis, or at least fit the criteria for diagnosis, of somatization disorder, a disorder marked by chronic symptoms with no known medical basis, such as painful stomach and colon ailments or general pains. Our bodies react to trauma in considerable physiological ways. Bodies store abuse in their very cells, abuse that can manifest years after the abusive incidents have ended. I illustrate what it feels like to store, and then later remember, trauma in and throughout our bodies.

Our bodies talk even when we are unable to say the words. Many survivors develop courageous strategies to resist oppressive and terrifying conditions in their lives. I discuss some of these strategies in terms of how the body is utilized to fight back. In the final section of this chapter, I discuss several important body therapies, therapies that can have a transformational effect on the individual's mental, physical, and spiritual well-being. By learning to move, feel, and experience the body in positive and loving ways, we release the toxins created during traumatization. It is through this process that we are able to regain our bodies and take back what rightfully belongs to us.

Recall Memory and Lost Time

The personal narratives and memoirs of survivors of severe child abuse illustrate the complex relationship between the mind, body, memory, and violence. Some of our collective scars are obvious and visible. I am reminded regularly of the abuse I've suffered every time I look in the mirror and see my discolored lips from forced and repeated oral sex as a child. I am permanently scarred by sexual abuse, and although I know there are people who become permanently disabled by abuse, I am still deeply disturbed by how the abuse remains with me today. The bodies and minds of people who've been abused store and remember violence and trauma in many complex and elaborate ways. Certainly most of our scars are not physically visible to others.

One of the most profound ways traumatization affects us is through our memory. Repetitive trauma in childhood often causes partial or full memory lapse of the traumatic events. Also known as "repressed" or "recovered" memory, memories of abuse can surface months, even years, after the incident occurred. Extensive and compelling research has been conducted in the past decade on trauma, dissociation, and memory, and in the following pages I present some of the major findings.[1] There are five kinds of memory: recall memory, imagistic memory, feeling memory, body memory, and acting-out memory.[2] Recall and body memory are most important to explanations of multiple personalities and severe dissociation.

Recall memory is what most of us think of as "memory." We are conscious of it—that is, the memory includes having the mental image, feelings, and sensations related to the experience, as well as having the sense it was you. For example, I might remember a graduation I attended last year. I can recall the enormous stadium, the graduates marching in their robes, the boring speeches, and the energetic ovations of the crowd. The experience is set in a context of space and time, and I know it was myself who was present. Recall memories are developmental—that is, they develop through maturation and become better as we get older. In other words, a two-year-old has less recall memory ability than a twenty-year-old. This is why memory distortions for children are so common: a child's recall memory has not developed fully. But age alone does not explain the phenomenon of repressed memory.

Repressed memory can happen when a person is severely traumatized. This is how it works: the brain, both physiologically and psychologically, stores nonthreatening information differently than traumatic stress.[3] As a traumatic incident occurs, dissociative strategies are utilized to cope with the situation. The brain cannot fully handle what is happening, so it dissociates, or separates from reality, in order to handle it. Dissociation during traumatizing situations manifests in various ways, on a continuum from mild to severe. Time might warp by slowing down, or we might believe what is happening is not real. There may be confusion and an inability to remember the ordering of events. Sensory perceptions might be altered, such as getting tunnel vision or feeling physical sensations unrelated to the incident. One might be able to witness what is happening but be emotionally numb while it is going on. On the more severe end, one might float mentally to a ceiling or become enmeshed in a wall. People can create invisible barriers or shields to protect themselves from the situation. The more we dissociate from an experience, the more recall memory is impaired, since we are less mentally conscious during the experience. This is why recall memory can become so severely impaired for a child abuse survivor.

When traumatic events are repetitive and extreme, conditions are set for alter personalities to be created—the child cannot bear what is happening, so mentally escapes to the point where an entirely new person emerges. Jane Phillips explains:

> As a multiple, I can be said to have been born more than once. The first time I was a standard-issue but much-wanted baby girl. Each trauma that followed was another birth. Terror cut the strings of my identity; over time, I blossomed into a full-blown multiple the same way a handful of escaped balloons rise and scatter in the air.[4]

While the body remains visibly intact, the mind has gone, sometimes in many directions, to other spaces and places, and literally split apart at the seams. The host, also called the primary or original personality, can go away for minutes, days, even years at a time while this new alter deals with the traumatizing experience.[5] As new traumas become too intense and unbearable, additional alters are created. This is how a person can develop many alter personalities.

Everyone dissociates to some degree in everyday life, yet people who develop multiplicity tend to be severely dissociative as a matter of course. Experts Steinberg and Schnall offer a helpful explanation:

> For most people, brief, mild episodes of dissociation are part of everyday life. Take memory, for example. Automatically driving a car and not remembering the ride, because only a split-off part of the mind was on the road, probably happens to normal people every time they drive home from work. Another common experience is the frustrating "tip of the tongue" phenomenon. When pressed, we can't recall a familiar name, only to have it pop back into consciousness when we're *not* thinking of it. . . . Multiply these quirks a thousandfold, and you might get some idea of how the memory of a person with a dissociative disorder has been impaired. People with DID may look whole on the outside, but inside their sense of self and connection with the outside world has been splintered into bits and pieces. Every day is a quietly heroic struggle, not only to keep unthinkable memories hidden from the consciousness, but also to conceal frightening symptoms from others.[6]

People with DID have seriously impaired recall memory because of severe dissociation. In fact, significant memory lapse is one condition necessary for a psychiatric diagnosis of DID.[7] Multiplicity represents the profound ability to survive extreme trauma.

As the trauma intensifies and more alter personalities are created, the mind develops what is called an internal system, or a system by which alters can operate and live. The internal system can be referred to in various ways: a family, parts or people inside, the insiders, the flock, houses, or troops. Each person who experiences multiplicity has a uniquely personal, and profoundly private, internal system. The internal system has many characteristics. For example, the average number of alter personality states for a given person ranges between ten and fifteen, but there can be as few as two to as many as one hundred or more.[8] Over 85 percent of those diagnosed with multiple personalities have four prominent personality types: child personalities, different aged personalities, protector personalities, and persecutor personalities.[9] Sixty-two percent of those diagnosed with DID have a personality of the opposite sex. Alters tend to be stable over time—that is, they continue to perform the same particular functions throughout the individual's life. As much as there are commonalities among the internal systems of those with multiple personalities, everyone has a uniquely personal internal system.

I have a total of nine alters, six of whom are female. Seven of the alters range in age from three to fourteen years, while one is much older than myself and another is my age. When I was four years old, a seven-year-old alter was created who took on my oldest brother's and half brother's characteristics; as we aged, he later became thirteen. He emerged to deal with sexual abuse perpetrated by my brother. He became a protector personality who kept charge of the internal system. He knew of all the other alters inside and "gave permission" for each to come out, or share our body, at a specific time. He also kept vigilant at night especially and would stay awake to make sure he would be prepared for any new assault or violation. Clara was created at age eight to deal with sexual abuse perpetrated by my great uncle; she remained this age until recently. Clara made our life better by being good and unabashedly optimistic. She is very responsible, organized, and smart, and she took care of us by making meals, keeping the house clean, and making sure we remembered things. I have another alter, Keys, who was created when I was four, and he aged as I did until the age of seventeen when we moved away from our biological family. Keys was created to protect three other alters who experienced terrifying and grotesque ritualistic abuse. His job was to keep these three alters hidden and silent from everyone, including myself, the other alters inside, and those on the outside, e.g., family, friends, and teachers. By maintaining secrecy and silence, the alters kept me from going crazy or killing myself. They kept me from being abused by more people, and they kept my siblings safe. Keys especially knew that more people would be harmed if he talked; silence was the only option. As anyone can imagine, making sense of the internal system is highly complex. Rarely is a child even cognizant that multiple personalities have been created. Even in adulthood we don't realize the extent to which our minds have become so severely fragmented. For many, such as myself, it takes a mental breakdown before we comprehend how split we are.

People often wonder how alters communicate with each other. It varies significantly from person to person, and the process is usually very private. I remember the first time I was hospitalized, the psychiatrist asked me if I heard voices in my head. My immediate thought was that if I told her what was happening, she would think I was crazy. At the time, I heard constant conversations in my head. Sometimes they were quiet; often there was screaming. The more difficult daily living became, the louder the conversations got (or vice versa—I'm not sure which caused which). I learned later this is how my alters communicated with each other and with me. When alters know each other, they can communicate.

The internal communication system is even more complex for those who have alters who are unaware of each other, even unaware of the host personality. Some describe the internal system as having adjoining rooms where some windows have two-way mirrors whereby those in one room may not be able to see out, yet others can still see in. Some people with DID develop intricate systems inside where alters are grouped, not all groups knowing about the others. In her memoir, *When Rabbit Howls,* Truddi Chase captures the complexity of the internal communication system for those with multiple personalities. Through intensive therapy, ninety-two voices were discovered, living out as "the Troops" in various networks and groupings. The more shattered one's mind, the more the host and alters are unaware of what happens when they are not out in the body or co-conscious.

Perhaps the reader can understand now why recall memory for the person experiencing multiplicity is so critically impaired. Alter personalities are developed specifically to deal with traumatic or stressful events. The result is that the host personality is unaware of the traumatic episodes. If you are unaware of an incident, then obviously you have no recall memory of it. Through intensive therapy and healing, the host personality and other alters may learn the full extent of the abuses suffered. But coming to terms with this information and acknowledging it happened to *you* is painfully difficult. There remains for a long time the sense that the abuse happened to someone else. It takes great courage, determination, and hard work to admit that the things that happened to an eight-year-old alter happened to oneself.

Yolla Hogan, a survivor of childhood abuse and a woman living with multiple personalities, explains what it is like to remember fully an event:

> So I might be able to tell something about a trauma but with essentially no sense that it's "my" story. Because "I" am not the one who experienced it. I'm not the one who went through the abuse. These other folks went through the various aspects of the abuse. I'm not the one who was mad. Even the one who went through the abuse wasn't the one who got mad. So what is it for a multiple like me to regain an event? I have to go back to this one [alter] and figure out what this one's experience of the event was, and then this alter's experience, and then this alter's experience, and try to bring them together—almost at the same time in the same place, so that then the event feels like it truly happened to me. Only then can *I* decide to let it go and not be tripped up by things that aren't true.[10]

It may take years for a person experiencing multiplicity to remember a single abusive experience. Like Hogan says, the entire internal system must work together in order for memory to be even partially restored. All of these reasons help us to understand why memory distortions are so prevalent for the person who has survived severe child abuse and developed multiple personalities.

There are several explanations for why certain people develop alter personalities to cope during severe trauma and others do not. The most commonly accepted reason is having a genetic predisposition to dissociation, while other explanations include psychobiological factors, neurological factors, seizure disorders, and environmental effects.[11] The end results are the same regardless of the reason. Severe dissociation brings on amnesia, which can include complete memory loss or partial memory distortion of the traumatic event. In other words, the person was so frightened that she cannot recall exactly what happened either prior to, during, or even after a traumatic experience. Memory loss can include not just the memories of actual events, but the feelings associated with the events as well. A person might remember being tied to a chair and beaten with a belt but not recall feeling terrified or physically pained while it was happening; the memory is devoid of feeling. Conversely, one can remember feeling terrorized by something that happened in a basement but not remember exactly what happened. Dissociation and the resulting memory lapse becomes a survival mechanism in the midst of traumatization.

Dissociative strategies are utilized regularly by those with DID, even in nonthreatening situations; dissociation becomes a way of life. It is understandable, then, that people experiencing multiplicity tend to have scattered and sporadic memories of their past and even fewer memories of the actual abuse. The level of amnesia varies from person to person; minutes, hours, days, even years of time can be unaccounted for. Just two weeks after my initial diagnosis of DID, I wrote the following:

> – IMAGINE HAVING A LIMITED MEMORY where, when you recall having lunch with a friend, you remember her memory because she retells the story on another day. And later, you don't know if what you remember is her memory of the event or your own, or even having two different memories of an event because you're not quite sure what really happened. Imagine slow dancing with someone you don't know and you don't remember how you got there. What if your memory was so distorted that you really don't know much about what transpired for over 30 years of your life. It's a complete fog where you're an invisible by-stander.

For years I used to say that Helen, my little sister, held all of my memories for me. Although we endured similar traumas, Helen did not experience memory loss in regard to daily living. Yet I could never remember things, even things that happened the previous day. So I would rely on Helen for recollecting information. It is extraordinary how my memory lapses were just absorbed and taken for granted by myself and those around me. They became rationalized as a personality trait of mine—I was forgetful, an "airhead." Helen would laugh at me, "Geez, how could you forget that?" Memory lapse was the norm for me; it was all I knew.

Even in the worst of my amnesia, there are others who have suffered much more extensively and who have years of their life completely unaccounted for. Truddi Chase describes an incident with her psychiatrist when he was puzzled by her lack of memory of her past: "I told you. I have four or five memories and a lot of flicks against my mind. I'm in real estate because that makes me self-employed. I don't have to face job applications full of questions that I can't answer."[12] Chase literally had years of her life for which she was unable to account. These few memories were the *only* memories she had of her past. People who experience multiplicity must work very hard to rationalize and cover up memory lapses by avoiding situations in which, like Chase, we need to recollect our memory. Many of us "lose time" regularly, becoming partly or even fully amnesiac of our lives, yet it is genuinely unconscious.

People experiencing multiplicity lose time in other ways. For Chris Costner Sizemore, the woman who was "Eve," her memory would start over each day:

> Despite the outward chaos, my inner experiences with recall were systematic and ordered. Beginning with the age of two, my life passed in review. Day after day, week after week, era upon era, it was virtually a ceaseless envisioning of who I had been, of those whom my former alters had known, and of the things the alters had done. As well, it was chronological, with few regressions or repetitions of scenes: Once I recalled a spot of time, I would not see it again.[13]

Literally, whatever happened the day before was wiped away, and Sizemore would start all over again each day with a clean slate. It is unimaginable for many. Yet this was her experience; it is the only thing she knew. Sybil Isabel Dorsett, the pseudonym used for the book and movie *Sybil,*[14] would lose several days at a time. Flora Rheta Schreiber, the author of the book, describes an incident where Sybil remembered leaving a chemistry class at Columbia University in New York and "waking up" five days later in Philadelphia, having no recollection of what transpired between time.[15] Such time lapses are extremely frightening and confusing. People who live with multiple alter personalities find extraordinary ways to cope. It remains amazing to me how much of this goes on without anyone realizing what our collective amnesia really signifies.

A critical goal of therapeutic treatment is dealing with memory lapse in order to recollect the trauma that initially triggered the dissociation. Therapists believe that dissociation and post-traumatic symptoms diminish when enough of the original memories are retrieved *and* one has the capacity to deal with the emotions involved.[16] Memories often surface during a flashback, that is, images, thoughts, or other sensory perceptions brought on by environmental stimuli, including certain sounds, smells, sensations, or touches. Flashbacks can occur simply by seeing an event or object that triggers past memory. Flashbacks are different from nightmares in that the memories occur while the person is fully awake as if the original trauma is happening at the present time. Flashbacks are often unpredictable and are one of many PTSD symptoms that can begin years after the original trauma occurred. Memories can also be induced through hypnosis and EMDR (eye movement desensitization and reprocessing).[17] In whatever way memories are recalled, the work can be extremely painful and even last a lifetime:

– MEMORY RECALL IS EXCRUCIATING. most often it comes for me in the form of a sensation—something i see or touch. when i do have a new memory, often i only remember what happens prior to and right after the actual abuse. i end up having this picture, a snapshot really, of whatever took place. what becomes painful is both knowing and not knowing what happened in the middle. so sometimes i keep it blocked out for as long as i can. who split my lips from their penis when i was five? i'm not sure. who was the dark man in the doorway when i was four? the picture is usually black and white. sometimes i see red blood on my lips, though, and the blood itself stands out. in the doorway i see yellow light behind the man. otherwise it's dark, black. . . .

– is it really important what happened in the middle? does it really matter who it was or what exactly took place? i struggle with this. part of me doesn't want to remember any of it, whether it's in the middle or not. another part of me wants to remember the middle, can't get these images out of her head. another part wants to remember everything because until we do, we can't be free. so all the voices inside speak different and competing thoughts about what, how, and when to remember.

Memories surface as we are ready, or almost ready, to deal with them. The commitment and determination to fully remember past abuse has enormous consequences personally, professionally, and collectively.

People who have survived and repressed severe trauma frequently feel insane because we have spent years of our lives detached from the heinous events that made us forget in the first place. Chris Costner Sizemore shares a particularly painful period of her life when she needed constant care and daily sessions with her therapist. "My life—or more accurately, my *lives*—passed before my eyes. I thought I was going to die. It was terrifying, redefining the word *confusion.* And when it became clear that I wasn't dying, I thought I was going insane."[18] Many of us struggle to remember past events and doubt ourselves for having inconsistent and unreliable memories. "I doubted the memory and myself. I was far more willing to believe that I was crazy, that I was a pathological liar, that I had a sick and twisted imagination than I was willing to believe that my own brother had tried to rape me on a summer morning in the laundry room."[19] Jane Phillips's experience is similar to many others. We begin to think of ourselves as crazy before we will accept our memories, memories we have spent a lifetime trying both consciously and unconsciously to repress.

Perhaps the most compelling argument to support the authenticity of repressed memory is the body itself:

– SO WHEN PEOPLE (including myself) begin to doubt what's happened to me, all i have to do is remember the semen and blood in my mouth and i know i didn't make this up. it's real. i never considered myself a creative person nor until recently did i consider myself crazy. nor have i considered myself to be transcendental or zen-like. i'm not creative or crazy enough to fabricate all this. i can't make my body move and feel things that haven't happened. and if all these physical feelings aren't enough, the scars should be. some people will want to explain this all away, but you know what, there's just too much information to deny. i'm the survivor of some really ugly and horrifying abuse. . . . i can FEEL it!

Our bodies speak a certain truth that corresponds to our compelling yet unbelievable stories of horrifying and fantastic abuse. For those with DID, despite the suffering we experience throughout our bodies, many find the body's voice validating. Our bodies speak a certain truth quite loudly and clearly: we have been violated, tortured, and exploited in despicable ways.

Body Memory

The memoirs and personal narratives of those with DID illustrate the extent to which our bodies store memories of horrific abuse years after it has ended. Overwhelming scientific evidence in the form of physiological and psychobiological research indicates the veracity of body memory. Our bodies store traumatic abuse in their very cells, and this manifests for survivors in alarming ways, such as abnormal brain waves, abnormal hormone secretions in the brain, immunological effects, heightened arousal, an exaggerated startle response, and disturbed sleep.[20] So while we may be able to numb ourselves to torture, our bodies remember; they hang on to whatever harm has been done to us:

– I KNEW A YEAR AGO that choosing to live means choosing to feel. i knew that being disconnected from my body meant that part of my body had been dead to me. i could feel the difference between when my body was alive and when it was dead. so living means i have to feel . . . and my body hurts like hell from all the years of abuse.

Our bodies react to everything that happens to us, and body memory is the physical manifestation of a past incident. The more significant the incident, the greater the impact on the body. People who have been tortured and beaten into submission mentally and physically have profound scars and bruises throughout their bodies. Frequently the most profound damage is invisible, such as emotional scars, damaged cells, or continuing to feel physically and mentally battered thirty or more years after the abuse has ended. These scars can be more acutely alive and real than any visible physical ailment or scar. Our bodies are scarred and tattered within.

The process of uncovering or experiencing repressed body memory becomes just as significant and potentially shattering as recollecting mental imagery or flashbacks. I have been physically, sexually, and emotionally abused by my father, brother, mother's partner, and at least one uncle. I was involved with ritualistic abuse perpetrated by, most probably, neighbors and a close family member. My body and soul have been exploited and violated to a degree that is insurmountable. I sometimes believe that the worst of the torture was the wait—waiting at night for someone to enter my room, waiting for someone to lose their temper, waiting for someone to harm me or one of my siblings. Like so many others who have experienced this sort of abuse, the inconsistency and unpredictability of the abuse made it so I had to be hypervigilant and inconspicuous, a virtually impossible task in a chaotic household. It leaves one fearful, walking on eggshells, in an always tenuous situation. The fear of waiting is learned, and for me it is felt throughout my body as part of my everyday existence.

That feeling became acute during an EEG exam (an electroencephalogram measures the electrical activity of the brain). In an EEG, electrodes are fastened to your head, and what seems like little lights are flashed randomly with intermittent time intervals. The brain scurries to make logical sense of the flashing lights, but there are no discernable patterns. For most people, the EEG is merely uncomfortable. It induced in me, however, the same physical and emotional feelings I had while quietly waiting in my bed at night, the anxious anticipation of when and how the next person would enter my room:

– THE EEG was horrible. I had a bad flashback, memories and feelings about what it was like to sleep when I was growing up, always waiting for something bad to happen, trying to anticipate when it might. It was so upsetting . . . my insides were curling and

> I wanted to squeeze my legs together real tight so no one could get in. But I was frozen, unable to move. My legs lay paralyzed on the table where the tech asked me to put them. I wanted desperately to move but I couldn't. I thought I might really be paralyzed this time. I could feel the tears slowly trickle down my face, and I began sobbing. The tech wanted to know what was happening to me, but I could hardly open my mouth to speak. Finally all I could mumble was that the exam itself was like sleeping, just waiting for something awful to happen. My words sounded like little dust bits floating on the air . . . lifeless and meaningless.

For years someone had whispered to me, "Lay still and be quiet." Out of survival, my body learned, literally, to lay still and be quiet. So during the EEG, I lay there paralyzed, unconscious until that very moment how profoundly powerful body memory can be.

Flashbacks can feel like you have been run over by a semi-truck. Many abuse survivors understand that a mental picture of an abusive incident isn't necessary to have a full-on sensory flashback. Flashbacks of the abuse in the form of body memory are more real to me than any mental imagery I could have. Our bodies talk when our minds are unable to grasp or cope with what has happened in childhood. Despite our disjointed recall memories, many trauma survivors have very loud and unmistakable body memories. You do not have to see bruising to *feel* bruised. Anyone who has been in a car accident knows this. Your neck might be sore or your knees hurt the next day though there are no scrapes or bruises. Multiply this experience 1000-fold and you can begin to get a snapshot of someone experiencing severe PTSD. The body of someone with PTSD is often severely battered and bruised on the inside, and much of the pain is felt both internally and externally—it is just that no one can see the bruises.

Body memory is extremely powerful. Our bodies and cells compensate and store the memories of abuse for what our minds are not capable of remembering. Cameron West, in a memoir of his multiplicity, describes an incident during his recovery with traumatic memories:

> I awoke, startled, drenched in sweat, and shook my head hard. *What just happened?! White pubic hair? Vagina? Oh, my God.* My

> stomach felt like I'd swallowed a dozen riverbed stones. Horrified, my eyes wide open staring blankly at the ceiling, not wanting to close them even to blink, I steeled myself to open the squeaky faucet in my mind just enough to let the terrifying images trickle in. In a millisecond, the trickle became a torrent and the torrent a raging flood. My face flushed and my body started to convulse. I sprang from the bed and, doubled over, I stumbled to the bathroom. . . . I turned on the shower so no one would hear me, dropped to my knees in front of the toilet, and threw up every meal I'd ever eaten. Exhausted, I wiped my mouth with the back of my hand and caught a glimpse of my fingers. The horrible images rushed back in an ugly wave. And right behind it another wave of nausea crashed and I retched again, my empty stomach rippling, nothing coming up but a sour liquid, tearing eyes clamped shut to lock out the disgusting view.[21]

Memory recall is quite physical and literal. Felt throughout our bodies, recollecting memory of past abuse is painful and revolting physically, emotionally, and spiritually.

Emotions can be experienced physically to the point where we develop mild to serious medical conditions. From rage and grief to shame and betrayal, bodies react to the emotions we feel. Bodies react harshly particularly when we are unable or unwilling to express emotions.[22] In mental health circles, this is known as "stuffing" or denying our feelings. Many times one does not become fully conscious of how the stuffing of emotions impacts the body until one is diagnosed with a serious illness. Emotions can become toxic if they stay in our bodies too long. When abuse is repeatedly directed at someone over many formative years, major medical problems can result.

Think about this another way. Ordinary people depleted emotionally and under stress might come down with a cold, develop ulcers, or develop more serious medical conditions. So imagine what can happen to people who are brutally assaulted and abused from the time they are three years old. People with DID are "highly somatizing"—that is, their bodies develop somatic symptoms or pains as the result of traumatization.[23] Trauma can be toxic, and the physical body becomes the receptacle of toxic waste. Given this perspective, the serious physical conditions of many people diagnosed with DID and PTSD are not surprising. It is common for people diagnosed with DID to have irritable bowel syndrome, serious stomach conditions, gynecological problems, and chronic migraines and headaches. A disproportionate number of people have secondary and tertiary diagnoses of severe sleep disorders, eating disorders, and anxiety disorders, each disorder having a profound and cumulative effect on the body and mind. During an in-patient group therapy exercise, seven patients, including myself, were asked to state our current somatic symptoms and medical problems. The therapist began writing on the board what each patient called out: fibromyalgia, migraines, depression, anorexia, autoimmune diseases, skin disorders, ulcers, irritable bowel syndrome, scoliosis, gynecological problems, arthritis, colon problems, miscarriages, bulimia, kidney stones, back problems, hormonal irregularities, low and high blood pressure, severe allergies, heart murmurs. I counted the board afterwards, and there were forty-three things listed. Seven abuse survivors aged twenty-eight to forty-five years old with a lifetime of serious medical problems. I was thoroughly overwhelmed by our collective responses. Dissociative identity disorder is not only a serious psychiatric condition but also a potentially debilitating medical and physical problem.

Our bodies store and remember emotional, physical, and spiritual suffering. Each abusive incident buries the pain that much deeper. It is not surprising, then, that survivors of severe abuse hear and feel their bodies crying out in pain. There was a time when it felt like much of the internal pain of my childhood abuses was lodged into my shoulder blade. With every flashback and new memory, I would feel the burning layers of pain. My shoulder was a physical reminder of the abuse; it became a self-protective mechanism to cope with horrific abuse:

— THE GLASS PIPE is slicing through my shoulder blade, slowly twisting and turning working its way in deeper and deeper. burying itself inside me just enough so it won't break through to the other side. i can't pull it out because part of the pipe is busted; pulling it out would mean severe damage and blood. a permanent hole would be left. the shattered pipe burns, reminding me of the abuse, reminding me not to relax, not to surrender myself to anyone or anything. constantly on the move, never resting. it beats hard, pounding to the rhythm of my heart. And when i try to get inside my burning shoulder blade, what i feel is this deep, uncontrollable rage.

Only when I started to express the rage I felt for being terrorized as a child did my shoulder pains begin to lessen. The more we address the suppressed emotions within our bodies, the more our bodies can heal. Our bodies remember and store abuse in the same way it stores the trapped feelings and emotions from terrorizing events. To heal means feeling our bodies—bodies that have stored a lifetime of trauma.

Emotions can be experienced in subtle ways as well. Shame and rage can lodge into dark and hidden places in our bodies, making us feel exposed and dirty. Our bodies experience the feelings of shame even when we are unable to speak the words aloud:

– I FEEL SO FILTHY, so dirty on the outside and inside. i don't even want to shower. i don't want to take my clothes off, get naked. i feel exposed and raw even with all my clothes on. taking them off will only make this feeling worse. if i could show outwardly what this dirtiness feels like on the inside, no one would recognize me; i'd be smothered and gurgling in a pool of sewage. i wish this dirtiness would just wash away. but no amount of showers will ever make me feel clean again.

Shame can feel like a blanket of dirt that won't come off with even the most diligent scrubbing. I believe the more shameful I felt, the less I felt the rage inside; it was easier to deal with a dirty self than to experience the burning, uncontrollable rage I felt for being beaten down and abused for so many years. Shame and self-loathing kept me from becoming out of control, the very thing I so deeply despised about my abusers. Survivors of child sexual abuse can find creative ways to free themselves from shame. Artemis writes:

I'd worn that cloak of shame and it branded itself into my skin. But I found out that I could take it off, even if it meant taking

> my skin off along with it. I could grow back new skin that was healthy and good. What helped me do that was allowing myself to be deeply loved. I allowed myself to be loved in the places where I felt the ugliest and most ashamed of myself. And I don't mean physical places.[24]

Taking off a layer of skin is both metaphorical and literal to explain how one heals from devastating abuses. Our bodies *feel* the skin coming off. Yet, just as wounds develop scabs and heal, so, too, can our psychological scars heal.

Multiplicity, Alters, and the Body

Certain aspects of multiplicity profoundly affect how we relate to and with our bodies. From how we experience alter personalities to the physiological aspects of switching, i.e., moving from one alter personality to another, the body becomes enormously significant for people living with multiple personalities. In the following pages, I illustrate many elaborate and multifaceted ways that people experiencing multiplicity relate to their bodies. Alter personalities frequently have their own mannerisms, styles, habits, and preferences that affect how the body is experienced. A goal of therapy is to become more aware or "co-conscious" of alters in order to learn, and simultaneously appreciate, the reasons for their existence. Paradoxically, the more we become co-conscious with our alters, the more we experience our bodies and minds through the alters' perspectives. This can force a person to feel and experience what she desperately wants hidden and forgotten. Even the act of switching between and among alter personality states can take a toll physically and emotionally on our bodies.

Switching is both a psychological and physiological aspect of multiplicity. Psychologically, the switching of alters might cause people to regress, get lost in the past, or struggle to maintain consciousness and in touch with current reality. Switching can be frequent and is often uncontrollable, particularly during stressful or threatening situations. People who don't experience multiplicity often wonder how one alter appears but not another. Arthur, an alter of Billy Milligan, explains what happens when one of his alters comes out: "It's a big white spotlight. Everybody stands around it, watching or sleeping in their beds. And whoever steps on the spot is out in the world. Arthur says, 'Whoever is on the spot holds the consciousness.'"[25] For Arthur and the others living inside Milligan, it was a spotlight. I sometimes experience alters riding on my shoulders, and depending how far out of consciousness I am, they either stay on my shoulders (meaning we are co-conscious) or come out fully in my body.

The actual physical experience during a switch from one alter personality to another differs significantly for each person. It can be extremely painful or completely unnoticeable. Switching can be as quick as a fraction of a second or in some cases last several minutes. Most of the public has no idea when they are dealing with a person with DID. Switching frequently happens so quickly, no one would even notice. People who experience multiplicity can go through most of their lives without anyone ever noticing or even suspecting they have alters inside.

Once certain friends learned of my multiplicity, however, they began to notice the switching, even before I did. My mannerisms and voice would change, and they would observe me behaving differently. One friend noticed my forehead and hands change. Another friend noticed my mouth and could tell when I was switching because I would clench my teeth. Others said my eyes changed. I would notice my voice change, but it was usually after the switch had already occurred. Only when the switch was severe did I even notice. Then I would get an excruciating headache on the top of my head that could last for several minutes.

It is not uncommon for people who experience multiple personalities to become "stuck" during a switch between personalities. Getting stuck between alters also can occur during periods of rapid switching, also known as "rolodexing" or "the revolving-door crisis." Usually the result of a specific crisis, rolodexing can be terrifying, physically painful, and confusing. One might switch through five different alter personalities in the span of a few minutes and simultaneously experience a multitude of behaviors, thoughts, physical sensations, and emotions. In clinical terms, rapid switching occurs when alters may be struggling with each other to gain executive control over the system or, conversely, when there is an abandonment of control whereby no alters are willing or able to be in charge. Getting stuck between alters can happen when no alter is able or willing to come out and the host personality is unable to control the system inside. Perhaps the most frightening aspect of multiplicity is the inability to control the internal system.

Being stuck between alters is akin to a computer freezing up when it is trying to process too much information at once. So much movement is going on in the mind and brain that things literally seize up. And like the computer whose hard drive is working triple time to catch up but can't, the mind scurries to put things back in order. But sometimes it is unable to. I was rushed to the hospital because of a severe migraine and had a frightening incident of being stuck between alters in the hospital parking lot. I was terrified to go to the hospital, and at the same time the migraine was agonizing. It was extremely difficult to stay mentally present, and alters were coming in and out of consciousness not knowing what to do:

> – WE WERE IN SO MUCH PAIN. she just came out [a four-year-old alter] and sat on the ground beside the car, holding her knees, rocking and muttering to herself. but we wanted a big person out to handle all this. there was so much chaos and screaming in my head. someone was screaming inside, "move! do something!" but i couldn't move and my feet were stuck to the pavement, and the only words that came out of my mouth were gibberish. "make it stop!" someone else screamed. the pain hurt so bad and nobody wanted to come out for this. so the little girl was pushed out. she couldn't even talk, only mumbled, and was scared to death. how cowardly of all of us to make her come out. but she doesn't feel headaches like the rest of us. so we froze in time and space, paralyzed to stop what was happening. we stayed huddled in the hospital parking lot experiencing complete internal madness, terrified we'd never come back to this world.

To be stuck in the midst of personality switching is the epitome of being outside yourself. One watches herself in agony at the inability to move, speak, or change the paralyzed state. It is a living nightmare.

The switching between alter personalities can feel very familiar; some refer to it as a habit. Through healing and intensive therapy, one works to gain executive control or to be in charge of the system, to become co-conscious while an alter personality is present. But becoming co-conscious means we have to feel physically and emotionally what the alters experience. The physical experience alone can be terrifying because our bodies feel like the possession of other people—this is the experience of having multiple personalities.[26]

> – SOMETIMES I LOOK at my hands and they seem so far away, like they're not even attached to me. it's the strangest feeling. like the other day in the restaurant when my hands didn't even look like mine. it felt like they belonged to someone else. they seemed little or something, so fragile, like a small child's hand. these hands definitely weren't mine. the feeling finally went away and i was so relieved. i don't like when these things happen . . . not recognizing myself or parts of my body. it's creepy.

When I first began experiencing Clara, a young child alter, she was disturbed by the large size of my hands. She did not understand how we had aged so much without her knowing. When she would be out in the body, co-conscious with me, I experienced my hands the way she did: they looked old and unfamiliar. It really does feel like multiple people are inhabiting your body. The experience of multiplicity can be very frightening and disconcerting, and it leaves one feeling vulnerable and isolated, ashamed to share with others what is happening.

There can be immense shame in lacking control over your body and mind. Simply the *possibility* of switching can leave one feeling ashamed: for not being able to stay present and coherent in front of others, for acting inappropriately, and for feeling terrified and uncertain about what the alters might do or say. The fear of switching personalities petrified me to the extent where I would not leave my home. Over time I would venture out, but even when I became more stable, I remained mortified that others would notice. When I finally left the house, I hid my face and my hands and refused to look people in the eyes for fear they would notice my disorder. And I suffered in silence because I was so ashamed of my behavior and my very self. A close friend asked me once why I had not told anyone about my fear of switching. I tried to explain that in order to share the experience with someone, you have to first admit that it is even happening. Part of my problem was that I was ashamed of it happening—i.e., the alters, the switching, everything—and the last thing I would do is *tell* someone about it. Once you admit to the experience of multiplicity, including the switching that occurs, you have to be able to listen to what the alters have to say. What they have to say may be too much to bear. There were times when I felt like a freak and was so ashamed that I was not able to stop the switching. My shame and rage kept me from letting close friends know how terrified I was. But I was also frightened of the possible inappropriateness of my alters' behaviors. So I withdrew further, both physically and mentally. There were times when I must have looked like a turtle trying to hide my head in a shell that couldn't protect me; I certainly felt that way. Multiplicity is simultaneously a psychological and physical experience; it has a way of taking control of your entire being.

Our body changes as we switch from one alter to another, and each alter relates differently to the body as well. Things always look different through my alters' eyes or maybe my eyes; I do not know. That is the part that gets confusing. Most of the time I do not know who is disturbed by the changes and differences with our body. There have been times when someone inside gets extremely angry about the changes they experience, like when a male alter would get so frustrated that we're a girl and have to deal with monthly "female stuff." When the little ones (I use the term "little ones" to describe my three youngest alters) finally started to come out, they didn't recognize our physical body at all. They thought that somehow they had been transported to another person's body and that one day soon they would be magically transported back to their own. How horrible it was for them; they felt cheated for missing out on our growing up. It was overwhelming to face the fact that bunches of people were living together in one body, my body.

People who experience multiple personalities differ from those who do not in many other ways. Everyone must see themselves aging in the mirror, see the lines and the contours of the face change. People who experience multiplicity might have recurring experiences where they are completely unfamiliar with the reflection in the mirror or where parts of their bodies are not recognizable. This phenomenon has varying dimensions. One woman I met sees nothing in the mirror, no reflection, nothing; there is a complete void. I had a different experience. I asked my boyfriend one time, "Do you ever see your sister when you look in the mirror?" "Huh?" he replied. I often asked him questions like this. I am certain he thought I was nuts, the rambling of some hysterical, crazy woman. Before I ever knew of my multiplicity, I would pass by the mirror and see my brother. I would see him so clearly it was eerie. It wasn't similar characteristics I saw, but him, in the flesh. I would do double takes as I passed by the mirror, just to make sure he wasn't *really* in the bathroom. I had no contact with him and he lived two thousand miles away, so it was highly unlikely he would ever be there. But I still looked. I would also see a teenager reflected back in the mirror whom I did not recognize. She had real cool hair and hip clothes; she seemed like a bad-ass. I would joke with friends that Harley Girl was my alter ego. My friends didn't realize though that I actually *saw* Harley in the mirror. Ever since I can remember, looking in the mirror has been like something from a sci-fi film. There was always someone looking back at me, and it wasn't me. Most everyone who experiences multiplicity has similar stories. Multiplicity affects every aspect of our being; it is a reflection not only of the horrific abuse we have suffered, but also of the many courageous ways we learned to protect and save ourselves.

Resistance and the Body

As much as the body becomes a conduit and target of heinous violence, survivors find courageous and creative ways to resist. Victims of abuse act in self-defense against their assailants in many different ways. Memoirs of the abused illustrate the complex ways people use their bodies during conditions rendering them powerless—refusing to eat or overeating, kicking and biting, self-mutilation. When small children attempt to resist, it is an act of bravery and courage beyond compare. Sarah Olson writes of her own resistance, "Throughout the years, I resisted Ron's brutality in every way imaginable. I bit him, kicked, screamed, and ran away at every opportunity. This resulted in my being tied up for hours. . . . I resisted in ways he would never discover but were meaningful to me."[27] Sometimes all the survivor has left is the knowledge that she at least tried to resist the violence and terror. "There is a freedom in knowing, regardless of the result, that I did everything possible to not be a victim, and to maintain some small form of control in dangerously unpredictable circumstances."[28] Many of these responses and resistance strategies have the effect of harming oneself further, but they can simultaneously bring relief, however temporary.

In the following pages I discuss some of the most common forms of resistance utilized by both children and adults to fend off or ease abusive situations. Sometimes these strategies are used unconsciously, and it is only in retrospect that we can understand the various ways we attempted to resist abuse.

Overpowering the aggressor and using weapons are but a couple of ways to resist assault. One way to understand the ways females particularly resist oppressive conditions in their lives is to put into context how females are socialized to act. In our culture (and many others), females have been trained to "freeze" as both a fear and anger response.[29] In other words, females are frequently taught to suppress anger and fear, whereas males are more apt to be taught to defend and protect themselves physically. The effect of these social norms is the increased likelihood that females can be victimized, since freezing is tantamount to immobility and potential greater harm. At times, however, this initial act of freezing may actually save someone's life. Remaining silent and not moving are the very acts that kept me from being suffocated by my brother and tortured by the adults in the basement. When I split off mentally during the abuse, part of me stayed trapped and immobilized through the assault, while other parts of me actively worked with the aggressor to minimize and eliminate the pain. Freezing became an active form of self-defense; it was a way for me to feel power in a terrifying situation. Gaining more power through our bodies, however we do it, is a courageous act of survival and determination.

People use their bodies to resist abusive conditions in other ways. One seriously compromising effect of childhood trauma is self-mutilation. Self-mutilation takes many forms, such as starving, cutting, beating, and maiming ourselves, each an attempt to gain control over paralyzing and frightening situations. Such behaviors can be, paradoxically, a way to self-soothe and a form of self-punishment. In most cases, it is a means to leave the reality of the physical body. Sue William Silverman explains the relationship she had with her body from a childhood filled with incest:

> I have an eating disorder and a sexual addiction. With food, I'm mostly anorectic, addicted to starvation in order not to feel, to numb-out. I watch my body grow thinner than light. No one can touch it or see it. It's a gray wisp, barely visible, refracting particles of light. I have no limbs, no torso, no heart, no stomach, no mouth. I can sleep inside a leaf or between petals of a flower. My body becomes a curl of wind. Yet if I *am* the wind, I command the leaves and flowers, direct their course. By starving, I believe I am strong, not weak. I am the only one who can control what I will eat. I am the only one who will control the fate of my body.[30]

It is understandable that people who have been severely abused are prone to self-mutilation. Eating disorders, particularly for females, are a likely result.[31]

Many people diagnosed with DID begin cutting, a form of self-mutilation where a person cuts on herself as a psychological and physical escape from what's happening inside. People with DID exhibit high rates of cutting. I wrote the following about cutting during a psychiatric hospitalization:

> – SOMEONE'S CRYING, tears of profound grief, tears of horror, intense and utter pain. So much catastrophe, unbearable chaos. So much anger and rage, so much hatred and so much of this directed at self—self disgust, contempt, pure loathing for surviving and not having the courage to end it, loathing for remembering, loathing for learning to cope, complete disgust for escaping without anyone knowing. It's being so good at the game that you aren't even aware of it.

– We are survivors. Yet we hate ourselves and we hate what we've become. We hate our very existence. Such a paradox because we worked so hard to get through it, to withstand the torture and humiliation, to try to win an unwinnable fight. Yes, we survived. But we hate that we made it, hate that we continue to fight. Because part of us wants it all to end, to end not just the struggle of dealing with all this, but the fight itself. Because the fight is almost as bad as what made us this way in the first place. We're all reliving a hell, a nightmarish existence. Yet we still fight as if we can ever really win. And we hate the world, hate ourselves, all the way through it. We've learned to hate because for us love was distorted, always with a cost too high a price to pay, a price we paid anyway. We kept paying, hoping we'd get the love we saw on T.V., read about in books, saw in other families. We paid with our bodies, our minds, our selves and our very souls. We keep asking ourselves, "Why me?" and never find an answer. The depths of our beings believe, without any doubt, it all could have been different.

– So why do we cut ourselves? We could have ended the torment long ago with a real good slash of the wrist or a gun shot through the head. But because we chose to fight, wanting all along to be connected, feel connected, finally get the love from the very people who terrorized us, we also chose to take them on, to take their good along with their bad. They taught us how to hate ourselves, how to loathe our very existence, feel horrendous shame, complete disgust and deep despair. We cut ourselves to make it stop. We cut ourselves because we've learned to hate. We cut ourselves because it's the ultimate choice we have in this world—to live or die, be in our bodies or not. Because parts of ourselves left, created new people and voices. Cutting is a way to bring it all back, make us bleed, make us be one. It's the ultimate act of Self. Of course we cut ourselves. Because there is constant conflict about what to do and how to do it. And there will always be resentment that we lived,

that we endured. As much as some of us take pride in this endurance, we despise our survival. We try to harm ourselves to keep the balance. It's yin and yang, cause and effect, the teeter-totter principle. As twisted as it is, we both love and loathe ourselves. And our actions reflect this.
– For me cutting seems like cocaine: once you get started it's hard to stop and you just keep wanting more. Talking with women who cut, carve, and engage in other potentially lethal behaviors I learned that, for a brief moment, it does relieve pain and even feels good. And it's a rush. It brings on the feelings of oneness, and for a time it makes them feel like they really own their bodies. Things we never had growing up. I fear what cutting could do to me: its possible irreversible effects and becoming addicted. And while sometimes the most powerful thing we can do is to take our own lives, to make the pain or voices stop permanently, I choose every day to live, to not even tempt the fates that cutting might bring. I, too, sometimes want to end this tormented existence in which I find myself, really finalize it because sometimes it's just too much and the fight just doesn't seem worth it. But I'm addicted to the fight and I don't think I could stop it even if I wanted to. Cutting might stop that for me. A survivor's instinct you might say. Others of us are simultaneously addicted to self-destruction. And, for them, it is just as instinctive. Cutting scares the shit out of me, scares me because I don't know how much self control I really have, how much drive to live I really have, how long I can keep up this fight. Cutting makes sense to me, it's the teeter-totter principle. What makes less sense to me is those, like myself, who choose not to mutilate themselves through cutting.

The pain and chaos inside one's body and mind might be excruciating, and cutting, carving, and other forms of self-harm are ways to produce on the outside what we feel on the inside. Michelle in *The Courage to Heal* writes, "And so, sobbing, I just picked up handfuls of poison oak and rubbed it into my skin from head to toe. After doing that I felt better. There was always a release with the carving—and this time with the poison oak—because somebody on the outside could see the pain that was a constant on the inside."[32] Sometimes these self-inflicting acts seem like the only solution. Of course, this solution is only temporary, but more important, the effects can be fatal. Ultimately, such behavior is a letdown, taking a physical, emotional, and spiritual toll on the self.

Cutting, carving, and other forms of self-mutilation can help us to understand the depths of a survivor's torment. Yet sometimes these forms of self-mutilation aren't nearly enough. There are so many complex reasons why someone would want to kill themselves. But suicide isn't always about wanting to kill yourself. Some of us just want to go to sleep and not wake up again. Others want to hurl themselves out a two-story window or down a bunch of pills to make the pain stop. People living with multiple personalities have complex reasons for thinking about, attempting, or carrying out suicide. During a psychiatric hospitalization I was given a diagnostic assessment about suicide and self-harm:

> – THE PSYCHOLOGIST just asked me a bunch of questions about suicide. Her list was so detailed—how, when, why, under what circumstances. I was shocked and terrified by my own answers. I don't want to die. But I know I'm capable of harming myself, killing myself. And I'm scared because I know what it feels like to want to cut off all my hair, stab myself with scissors, jump out of a two-story window and hope my neck snaps. The feelings are so intense—the anger, rage, repulsion, self-hatred, the anguish and despair. It gets so loud in my head, so much noise. And my skin hurts. So I furiously and frantically fight to get out of my skin, escape the torment and terror. I yank my hair to feel myself, because I'm far away and I want to come back. I want to hurt myself to remind myself I'm alive, make me come back from wherever it is I've gone. Because I go to a place that's far away, a place that's very scary where I'm alone in the darkness. I can't hear anyone, see anyone,

can't touch or smell anyone. Completely lost and alone, completely outside myself.

I realized then that suicide was an option for not just me but for several of my alters as well. It wasn't about killing myself, but about trying to make the excruciating pain stop.

While many of us engage in self-mutilating behaviors, we simultaneously learn how to numb ourselves to pain and torture. In adulthood, numbing ourselves can become a necessary coping mechanism during times of stress but can also become part of our day-to-day life. Staying numb is a way to avoid the feelings and deny the extent to which abuse is affecting our lives. Sometimes, however, staying numb is a way to avoid further physical traumatic stress reactions. For me it has been a constant battle to balance the numbing feelings with all the chaos in my head:

– I HAVE WHAT FEELS LIKE STATIC going on in my head. it's all the time and i'm afraid to tell anyone about it. it's not like i hear voices or anything. but there's static as if someone is trying to converse with me, sending me cryptic messages from far away places. plus the noises in my ears and the constant ringing are so loud. sometimes it even hurts like i have an earache. and my poor head. the top of my head is constantly bruised and often feels like it's in a vise being flattened like a pancake. people wonder how i can numb-out so easily. try feeling what i feel for a minute or two and they'd know why. numbing is a hell of a lot better than this shit.

At times I invite and embrace the numbness because the pain throughout my body and the chaos in my head are just too agonizing to bear.

Numbing isn't necessarily thorough or complete. Parts of the body can be dead or feel dead, while other parts may be lying dormant and waiting for the opportune time to strike. Other parts of the body may be numb and completely disassociated. I simultaneously can feel each of these sensations at any given time. It takes an immeasurable amount of concentration for me to feel and experience my body. And even when I feel it, it is only parts and still not even most of it. At other times I get disconnected from certain parts of my body. For example, I may be cut in half at the waist and unable to feel from the waist down. Or maybe I won't feel my legs or my back but still feel the chill in my feet. Sometimes my head gets completely cut off, and other times just the top of my head goes numb. Disembodiment is felt literally for people with DID—by definition this is multiplicity. It is during these times that I wish I could feel more pleasure and more complete in my body. Part of what helped me to regain positive and pleasurable tactile and sensory experiences was a committed effort to reclaim what rightfully belonged to me: my own body.

Body Therapies: Finding Relief, Gaining Solidarity

In addition to psychotherapy, body therapies are an important therapeutic aspect to restoring the damaged cells caused by trauma.[33] Therapeutic massage, biofeedback, yoga, martial arts, swimming and light exercise, and sessions with a noninvasive chiropractor provide opportunities for increased connection with our bodies. And sometimes we just need relief because we feel so battered and sore. Even the simplest acts like taking a bath or going for a swim become excruciatingly difficult. I remember the first time I went swimming after a couple of years. A friend invited me over to her pool because it was a really hot day. It was a grand achievement getting in my swimsuit and an even greater achievement getting in the water and moving my body. It felt so wonderful to move so freely, and I cried at the simple delight of it. Our bodies feel like toxic waste dumps that we want and need to discard and avoid. Reconnecting with ourselves becomes profoundly necessary and even lifesaving.

Post-traumatic stress symptoms might leave one feeling vulnerable and on sensory overload. Bright lights, touches, and every sound may feel extreme. The last thing you might want to do is accentuate any aspect of your body, such as get in a swimsuit or let a massage therapist touch you. And when you've been taken advantage of and abused for most of your life, it may be difficult to accept love and intimacy from another, even if the person is compassionate and trustworthy. On top of all this, healthy personal boundaries are rarely learned in severely abusive and dysfunctional families. Even in situations where the abuse took place outside the home, the survivor may not learn what healthy boundaries are. Any touch can become magnified and alarming. We doubt our intentions and desires, and we doubt even further our own judgments and perceptions about trusting others:

> – MY BODY WAS STOLEN FROM ME all my life, in my home, with boyfriends, in my workplaces. what does it mean to touch someone in a healthy way, to have appropriate touching? i try now to hear my body when it can speak. mostly it stays numb though. mostly i can't listen because i'm afraid of what it will say. mostly when it speaks i feel the pain in my stomach and back from being pinned to linoleum tile, the horrid taste i have in my child's mouth from a man's ejaculation. sometimes my body is quiet though, and it wants to be touched. not sex kind of touching, just gentle caresses. like someone should have done when i was growing up. but how am i supposed to trust anyone to touch me like that?

We stop trusting our intuition and get involved with people who continue to harm us because we are unable to discern and create healthy boundaries. The suffering of many survivors is exacerbated by the fact that they never learned how to reach out to the right people or how to love and take care of their bodies in healthy ways.

Discovering healthy outlets for the many emotions we experience in a given day can be extremely beneficial and especially healing to our battered and worn-out bodies. Every time I move in healthy ways, another toxin is released from my body. This knowledge helps keep things in perspective. Bodies need to heal, just as our minds and spirits need to heal. Yet healing does not have to happen in isolation. The physicality of the body, through gestures, touch, and other actions, can bring people together and link them in solidarity, just as it can tear them apart through violence and fear. But sometimes our life experiences don't lend themselves to simple intimacy with others. Fearing hugs by a fellow patient, Marya Hornbacher explains, "Contact with another body reminds you that you have a body, a fact that you are trying very hard to forget."[34] Yet it was this very physical contact and gesture of intimacy that helped Hornbacher survive during a hospitalization for her eating disorder. Although Hornbacher herself wasn't a victim of child abuse, the trauma she suffered with having a life-threatening eating disorder was immense. Her situation is similar to many who have been severely traumatized: it becomes excruciatingly difficult to accept even a simple touch by another.

Kindness and the intimacy of soft and caring touch can have the effect of building community and solidarity in situations that are extremely isolating. Libby K. in *Multiple Personality Disorder from the Inside Out* explains:

> I would have others know how even the smallest kindness, the softest, seemingly meaningless touch of a hand, can actually mean the difference between life and death. . . . I want others to take an unflinching look at the reality of our past and present lives and be willing to stretch out a hand. That hand might, in the moment, mean the difference between being able or not being able to continue the battle against the dragon.[35]

Community can be found in the most unlikely places.

Isolation is not just an individual problem; it is a serious social malady whereby scores of abused people are ignored, silenced, and disregarded regularly by major social institutions. Shamed by the stigma of multiple personalities, silenced by society's ignorance, and fearful of negative reactions from others, hundreds of thousands of people with DID are completely isolated in their struggles to survive and heal. Many lack support of family and friends, have totally inadequate or no professional help, are unable to care for themselves on a daily basis, and are unable to afford decent housing or necessary medications. Far too many lack the political, social, and economic power or resources to make significant changes in their lives. To make sense of how people with DID are treated, we must understand the role of social institutions in creating such conditions in the first place.

4 Women, Children, and Trauma

A Societal Perspective

> I believe there is a cultural denial of incest as strong as my personal one. . . . This cultural denial exists for many of the same reasons that my denial existed, to protect the perpetrators, to protect the power system, to protect ourselves from facing ugly truths, to create a comforting fantasy for ourselves that "People don't do such things," or "We don't have these problems." . . . No one who has been through incest or rape wants to claim a past that makes her feel so personally soiled and victimized.
>
> —Helen Bonner, *The Laid Daughter: A True Story*

Scores of people, especially women and children, are currently living in terribly abusive conditions. Millions more remain haunted by their painful pasts. Many theories attempt to explain how and why so much violence and abuse is directed at women and children. In this chapter I offer an explanation that has been extremely beneficial to me in my own recovery: Violence against women and children is possible because social institutions perpetuate practices that degrade and harm women and children in such a way that masks the insidiousness of the problem. Social institutions are established structures that help keep certain behaviors and practices organized and operating. The government, the media, schools, the medical establishment, and religious organizations are social institutions. The family is another major social institution. While there may be many different types of families, e.g., single-parent families, foster families, or two-parent families, the family is considered the primary unit of social relations; it is an institution. Institutions engender shared values and practices. Practices such as the inequality between the sexes, inequality between adults and children, and cultural shame and denial lay the foundation for millions of people to be abused and silenced each day; it is the basis on which trauma-related psychiatric problems develop.

When we can step back from our own personal struggles to see a bigger picture, that is, the societal context in which we live, we can then understand better why so many of us are suffering:

> — I CAN'T BELIEVE no one knew. all the teachers and scout leaders, my mom's friends, neighbors, our relatives, friends' parents, our family doctor. how could five children be subjected to such cruelty without anyone knowing? it doesn't make sense. at least one person had to suspect something. but where were they and why didn't they help? instead we were forced to do really ugly things, forced to watch each other get screamed at and beaten, forced to keep quiet, forced to pretend everything was fine. well, it wasn't fine. and all you adults out there who may have thought something was wrong but didn't do anything, well you're to blame, too. because you let these things happen to me, my brothers and my sisters, and you didn't do anything about it. your silence kept the abuse happening. what a horrible society this is for not teaching people any better!

Child abuse in individual homes, and behind closed doors of day care centers, rectories, and teacher's classrooms, happens when we, as a society, tolerate it. Individually we are socialized to consider certain behavior private. What happens in homes, for example, is considered by our government and other social institutions to be private family matters, with the result that little children are beaten and tortured without anyone noticing. In rectories we expect priests and ministers to protect and care for our children. Individuals are given little room to question those in authority or to intervene when we even mildly suspect abusive conditions in someone's life. Child abuse is a deeply disturbing societal problem needing immediate solutions from each institution.

Personal experiences of abuse aren't just personal after all—they are political and far-reaching. Child abuse isn't just about an abuser and the abused, because everyone who comes into contact with either of these people is affected. The harm, betrayal, and lies extend throughout individual families into our neighborhoods, communities, and social institutions; abuse spreads like wildfire. What happens to one person, or in this case millions of people, happens to all of us either directly or indirectly. Personal healing is similar in that as one person heals, others are positively affected as well. *As we learn to heal as individuals, we can then realize our personal healing is very political: we heal for the many lost and abandoned souls, and we aid in the healing of society.* This perspective can be empowering, and it is for this reason alone that this chapter is paramount.

Millions of people each year suffer from trauma-related disorders because of severe childhood abuse, including dissociative identity disorder, post-traumatic stress disorder, eating disorders, and depression. The majority of people who develop PTSD, a condition most of us relate to combat veterans, are female rape and abuse victims.[1] The primary cause of DID is extreme, repetitive, and prolonged child abuse. However individual PTSD and DID may seem—and by this I mean that people individually suffer and live with these conditions—trauma-related disorders are, most acutely, a collective and societal issue. *Such conditions are the result of the systematic degradation, violence, and exploitation of women and children.* Systematic means the cruelty is not isolated or random; it is purposeful and direct.

It is understandable that survivors of severe child abuse frequently ask, "Why me?" Unfortunately, there is not an adequate answer to the questions "Why me personally?" or "Why my family or neighborhood?" But there is an answer if we can frame the question differently: "Why *all* of us?" It is not sufficient that we ask and demand answers solely about the conditions of our own personal lives. We must begin to recognize the *systematic nature* of violence, trauma, and psychological distress among the millions of survivors of these atrocities. There are specific reasons why females especially are at high risk of violent assault and sexual abuse, and that children are the target of adult and older youth aggression. In this chapter I demonstrate how three major social institutions in society—the government, religious institutions, and the medical establishment—perpetuate and even cause the suffering of scores of people every day.

There is a direct connection between the conditions in society that create and sustain widespread violence directed primarily at women and children and the horrifying personal accounts of child abuse survivors. In "The Rat's Nest," Lisa Poupart writes of her own familial abuse:[2]

It's ok if she pulls my hair
it's only a rat's nest

Go on
Admit what you do

Slap them in anger
Shove them in pain
Hurt your poor babies
like they did to you
calling them
stupid
  worthless
    no good

Throw them in
showers
crack open their heads
seven stitches
an entrance for hate
like you carry
      for
        those
          who hurt you

Make pageant costumes
send cookies to school

buy another puppy
to cover your trail

While you beat with
wire hangers
red welts
across backs

When you pick up
the belt
that lashes their souls
do you ever think twice
about wounds beneath bruises
the source of the screams

deny it
until my clone
starts a fire
runs away from your home

Maybe one day you'll feel it
when she sits at twenty-six
writes a poem of rage
or beats your own grandkid
for burning her toys
while you made her watch

Will you wonder
when they have grown old
why they never come back
to the kitchen of lies
terrorizing with
  hands
    words
while baking fruit pies

Abused repeatedly by her father, told she was worthless and stupid, a mother pulverizes her children because she cannot bear the pain and torment of her own existence. There are so many families living double, or even triple, lives: the public face of a loving nuclear family, the private face of brutality, rage, and fear. Economic expectations, social standing, and misguided beliefs about what it means to be American—the conditions that foster abuse against women and children—continue to escalate.

Abusive conditions happen in a context: a society that allows violence and degradation to be a part of millions of people's everyday lives. The ideologies and cultural practices that support the inequality between females and males, and between children and adults, are the norms that allow child abuse and family violence to occur. Such norms force abused women and children into dark, secret places, unable to disclose the horrors of their lives. To understand the role of society in maintaining conditions of abuse, we must first explore the unequal relationships between females and males, and between children and adults.

Inequality between the Sexes

We live in an unequal society where men hold and wield the majority of power. What do I mean? Men own and control every major political, economic, and social institution. As of 2002:

- Women held less than 14 percent of the seats in the U.S. Congress, yet made up half of the general population.
- Men were the CEOs of all but two Fortune 500 companies, even though women made up almost half of the labor force.
- School principals and boards of trustees were disproportionately male.
- Medical schools, hospitals, and hospital boards were predominately male-owned and operated.
- Mass media, including television, print, and radio, were overwhelmingly male-owned.

Men have access to political, social, and economic power in a way that women do not. Racial and class differences exacerbate this inequality.

In other words, it is primarily *white men* that hold key leadership positions; women of color and the poor, especially, are disadvantaged.

It matters that men are in charge because research shows significant gender differences in how men and women are socialized to behave, think, and express themselves.[3] When more than half of the population is left disadvantaged economically, politically, and socially, they become vulnerable and susceptible to abusive conditions. An individual mother and her child are much more vulnerable in an abusive household where the husband is the primary breadwinner. Economic conditions and the reality of poverty frequently force women to stay in abusive situations, or in some cases to participate in illegal acts, because they are unable to afford to live alone.[4]

White men hold the majority of power and have control over major institutions because as a society there are unequal relationships between men and women, between whites and people of color, and between the rich and poor. This does not mean that some women don't have control over men or that some men aren't battered and hurt by women. Inequality between the sexes means that females, *as a group of people and by virtue of the fact they are female,* are considered less essential than and subordinate to males. Females are hurt *because* they are female; in many cases they are hurt because they are also poor and of color.[5] Females are significantly disadvantaged by institutions in many ways, and this hurts all of us. The following are a few examples:

1) *The workplace:* Women receive unequal pay for the exact same job; there are fewer numbers of women in key management positions; females receive fewer workplace benefits; and labor continues to be segregated where men's work is paid more. According to the U.S. Census Bureau, women working full-time earn seventy-three cents for every dollar earned by men. African-American women earn sixty-four cents, and Latinas earn fifty-two cents for every dollar paid to their white male counterparts.[6]
2) *Mainstream television:* Television shows and movies continue to depict females as helpless and vulnerable; females are sexualized and degraded in the name of humor; and sexual violence against females continues to be a predominant theme. So while we tell girls they can do anything that boys can, they are reminded regularly that this isn't the case.[7]

3) *Schools:* Teachers continue to promote gender stereotypes in the classroom; fields of study are promoted differently for girls and boys; and sexual harassment of girls at school is commonplace. Studies show how teachers continue to spend more time with their male students and call on boys first and more often. As children age, gender discrimination increases. Unequal power relations between males and females, and between adults and children, provide the basis for systematic mistreatment, inequality, and abuse.[8]

Gender inequality has been going on for centuries in most parts of the world.[9] In the late 1700s, nonindigenous women were considered personal property of men and denied many rights: they were not able to go to school, own property, vote, or even speak in public. Men, by law, were allowed to hit women and children. Women were denied access to political, social, and economic resources. Social change for women has not occurred without massive grassroots and national movements by dedicated, impassioned people. As a result of this activism, in 1920, about 150 years after the Declaration of Independence was signed, the Nineteenth Amendment was finally passed, guaranteeing a woman's right to vote and hold major office. The 1960s saw another wave of feminist movement and the political organization of hundreds of thousands of women. More and more women made their personal lives public by demanding "the personal is political." Laws were passed, although not the equal rights amendment, to allow women more economic, political, and social opportunities. Despite all this work, females continue to be disadvantaged and violated in insidious ways. When an entire group is considered less important or worthy than another, horrible things can happen repeatedly to the group without much notice or concern. And even when there is concern, the values that keep this group subordinate remain intact.

When females and males have a more equal footing with each other, there will be less violence directed at females *because it will no longer be tolerated.* Females are hit and beaten on a regular basis by men because we, as a society, do not regard females with the same sort of esteem and respect as males. This is not to say that males aren't also violated or that females aren't abusive themselves. Nor does this analysis suggest that battery and assault is absent from same-sex relationships. It means, instead, that *the violence directed at females is systematic and purposeful; it happens because they are female.* While most people would say that women and men should have, or already do have, equal rights, it is not part of our collective conscience. In other words, in the back of our minds, many believe females are weaker than males and are dependent on males for protection. This consciousness translates into females seeking dependency from males and males wanting to protect females, however unrealistic this may be. It is part of how we think as a mass culture and, therefore, part of how we think and act as individuals. It is fostered in our government through current social welfare laws that discriminate and harm single mothers and poor children. Sexual inequality provides the basis by which so much violence can happen in the context of families and against children.

Children are denied equal status with adults by virtue of their age and size alone. Anyone who has been abused in childhood probably recognizes that children as a group are disregarded and violated by adults regularly. More than likely she understands that the abuse happened because she was small and vulnerable, completely dependent on adults, and, for too many reasons, no one was either willing or able to stop the abuse. Repeatedly molested by her foster father, Bella Moon describes herself as a child through the eyes of her older self:

> Obviously the child had been frightened into lifelong silence, not only by the thing upstairs but by a suspicion that she had had something to do with all of it, something sinister within herself, an alien presence that was herself. Yes, the silence was collusion with the adults who had violated her. She was protecting them. Already, at age six or seven, she knew the politics of survival. In order to survive, keep quiet, and remember—you saw it, and said nothing; you submitted, and said nothing. You did not raise a hand, you did not run. Above all, you do not tell your mother. The old woman wants to clasp the child and run. But there is no place to run to. One must stand in the sunshine and bear it.[10]

Children must "bear it" because there is little or no alternative; they are fully dependent on their caretakers for most, if not all, of their basic needs.

Child abuse continues because each institution condones and sometimes even applauds the violation of children. Most often done in the name of discipline or love, children are beaten and tortured because people think it is necessary. And although perpetrators of violence and abuse might feel guilty or ashamed of their actions, they justify it to themselves as reasonable and acceptable. Laws and moral edicts in certain religions support this justification. Children are disregarded and disrespected not only by their abusers but by most of society as well. Just as there is a long-standing history of the inequality between the sexes, there is a continuous history of the subordination of children. *Every institution in society is responsible for the creation and maintenance of conditions that make child abuse possible.*

In the following pages, I illustrate how three different social institutions are culpable for child abuse and violence against women: the government, religious institutions, and the medical establishment. Through these examples we can begin to see patterns in the ways females and children are regarded and treated by powerful institutions. Such analysis allows us to think more critically about our individual lives and how these patterns affect us personally. The examples I provide are not isolated themes but happen each and every day throughout every institution. When we ask ourselves how a single doctor can be treating us so badly, we are also asking how the profession itself is treating scores of other females in a similar way. We empower ourselves anytime we can step outside our own personal situation to see a bigger picture; ultimately, we become conduits for social change.

The Federal Government

Violence is a practice widely condoned throughout every major social and political institution. Our federal government declares it unlawful for individuals to murder people, yet the government itself is not held to this standard. There are instances, such as the death penalty and police shootings, when killing someone is permissible.[11] So as we admonish certain forms of violence, as a society we support others. The examples are endless: sports violence, corporal punishment in homes and schools, military aggression, television and movie violence, and the legality of guns. There are marked inconsistencies with how, when, where, and under what circumstances violence is tolerated or even applauded. We condone violence by failing as a collective society to stop all forms of it. *We accept a level of abuse and violence in our everyday lives, and this is adversely affecting our children.*

In this section I discuss the history of child welfare and argue that the state of abused children today is a reflection of that history. The government has failed to adequately care and protect dependent children, i.e., children for whom the government is responsible, such as those in the foster care system, juvenile detention, and prison.[12] When the government is unable or unwilling to adequately protect its most vulnerable citizens, it says something outrageous about its social and political priorities. Family violence, particularly child abuse, provides evidence of a society that condones violence and the oppression of children.

Child Welfare

Certain attitudes and practices within all major institutions, particularly the government, adversely affect the welfare of children. The government, through laws and social policies, sets the standard for how citizens are treated. In the U.S., we have federal and state systems to help fund and treat abused, neglected, and abandoned children. We can learn a great deal about how children are viewed and regarded by specifically examining the foster care system.

This country has a long-standing history of child welfare, orphanages, and foster care.[13] The first U.S. government–sponsored institutions for the poor, sick, and mentally ill were called almshouses and first opened in the late 1700s. Initially, almshouses cared for mostly women, including pregnant women and girls abandoned by their husbands. Over time, the number of children residing in almshouses increased as poor and sick parents with children had nowhere else to go. During the period 1880 to 1920, over seventy-five thousand children resided in almshouses.[14] The conditions of many almshouses were horrible—the sick failed to receive medical treatment, people went hungry, and the buildings themselves were not kept up. Almshouses became repositories for unwanted, neglected, and abandoned people, mostly women and children.

Poor and abandoned children were also found in children's asylums and orphanages. Considered temporary housing until children were placed into foster homes, by 1900 an estimated ninety-three thousand children lived in orphanages, primarily because of poverty.[15] The number of children living in orphanages reflected a particular mind-set: poor children were salvageable if taken away from their indigent parents and placed in orphanages where they could be nurtured and educated better. Ironically, most orphanages were in poor condition; kids were beaten and maltreated, forced to go hungry, and were not adequately cared for. Lack of funding and concern kept orphanages from functioning the way they were intended.

Foster care, or the placement of children away from their parents or guardians, has been practiced since the 1800s, but was rejuvenated when orphanages were found to be failing. Foster families would be paid a stipend to raise, care for, and educate impoverished and orphaned children. Initially, however, many children placed in foster homes were indentured, meaning they were expected to work for their keep, sometimes in horrible conditions. Moreover, placements became long-term rather than temporary. The mind-set about the poor continued, and the majority of those placed in foster care had parents and families living elsewhere. Racial minorities failed to be placed at all and remained in the worst kept orphanages. The presumption was that out-of-home placement and orphanages were better than children being raised by indigent parents.

By the early 1900s, a shift occurred when the federal government began to understand the importance of family preservation, i.e., keeping families together, and the inadequacy of current almshouses, orphanages, and foster care. In 1909 President Theodore Roosevelt convened a White House Conference on Children. The first of its kind, the convention focused on improving the lives of children, including offering mothers pensions with the idea that they should stay at home with their children. Three years later, with urging by the president, a Children's Bureau was created to combat the exploitation of children. The Social Security Act was enacted in 1935, establishing a national welfare program to provide funding and assistance to needy families, and Aid to Dependent Children, later renamed Aid to Families with Dependent Children or AFDC, was established. The government determined that poverty alone was no longer grounds to remove children from their homes; welfare allowed families to stay together. However, identifying and preventing child abuse, another important goal of the Social Security Act, became less of a priority.

It took decades for dependent and abused children to be prioritized on the national policy agenda. In 1974 significant federal legislation was passed, the Child Abuse Prevention and Treatment Act, to further assist abused and neglected children. Federal money became available to identify, prevent, and stop child abuse. The Adoption Assistance and Child Welfare Act of 1980 helped to increase the number of children being adopted and to help keep struggling families together. For a brief period, it appeared as though children's rights had become a national priority.

With the election of President Reagan, however, America began to assault single mothers and poor families through legislation and severe cuts in federal aid.[16] These government cuts caused hundreds of thousands of single mothers and their children to lose AFDC benefits, the primary source of funding for poor families. The effect was increased homelessness, poverty, and abuse. In 1996 the Personal Responsibility and Work Opportunity Reconciliation Act essentially abolished welfare and created Temporary Assistance for Needy Families (TANF).[17] Federal funds, in the form of block grants, are now provided to states under the TANF program to develop and implement their own "welfare" programs. What does this mean? More than five million children are affected by TANF annually, and less than two million are in proper day care because parents, mostly single mothers, are unable to pay for it. TANF work requirements are such that although scores of people are now in the workforce, families' earnings are below poverty levels; people working full-time jobs are unable to clothe, feed, and care for their children. The Welfare Reform Act has thrown more single mothers into poverty and has put them at risk for domestic violence situations and incarceration.[18] Woefully lacking in this legislation are additional supports necessary for those who work in poverty-level jobs, such as child care, transportation, and educational assistance. So while our nation may embrace the importance of families, single mothers and their children are undeniably excluded.

The foster care system continues to be ineffective and inhumane for thousands of children. The current system works to assist troubled families by temporarily placing children into foster families or group homes. The conditions of many foster homes continue to be appalling. Children are battered and abused and shuffled from one foster family or home to another. Children are placed in foster care for various reasons. Parents may be unable to care for their children because of homelessness or drug addiction, or they may be abusive or neglectful and need help in parenting. Discrimination persists, and children of color and the poorest of children are more readily taken from their homes. Many children spend years in foster homes, never living with a "family" again. Others are placed as many as a dozen or more times in foster families, where they can be transferred to a new family or back in a foster home at any time without notice. In a recent study of California's Department of Social Services, the agency responsible for administering foster care in that state, serious problems were found with length of placements, abuse in foster homes, and increased abuse when returned to families. Once taken from their families, California children spend over two years being shuffled between different foster homes.[19] Federal investigations into current foster care practices will undoubtedly show the massive abuse and neglect going on within the system itself. Unfortunately, we can see the cumulative effects of long-term placement of children: the numbers of youth in juvenile detention and adult prisons, the continued cycles of poverty and abuse, and the long-term psychological harm toward children in the system. Long-term placement in foster homes and the placement of kids in multiple foster families can have enormously devastating consequences for children. This was the case two hundred years ago, and it remains the same today.

When considered historically, the federal government has not been responsible for abused and dependent children for very long and the government's track record on protecting dependent children is seriously neglectful. Certain historical trends have persisted:[20]

1) Today, an estimated twelve million children live in poverty, where parents and guardians receive inadequate government assistance to afford decent housing, medical care, food, or decent child care.
2) More than a half million children were living in foster care as of 1999, with over one hundred thousand waiting to be adopted.
3) Racial minorities continue to be overrepresented in the foster care system. Of the children in foster care in 1999, 42 percent were black, 15 percent were Hispanic, and the remaining 43 percent were of "other racial and ethnic origins."
4) While African-American children make up 42 percent of children

in foster care, over 56 percent are waiting for adoption. In other words, white children remain the most likely to be adopted.

5) Foster care remains a long-term situation for scores of children; the average time a child stays in the foster care system prior to adoption is almost four years.

We have failed to learn and respond appropriately to our own history and neglect of children. When the government abuses children through neglect and inadequate care, so too can individual families. Government actions influence individual behavior.

The government's lack of attention and protection for dependent children and its tolerance for children in poverty is one indication of how children overall are treated and regarded. Ultimately, it is the government who is responsible for caring for children when families aren't able to. If the government is unable to protect children in its care, how in the world can it protect *all* abused and neglected children? Sarah Olson asks about her own abuse, "How did it happen that two sisters were systematically abused, tortured, exploited, and neglected for years with no one taking notice? In part, it was due to the randomness of it all."[21] While abuse on a personal level may seem arbitrary and random, on a societal level it is systematic, far-reaching, and constant. Governmental neglect is partly responsible for the condition of children, both historically and today. The government has a long-standing history of failing to respond adequately to children's needs and their suffering. This provides a trace of evidence that the eradication of child abuse remains a low priority for the federal government. Clearly, radical change is needed.

Female Battery

Through particular ideologies and practices, the government has also insufficiently responded to violence in the home. In chapter 2 I discussed several forms of family violence, including child abuse and sibling abuse. In this section I focus on female battery, i.e., violence perpetrated by males against females regardless of age, whether married or unmarried, or living together or not.[22] While all abuse is about unequal power relations, female battery is, by far, the most systematic of abuses between intimates. Female battery can take the form of physical abuse, emotional or psychological abuse, and/or sexual violence. Current U.S. statistics on female battery are alarming:[23]

1) Women are as much as ten times more likely to be victimized by intimate partner violence than men.
2) As many as two to four million women are assaulted by intimate partners each year.
3) Of the two million assaults that result in injury each year, close to six hundred thousand will require medical treatment, including emergency hospitalization.
4) Most assaults between intimate partners are never reported to the police. The primary reason the assaults are unreported is victims think the police couldn't or wouldn't do anything about it.
5) Forty percent of female victims of intimate partner violence live in households with children under age twelve.
6) Every day four women die in this country alone from domestic violence.
7) Women in the U.S. are five times more likely to be murdered than women in other industrialized countries; most of these murders are committed by a male intimate partner or relative.

These statistics force us to question how it is that so many females can be violated in their own homes without the government being more aggressive to stop it.

The effects of female battery and psychological abuse on women are severe, not only to the victim but also to those forced to watch it. Children forced to witness violence between caretakers frequently suffer with long-term behavioral, developmental, and emotional problems. For many it means an inability to form healthy relationships and the increased propensity for aggression.

Males can control females in battery situations because, in many cases, females are economically and emotionally dependent on them. Christine, an alter personality of Lynda Seeley, writes in a poem to a battered friend:[24]

There are no marks, I've looked
But then, a good lover
Never leaves marks

My muscles scream
The memory
Wrenched and taunting
Your emergency
Churns my brain
Burns

From the inside . . .

No suffocation compares
to a woman
too long in one body

the terror is

falling
before the fall

The suffocation a victim of abuse feels is both metaphorical and literal for far too many women.

Kathleen Ferraro, an expert and testimonial witness in wife battery cases, explains three distinct ways an abuser exerts control over his partner: increasing the isolation of the woman from loved ones, extreme possessiveness and jealousy, and monitoring her daily activities.[25] Psychological abuse is the most consistent and exacting way abusive males learn to dominate their partners. Females begin to feel helplessly trapped and perceive themselves as unable to cope on their own. Bonds develop between the victim and her abuser, making it all the more difficult to leave an abusive situation. Batterers capitalize on each of these forces to keep their partners in line. It is never as clear as, "He hit me, therefore I must leave." Not enough can be said about the courageous women who try to leave these abusive situations. Unlike popular myths about weak wives failing to leave their abusive husbands, *women do leave;* in most cases, however, women and children are threatened and further harmed if they go. Fear of retaliation makes it so females in battery situations are unable to leave.[26] Fortunately, there are thousands of domestic violence shelters around the country today, yet partly due to lack of funding, the shelters have substantial problems.[27] Millions of mothers and their children continue to remain in agonizing situations because help is unavailable or inadequate.

The government's response to female battery and sexual violence is abysmal. There are a limited number of legal options for those in such situations, including restraining orders and arrest, but many times the orders are ineffectual. Meant as a means to deter an abusive person, the order might antagonize an already volatile situation. Restraining orders are ineffectual in that threats, intimidations, and assaults continue despite the court ordering otherwise. So victimized women wait and hope that things will one day be better:

> – MY LIFE IS CONSUMED BY WAITING, waiting mostly for the next assault to happen. if there is one thing i know for sure, something bad is waiting around the corner . . . a punch to the groin with another flashback, a crowbar upside the head with petrifying night terrors. the waiting is torture. but there is something all-too familiar about it. it's waiting for another person to poke things up me, slap me around, smash a hand or pillow over my face, "shut up or you die."

Those with severe trauma-related disorders can understand the mentality of waiting. Most of us wait each day in the hopes that the next one will be better. As unrealistic as it may be, there is a continued sense, a feeling of hope, that surely things will change. But for the majority of women who find themselves in abusive situations, the violence only gets worse with time.

There often comes a point when the victim must decide whether to have her abuser arrested, and that decision can be excruciatingly difficult. Loyalty, shame, and guilt, the very emotions that keep children silent and trapped in abusive situations, also keep women from calling the police or soliciting help. Many women believe that the police won't or can't do anything. Moreover, battered women fear negative repercussions from their partners and their fears are well-founded. Although batterers may be taken into custody, very few are ever prosecuted; the result is increased intimidation, threats, and violence perpetrated against the woman.[28] When batterers are prosecuted, women and children are victimized further by the judicial system. Arresting batterers or getting restraining orders against violent and abusive people are only temporary solutions to wife battery. Why? Because the ideologies that allow wife battery and child abuse to occur remain intact. Illustrating how the government has yet to deal adequately with family violence is not sufficient unless we address *also* the underlying reasons why so much violence is perpetrated by males against females, and by adults against children, in the first place.

Theories abound about how to explain, address, and eradicate all forms of domestic violence, including wife battery and other intimate partner violence. Some explanations focus on perpetrator characteristics or the family itself. Other theories look at external factors that influence the family, such as stress, a bad economy, or the cycle of violence. Psychological explanations of sick perpetrators and dysfunctional families are important. We all know that the likelihood of abuse increases with an aggressive, angry, substance-abusing person. Most of us understand, as well, that children learn from their parents and caretakers, including teachers, priests, and other important adult authority figures. Experiencing violence, or even being a witness to it, increases the likelihood we will be abusive or further victimized (or both) in later life. We also know that stress and the inability to pay for essentials might influence someone to become abusive. But these sorts of explanations do not explain the systematic nature of violence in the everyday lives of females. The most compelling explanation to me to explain family violence is the cultural and institutional factors in society that allow for the systematic cruelty of millions of people to happen in the first place.

Family violence is symptomatic of a society that tolerates wide-scale abuse against vulnerable and less powerful people. As the ultimate system of law and governance, the federal government is responsible for ensuring that individuals are not violated and harmed. Child abuse and female battery occur because of attitudes and practices that continue to permeate major institutions. *Females are violated because they are female, children because they are children.* It is abuse against two often vulnerable populations lacking the economic, political, or social power to stop the terrorizing conditions. The government has yet to recognize its role in maintaining such sexist ideologies and practices, with the result that family violence is regarded as a low priority on the national agenda.

Many of us wonder how it can be that child abuse and female battery continue to escalate when government officials, e.g., police, courts, and legislators, know how pervasive it is. Sarah F. in *Multiple Personality from the Inside Out* explains how this can be:

> Many do not want to hear about the unspeakable horrors I have seen and heard, of the evil that is truly in this world, of the ABUSE. It makes them queasy, uncomfortable, unsure. Their eyes seem to glaze over. It is much easier to focus on the results of the ABUSE. Tell people you are a multiple and they are fascinated. Their imaginations unwind into fantasies of Eve, Sybil, Dr. Jekyll and Mr. Hyde, or demons and exorcism. The stuff movies are made of. Even so, multiples heal. But the cycle of abuse with its ramifications and ugliness remains firmly in place. As long as this present attitude abounds, there will continue to be multiples, because there will continue to be ABUSE. ABUSE we permit, by listening and not hearing, by talking but saying nothing, by not believing because it is unpleasant.[29]

Collectively we are remaining silent. Government inaction and ineffectiveness reinforce to both adults and children that kids can be disregarded and abused. People enact warfare and heinous abuse on children *because they can,* because no one is successfully stopping it, and because we continue to support ideologies that oppress children.

The government has the authority to prioritize issues and set the national political agenda for deciding what constitutes a crisis, an epidemic, or terrorist action. The federal government has called a war on drugs, a halt on illegal immigration, and more recently a war on terrorism. Billions of dollars are going out to these causes. Ironically, females in the U.S. are terrorized on a daily basis through physical violence, rape, sexual abuse, and the fear of assault, *yet there is no call against domestic sexual terrorism.*[30] Research has proven for three decades now that sexual assault and abuse are common experiences for most women and children, especially girls. For many it is fatal. When will there be a national call to stop the epidemic of child abuse and female battery? Clearly, current federal and state laws and policies are insufficient. By failing to protect children from abusive and terrifying conditions, the government helps to create and maintain the cycle of violence and abuse. Law enforcement, government social services, the courts, and criminal justice systems maintain conditions that make child abuse, and subsequent trauma-related disorders, possible. Who is to blame for the cycle of abuse? All of us, as Sarah F. points out, "By listening and not hearing, by talking and saying nothing, by not believing because it is unpleasant."

Religious Institutions

Religious institutions, such as the Roman Catholic Church, United Methodist Church, Southern Baptist Convention, and the Church of Jesus Christ of Latter-day Saints (Mormons), help to create and maintain conditions that allow child abuse to happen. Through the teachings of certain ideologies, religious indoctrination, and church practices, religious institutions have a tremendous amount of authority and presence in the lives of their congregations. Organized religions collectively are multibillion-dollar industries that help instill the belief in and conformity to particular philosophies, principles, and practices.

My primary religious experience is with the Roman Catholic Church. I was baptized as an infant, received my Holy Communion at age six, and was confirmed Catholic at age fourteen. I progressed through the sacraments like most Catholic children. I attended Catholic schools from second through fifth grades and all four years of high school. It was in high school when I realized I was not really Catholic. Perhaps it was the violent and class-oriented history of Catholicism or feeling brainwashed by anti-abortion videos. Maybe it was because I didn't think it right that my friends and I couldn't be altar girls or that women couldn't be priests. I think what finally did it were my readings on Eastern religions and philosophies that seriously challenged Catholicism. Needless to say, my Catholic upbringing has certainly left an impression on how I view all organized religion today.

There was a time when I felt very angry at and betrayed by the Catholic Church, holding it partly responsible for neglecting the abuses going on in my family. We lived in a small community, just one block from the Catholic school and one mile from the church. It amazed me that even the priests and nuns did not know something was terribly wrong in my family. It was a small congregation, so most everyone knew who we were. I was also angry because my uncle, a retired Catholic priest, molested me when I was a young girl. I later found out he abused my two sisters as well. My mother liked to visit Catholic churches when we were vacationing. I remember as a little girl standing in these huge, breathtaking cathedrals wondering how there could be so much poverty when the Roman Catholic Church was so wealthy. I held the church responsible for a number of things—poverty, child abuse, treating women badly. Some of these faults were rightly justified, others perhaps not.

I do not feel angry or betrayed any longer by the Catholic Church. What I am most concerned about today is how religious institutions and their practices and ideologies influence social, political, and economic conditions. Specifically, my focus is on how institutions, including religious institutions, affect abused children, their families, and child abuse perpetrators. The following examples demonstrate the many ways in which religious institutions as a whole can affect individuals and their families regarding child abuse. I want people to understand, too, that while my institutional experiences with organized religion are primarily with the Catholic Church, research shows that such examples can be found in most other religions as well.

Moral Principles Gone Askew

I used to be a good Catholic. I'd go to church each week, pray at night like I was supposed to, be a good girl, and go to confession. On confession day I'd stand there in line with all the other kids, waiting for my turn. I'd try to think of some new sin I committed, but it was tough since I really was a pretty good kid. So there were times I had to lie to the priest about what sins I committed since my last confession. Telling the priest I had no sins, or that my sin was lying in the confessional, was never an option. I would sit there squirming outside the confessional trying to figure out what to tell him. This particular day I decided to lie again. I confessed something like the following:

"I was mean to my brothers and sisters, and I said bad things to my mom." (This was one of my regulars.)

"What did you say to your mother?" He caught me off-guard because I realized I had nothing prepared about my mom; I had been ready to talk about my sister. Fortunately, I remembered an incident from the day before involving my brother and my mother's friend, one of our caretakers. In the most convincing way I could muster, I repeated to the priest exactly what my brother, Charlie, said to Maxine as if I had said it to my mother: "I hate you! Why are you so mean to us? Why do you hate us so bad?" I swear the priest chuckled.

"Hmm. You know, it's important to respect your elders, especially your parents. They're wiser than you, and take care of you, and they know what's best for you. Do you understand?"

"Yes, Father."

"Now, I want you to be a good girl and be kinder to your mother, OK?"

"OK, Father."

"Your mother works very hard to take care of you and things aren't always easy for her, you know that, right?"

"Yes, Father." At this point I am convinced he knows who I am; I feel humiliated and completely ashamed by my confession because now the priest thinks I hate my mom.

"Try to think good thoughts so things will be better."

"OK, Father."

"Say three 'Hail Mary's and one 'Our Father' and ask God to forgive you. . . ."

"Thank you, Father."

No priest ever asked me what my mother or any other adult did to provoke my saying I hated them. I even remember wondering why I could keep confessing the same things over and over without being questioned. Perhaps most adults assume kids are complainers and that they each, at some point, hate their parents or others in authority; or they assume kids are being melodramatic and overexaggerating the problem. Still, I came away from every confession feeling terribly guilty for so many things—for betraying my brother, for lying to the priest, for saying I hate my mom.

Confessions and sermons made me believe it was my duty to respect my parents and elders, no matter how abusive or demented they were. I believed that if Charlie was beaten by my father and Maxine, he must have deserved it. I believed good would triumph over evil. And I believed my good thoughts could change everything—that is what my mom *and* the priest said. The converse of this, of course, is that if things didn't change, then it was my fault since I wasn't acting or thinking good enough thoughts. The church instilled in me something much more terrifying than what my family did—the belief that I somehow controlled all of this. While the belief and practice of respecting one's elders may be moral and important, it may also have a deleterious effect on abused children.

Imagine the millions of abused children and adults involved with religious organizations who instill such similar principles. It is one thing to hear these beliefs from your own parents, a whole other to hear them from a minister or priest. For many young children, religious leaders are God themselves; they have an influence like no other. Think about all the other sorts of religious practices and ideologies that can affect the further oppression and abuse of kids: if you are loving, you will be loved; if you do good things, good will come back to you; men are the spiritual leaders of the family; virgins are pure; and hope can get you through anything. But having hope, for example, doesn't change the fact that a child is being raped by her uncle. It may only reinforce to her that the abuse is her fault, that she must not be hoping enough. I am not saying that all of these principles are wrong. My point is that uncritical submission to certain principles has the potential to exacerbate the suffering of abused children. Values, morals, and beliefs are learned predominately through religious indoctrination and then passed on to individuals through families. Religious institutions have a powerful influence over the everyday lives of hundreds of millions of people in this country alone.

The Policy of Silence

Religious institutions also maintain child abuse and the conditions that create it by certain administrative and leadership practices. In 2002 the Roman Catholic Archdiocese of Boston settled child molestation claims against at least seventy priests spanning over a decade.[31] John J. Geoghan, a priest in the diocese, was known by Church officials as a pedophile, yet was transferred several times to new parishes where he continued molesting children. More than 130 people to date have accused Geoghan of molesting them, and the Church has settled about fifty lawsuits totaling more than $10 million for Geoghan alone.

Now incarcerated, Geoghan molested many victims in a systematic and regular way. Perhaps the most disturbing aspect of the Geoghan case, as well as other cases involving clergy sexual abuse, is the role of church leadership in covering it up.

Nationwide, hundreds of victims are breaking the silence of clergy abuse. In New Hampshire, the Diocese of Manchester settled claims for seventy-eight victims involving over thirty-five priests for almost $6 million.[32] The attorney general of New Hampshire conducted an investigation into possible criminal charges against the Roman Catholic Church for violating state child endangerment laws. The Diocese of Providence settled a $13.5 million lawsuit involving thirty-six people sexually abused by clergy in various Rhode Island parishes.[33] Scores more child abuse cases are coming forward nationwide. Diocese officials knew of many of these molestations but failed to stop them. Worse, Church officials transferred suspected and known pedophiles to new parishes where they continued molesting more children. With the release of priest transfer lists and more alleged victims coming forward, the public has learned much more disturbing facts about the wide-scale cover-up involving Church officials. Sadly, we may never know how many molesting priests and victimized children were involved.

There are many complex reasons why clergy abuse remained, and continues to remain, silent. In some cases, the abuse was part of religious practice whereby children feared for their very souls if they told. In chapter 2 I discussed many of the reasons why children stay silent to the abusive experiences in their lives. When abuse happens by a holy person, the demand to remain silent is intensified. I was molested by my uncle, a Roman Catholic priest, on several different occasions. On one occasion, he led me into a bedroom:

> – HE LIT THE CANDLE and said I should come sit on his lap where we could watch Jesus on the cross. "Jesus died for us so we could be saved," he said very seriously. He told me I should always remember that. Gently he moved my hand to his pants and he had me stroke him above his clothes. He put me down on my knees while he still sat there. He moved his pants away and had me put my mouth around his penis to suck on him. It hurt really badly

> because my lips were so small and badly chapped. I remember closing my eyes thinking that maybe the next time I opened them it would be over. I tried to go far away inside myself. I don't think it worked because I was still choking and all I saw was his pubic hair and black priest clothes. All I could think was that if Jesus was nailed to a cross and died for us, then I should be strong and not complain about how bad it hurt.

Inspired by others coming forward with clergy abuse, I was finally able to disclose my own experiences just recently. I was not only molested by my uncle, I was molested by a *priest.* Clergy use their authority as holy people to molest children, and in the case of the Roman Catholic Church particularly, the practices are an insidious aspect of Church culture itself. The resolve to remain silent can feel like it is sealed by God himself.

Institutions foster conditions that keep these practices of denial and silence intact. In cases where parents confronted the Church, in some parishes they were persuaded and manipulated by Church leaders to sign documents stating they would not go public with the abuse. Out of loyalty toward the Roman Catholic Church, the pope, and even the molesting priests, victims and their families kept and continue to keep silent. Other institutional practices foster secretiveness in the Church. Church officials have, historically, seen themselves as above ordinary people; they are the servants of God.[34] Faith itself, and the belief in the power of the Holy Spirit to guide, reinforces the divine warranty of Catholic Church practice. Secrecy also becomes a means of self-protection: when one person is attacked or is having problems, the group closes in to protect its members. The Church is no different from other clubs trying to protect its reputation from becoming tarnished. Transferring priests to other dioceses was a way to protect itself from unseemly conduct by its membership. Moreover, it was a way to deny the worst aspects of Catholic Church culture.

Blaming and denial strategies also shed light on how powerful institutions can prevail to keep the norms of manipulation and irresponsibility in place. For example, the Catholic Church has attempted to blame gay priests and parents for priest molestations. By purging gay priests from service, the Church has taken a position that pedophilia within the Church would end. The Church gives itself absolution by blaming pedophilia on "deviant" homosexual priests with uncontrollable urges. Yet research is conclusive: pedophilia is not caused by one's sexual preference, i.e., whether one is straight or gay. Pedophilia is a psychiatric disorder characterized by sexual activity with prepubescent children.[35] People who are gay or lesbian are no more a threat to children than heterosexuals.[36] Moreover, blaming the problem on gay priests also ignores the scores of girls who have been molested as well.[37] Clearly, the child abuse scandal is not a gay priest problem any more than it is a problem of negligent parents. While it is unfortunate that many parents of abused children fail to notice the abuse, it is not parents themselves who molested and raped children in the Church rectory. These tactics of deflecting responsibility away from the leadership of the Roman Catholic Church are egregious and call attention to a much more insidious problem: the widespread abuse of power by clergy and a system that both condones and denies it.

The Church is facing hundreds of charges of priest molestation because, structurally, the Church has failed to offer children protection from harm. The system of allowing priests to molest children and then be transferred to other dioceses, forcing families into secrecy by signing away their right to speak, and ignoring the structural problems that allow priests to so easily abuse children has been exposed. While the Catholic Church has attempted to cast blame elsewhere, e.g., on gay priests and negligent parents, their tactics are not working. At least for now, religious practices are being seriously and publicly questioned.

The Medical Establishment

The medical establishment is a powerful multibillion-dollar industry in this country and includes corporate boards of prominent hospitals, medical schools, professional medical and psychiatric organizations, research institutes, and professional journals. The institution of medicine affects our everyday lives by maintaining practices that fail to regard and adequately respond to women's and children's complaints. It is not about whether individual physicians are good or not.

Nor is it about physicians failing to understand the importance of larger social issues. I think of the work of Dr. Henry Kempe who, along with several of his colleagues, led the crusade for the passage of the Child Abuse Prevention and Treatment Act of 1974.[38] Clearly, individuals and organizations within the medical field have made a significant difference in people's lives by affecting social policy. Structurally, however, the medical institution remains authoritative, rigid, and dismissive of certain people and certain conditions. In addition, the medical establishment, like other institutions, has a preference for individual pathology. That is, the focus is on individual complaints rather than the conditions in society that create ill health. When these complaints aren't taken seriously or are neglected, good health care becomes suspect or is absent altogether.

Two of the ways the medical establishment is culpable for the maintenance of beliefs that foster the subordination of women and children include gender bias in the diagnosis and treatment of female patients, and the lack of adequate and consistent response to abused children.

Gender Bias in Medicine

The medical establishment fosters the inequality and subordination of females in many ways. In this section I go into more detail about prominent ways gender differences affect psychiatric diagnoses and treatment.

Early medicine focused on the male patient as the standard for all patients.[39] Freud, for example, developed theories of *child* development, yet his work was almost exclusively with *boys.* Historically, when the standard of behavior or thought is based primarily on male experience, issues affecting females are considered abnormal or even pathological. Male behavior, thought, and experience are considered the norm. Male-focused research continues today. Prescription medications are based on an averaged-size man. Most methods of contraception remain harmful to female health, and in some cases fatal, despite the enormous resources to find healthy alternatives. Women have been notoriously excluded from research on certain diseases, including cardiovascular disease and hypertension. Various rationales are given for the omission of females from medical studies, including female hormonal variations, a lower rate of certain diseases, and fewer females in the sample.[40] Women are excluded because of their differences from men, an exclusion based on abnormality.

Another result of early gender bias in the field of medicine was to label females "hysterical." The history of female hysteria dates back centuries.[41] Considered a serious affliction affecting neurotic women, nineteenth-century investigators believed hysteria originated in the uterus. Hysteria "offered a scientific explanation for phenomena such as demonic possession states, witchcraft, exorcism, and religious ecstasy."[42] By the turn of the century, investigators agreed that the genesis of hysteria was psychological trauma; female medical problems were considered psychological in nature.[43] The ideology that female patients are hysterical and in need of psychological help for medical complaints remains with us today. For females diagnosed with psychiatric problems, hysteria is likely to be assumed.

From the moment I set foot in the psychiatric unit, I might as well have been told outright that I was hysterical. I was not considered a "good" patient because I asked too many questions and wanted too many answers. But not knowing or even understanding what was wrong with me, and wanting desperately to be active in my own treatment, my attempts to be a good, reliable patient failed. I was seen by a husband-wife pair of psychiatrists. "All you university people are the same," one of them declared, "You come in here voluntarily, but you refuse the help that's here." I was concerned about two of the staff and the "help" I was receiving. Most especially, I was appalled at a therapy group I attended and was expected to attend each day. So I asked the psychiatrist whether these two seemingly incompetent occupational therapists had the training to run psychotherapy groups. "What do you think?" the psychiatrist responded sarcastically. "This is a good hospital! We could be sued if staff weren't trained professionals." He ridiculed and dismissed me, then proceeded to tell the supervising nurse what I had just asked him in confidence. I could not help but get extremely frustrated and angry at the lack of information provided to me. It was all the more evidence to document my hysteria. While the word "hysterical" never came up in our sessions, the behavior of these psychiatrists and other medical staff made it clear to me they certainly thought I was.

My case is not unusual. In stories upon stories, women are not taken seriously by medical staff. Females, as it turns out, tend to ask more questions of their physicians, while physicians tend to provide less accurate and detailed information to their female patients.[44] This is the plight of many women who find themselves attempting to discuss their hypertension, stomach and colon problems, anxiety, depression, or sleep disturbances with a physician. More often than not, many of us become quiet martyrs not wanting to be told by medical staff we are hypochondriac or crazy.

People who suffer from serious psychiatric conditions in addition to having medical problems can find it extraordinarily difficult to make, and then go to, doctors' appointments. We never know if the physician will be sympathetic and knowledgeable about our conditions and experiences. I recently went to a physician for the first time and struggled with deciding how much to tell her about my DID and PTSD experiences. Forms ask you for current medications and hospitalizations, and recent and past medical problems. As someone who has lived with post-traumatic stress symptoms for many years and also developed serious medical problems as a result of abuse, I wasn't sure how many medical problems I should discuss with her on the first visit. I feared how she would react and was anxious about the stereotypes and misinformation she might have about multiplicity. Will she take me seriously? Will I seem like a hypochondriac? This doctor's visit became increasingly distressful for me.

Like many stressful situations, I was not certain I would even remember the answers to the physician's questions. People suffering with serious trauma-related disorders can get easily confused in a doctor's office because our memories can become distorted. Jane Phillips explains how memory affects one's ability to deal with medical appointments:

> Because different selves recall different chapters of my history, I do not have immediate access to medical information. The real answer to a doctor's question can take days to surface from some far-flung corner of my system. Worse, because I shift reflexively from part to part, I can't sequence the fragments of my history I actually do recall. Did the rash start before or after the fever? . . . Unfortunately, my parts track symptoms the same way incompatible and surly members of a committee might carry out their

work: in secret and with an air of martyrdom. I never get their clear, unified report.[45]

It is all too common for those who have suffered severe trauma to have broken memories of medical histories. Medical forms themselves can be confusing. Many do not know what, how, or when to tell doctors what is really happening. Perhaps everyone has difficulty going to doctors, particularly if they are dealing with an unpleasant or embarrassing condition. For some of us, doctors' visits can be excruciating. It is difficult to be a cooperative patient when medical forms and the process itself do not lend themselves to it.

We live in a culture where it is assumed that female medical complaints are overexaggerated and psychologically based. This becomes internalized by female survivors especially. Many who suffer from trauma-related illnesses are fearful to go to doctors because it is uncertain whether the discomfort is due to a severe flashback or a "valid" medical problem. It can be quite difficult to determine the genesis of any pain for a person living with severe post-traumatic stress or dissociative disorders. People with trauma-related illnesses frequently ask themselves if what they are experiencing is a new medical problem or a symptom of a flashback. Jane Phillips explains:

> My body pulls the same trick. My chest, my abdomen, a leg, a hand suddenly register physical sensations that are utterly real, utterly terrifying, and utterly breathtaking. Often I must decide whether the pain in my chest or leg or abdomen is happening now—or is it a phantom from the past? Do I see my doctor? Or talk with my psychologist?[46]

The fact that any of us need to make sense of these ailments on our own says a great deal about the inadequacy of current medical practices. Medical incompetence, ignorance, and stigmatization exacerbate an already seriously troubling situation. We internalize cultural practices and expectations of the hysterical female by becoming more ashamed and forcing us to suffer in silence.

The history of sexual inequality in the medical field, including the perception of females as hysterical, helps us to understand why physicians and others working within the medical profession continue to play into false female stereotypes. Unconsciously perceiving females as hysterical and overemotional has the effect of increased misdiagnosis, overdiagnosis of certain conditions, and the overprescription of medications to females. Females become pathologized by virtue of their gender and life circumstances. Rather than ask what is wrong with a society in which so many females are suffering with "emotional" problems, the female experience is minimized and invalidated. The fact that females are perceived as less credible and weaker than males only reinforces the degree to which female complaints are ignored and dismissed. *Our inability to be taken seriously by physicians is symptomatic of the many ways females are denied, ignored, blamed, and shamed for valid medical complaints and concerns.*

The Invisibility of Abuse

Children, perhaps more than any other group of people, are frightfully ignored in the health care system. Most prominent are the many distinct ways child abuse stays invisible and undetected. As a group, children's voices are silenced as a matter of course in society, and this includes within the medical establishment as well. We lack access to children's stories of abuse because they are never heard or recognized, and it is only in adulthood when we learn the truth. What we know is that there are vivid testimonies of adults severely abused as children and their experiences within the health care system. Jill Morgan was first raped by her father when she was four years old. The result was severe emotional and physical injuries:

> With no words and no warning, he spread my legs and entered me dry. My scream started the dog barking. I must have passed out, because my next memory is of the sunlit garden through the French doors to my right and the sound of the dog barking frantically in the kitchen. My memories here are sketchy. I really don't even remember the pain yet. When he was through with me, he dropped me on the floor like a discarded dishrag. Then with belt in hand he began beating me.[47]

Morgan spent the next several weeks in a hospital with a broken pelvis, and her case was not reported to authorities. While this experience happened decades ago, these situations continue to happen today.

Abuse remains intact when reporting procedures are inconsistent and ambiguous. The reporting of child abuse by health care providers is haphazard in that every state has their own, distinct criteria for reporting suspected cases, and every professional organization has different, and sometimes conflicting, standards of reporting. Nationwide, medical personnel were responsible for 11 percent of the two million cases reported to authorities for child maltreatment.[48] Yet many more suspected cases of abuse go unreported, while other cases go undetected altogether.[49] With so much discretion in the reporting of abuse, cases can readily fall through the cracks.

There are numerous reasons why child abuse is not reported by health care providers. Inadequate training in medical school and fast-held stereotypes and misconceptions of abuse keep cases from being reported. Many primary care providers are reluctant to report child abuse also because of negative experiences with state child protective service (CPS) agencies.[50] Others perceive the child may not benefit if they report suspected abuse. Many health care professionals continue to downplay the extent of child abuse by holding to stereotypes that "good" fathers don't rape their daughters. The cases most likely to be reported to CPS are the most severe cases of assault or when the parent is poor, lacking insurance or on Medicaid, or families of color. Stereotypes of abusers being poor and uneducated reinforce who gets reported or not; class and racial stereotypes lead to greater misunderstanding of the prevalence of abuse. When child battery is legal in homes and in schools, and standards of reporting are ambiguous, the detection and treatment of abuse will remain inadequate.

Another reason childhood abuse, for both children and adult survivors, remains invisible is a medical model that denies the holistic nature of people and their conditions. The Western medical model practiced today separates the mind, body, and spirit by perceiving physical ailments as separate from one's mental and spiritual health. In 1999 the surgeon general commissioned for the first time a national report on mental health.[51] An overarching theme of the report was the inseparability between the mind and body. The report found that physical health and mental illness are states that cannot exist in isolation from each other.[52] When a separation is made between the mind and body, this affects how child abuse is treated in the health care system. Chronic stomach pains, bedwetting, joint problems, and severe headaches may actually be conditions symptomatic of abuse and a suffering spirit. A denial of mind/body connection also severely limits how the mentally ill, especially, are treated in the health care system. The mentally ill are much more likely to be left untreated or be poorly treated because physical illnesses are not connected with serious symptoms of mental illness.

The fact that there is a separation of treatment systems between overall health care and mental health care reinforces an antiquated belief that the mind and body are separate. Examples of how the mind and body are one are numerous: brain research on memory, mental disturbances after major surgery, and conditions resulting from trauma. Symptoms of traumatic stress illustrate how mind, body, and soul are inextricably linked. When physical symptoms are treated separately from mental processes, signs of abuse and trauma can be easily overlooked. It is only when abuse is physically noticeable, or in many cases extreme, that it becomes detected. Nancy G. constructed a prison inside herself from so much mental dissociation from physical and emotional trauma. In "Abuse: A Trauma That Never Ends," she writes:

> We've always been locked in one prison or another. Our parents built the first one and we, eventually, through the timeless abuse, devised an even larger prison of our own. The only difference is, today we can see the steel prison bars of the jail. But our own prison bars are invisible to others. An invisible prison, few can understand.[53]

To view people holistically means we will begin to notice and respond to people suffering in their own invisible prisons. There are many obvious signs of abuse if one only has the background, experience, and willingness to notice.

Most anyone who picks up a book on traumatic stress and dissociation will likely find mention of several leading psychiatrists and psychologists currently in the field: Jon Allen, James Chu, Christine Courtois, Barry Cohen, Judith Herman, Frank Putnam, Colin Ross, and Bessel van der Kolk. Collectively, these experts are affiliated with most of the mental health trauma centers throughout the country, are current or past presidents of major medical and mental health organizations, are editors of prestigious journals, have published extensively, and have received millions of dollars in funding for mental health-related research and practice. These experts have a tremendous amount of influence within and outside their professions. When a group of people is able to significantly influence the direction and agenda of any practice or policy, there is reason to take notice; in this case, everyday lives are affected by what these experts do or say. Their work affects not only those in the medical and mental health fields, but also social service providers, policy makers, the academic community, survivors of trauma, and the public as well. Working together, these experts can significantly influence public policy and what is understood about trauma as well as the prevention, treatment, and visibility of child abuse more generally.

Severe trauma damages children in very direct and measurable ways. In chapter 2 I illustrated various ways severely abused children can develop medical ailments in addition to psychological, developmental, and behavioral problems. Abused children frequently display post-traumatic stress symptoms, including chronic infections, stomach problems and ulcers, bedwetting, depression, serious sleeping problems, and a look of terror or complete numbness. However, physicians typically lack the training and knowledge to detect trauma-related symptoms. The medical establishment sets the tone for how health care workers and those in authority respond to traumatic stress and illness. Establishing a model of medicine that denies the reality of certain "invisible" conditions increases the suffering of abused children. Lack of accurate information and knowledge keeps those suffering from severe childhood abuse from being properly diagnosed and treated.

A focus on individual pathology rather than the conditions in society that create ill health are costly for everyone. Rather than treat the scores of adults and children exhibiting PTSD and other trauma-related symptoms as a societal problem needing social, political, and economic remedies, the medical establishment treats each individual independently. One person's reproductive problems, migraines, and depression are hers alone to deal with. The situation is only compounded when an individual's complaints aren't taken seriously or are neglected. Yet individual problems are also *public* problems. A medical model is lacking that acknowledges the public and political nature of abuse. Survivors of abuse will be free from suffering only when institutions themselves promote values of respect and equality, and absolutely deplore any practices that condone violence and harm.

The Social Costs of Abuse

The social costs of child abuse are enormous, from social isolation to the economic costs of treating victims of abuse. Thus far I have focused primarily on how child abuse affects individual people. However horrific an abusive experience is for a child, and later for the adult survivor, the social costs are even greater.

As a society we pay substantially for the effects of child abuse. The economic costs alone are astronomical: billions of dollars in health care costs, costs for incarcerating abused youth and adults in prisons and jails, public programs and shelters dedicated to abuse victims and their families, decreased productivity in the workplace, lost wages, and underemployment. We pay in many other ways as well: social isolation, poor quality of life, fear of crime, mass intimidation, and widescale suffering. Perhaps the most egregious cost is the continued perpetuation of the cycle of abuse and violence. Every day thousands of children are abused in despicable ways. We condone child abuse by failing to stop it; our societal neglect is deplorable. What follows are some of the ways we pay as a culture for the widespread abuse and neglect of children and for the devastating psychiatric problems that result.

The most tangible costs of child abuse and violence are economical. Billions of dollars are spent each year on the medical and mental health treatment of childhood trauma victims. The following are current statistics on mental health expenditures:[54]

1) Of the $843 billion spent on national health care, direct costs for mental health care accounted for a small 8 percent, or $69 billion;[55] indirect costs of mental health services, e.g., loss of productivity in the workplace and society, amounts to $79 billion annually.
2) The government pays for 53 percent of the direct costs for mental health treatment, while individuals seeking treatment pay for almost one-fifth, or $11.7 billion, of their care.[56]

3) Hospitals admit millions of people each year for psychiatric problems; psychiatric admissions represent over 25 percent of all hospital admissions.
4) A quarter of a million people with mental illnesses were incarcerated in American prisons and jails, a rate four times the number of people institutionalized in state mental hospitals.[57]
5) Billions of dollars are spent on psychiatric costs prior to the correct diagnosis. For example, people with PTSD and DID can spend an average of six or more years in the medical system being treated for mood disorders, general anxiety, even schizophrenia, before being diagnosed correctly.[58]

Cost-benefit studies are clear: hundreds of billions of dollars could be saved annually if patients were diagnosed and treated properly. In many cases, preventive strategies could be utilized to avoid or at least diminish the symptoms of many forms of mental illness.

Misdiagnosis due to lack of education and training has enormous social and economic consequences. One study found that fifteen female patients diagnosed with multiple personalities spent $4.1 million on psychiatric health care costs—and this was over a decade ago.[59] These results indicate the absurdity of payments for psychiatric treatment for those living with multiplicity. I get very angry when I think of my own expenses. I believe the first indication that multiple personalities were becoming problematic for me was in 1984. Yet diagnosed with clinical depression, I was handed a bottle of pills and sent on my way. I stopped taking the pills after two weeks because of their horrible side effects. But I took the diagnosis of depression seriously and at least attempted to exercise, eat well, and take better care of myself. I didn't utilize mental health services again until four years later when I finally admitted to a therapist I had been molested by my father. After three years of intensive individual and group therapy, treated for post-traumatic stress and depression, I thought I was healed. I believe had therapists been more experienced and knowledgeable, my multiplicity would have been detected sooner. Throughout the next decade I would meet with therapists when things would get chaotic. Finally, in 1998, I was diagnosed with severe PTSD and DID.

Almost twelve years in and out of the mental health care system, I have utilized an abundance of services: three psychiatric hospitalizations; outpatient treatment with psychiatrists, psychotherapists, and group therapy; prescription medications; physician visits for sleeping problems, migraines, stomach problems, and other trauma-based conditions; and many holistic treatments, including acupuncture, herbal remedies, chiropractic treatments, and massage therapy. Indirect costs for me include loss of productivity and absenteeism in the workplace during the periods I suffered severe PTSD, loss of wages from unemployment, loss of hours from volunteerism and social supports to others, and financial costs for everyday care and necessities covered by friends. Overall costs for me alone probably come close to $1 million. The financial costs of childhood traumatization, including the myriad of long-term medical and psychiatric conditions that develop, are outrageous, particularly since these conditions are highly treatable yet frequently misdiagnosed.

Adult mental health care costs are astronomical. Mental health problems cost the U.S. billions of dollars annually in workplace losses alone through absenteeism, lost productivity, and lost earnings due to illness.[60] There are enormous insurance premiums and unrecovered costs of therapists and hospitals for clients unable to pay full fees. There are millions of visits to physicians, therapists, and other mental health service providers each year for mental health–related problems. According to the National Center for Health Statistics, in 1999 the number of annual office visits to physicians for mental disorders was 24.5 million, including 9.7 million visits for depression, and another 4.8 million for anxiety.[61] It is an outrage that psychiatric costs for the treatment of trauma-related disorders are so enormous. Entire industries profit from mental illness and instability, though this fact often goes unrecognized. It is an understatement to say that mental illness caused from human cruelty is economically costly.

There are other costs due to abuse, perhaps not so visible as expenditures, which harm the very fabric of our society. One major cost is the enormous social isolation that often results for the survivors. Trauma can be chronically disruptive and life altering.[62] Feelings of isolation come both when trauma victims withdraw from others, as well as when others withdraw from the survivor, each out of desperation, denial, avoidance, and fear. Many of us withdraw not only because of the abuse experiences themselves, but for what it does to our identities and minds. A few months after my first psychiatric hospitalization I wrote the following:

> – I MUST LOOK THE SAME to everyone. my hair is the same. i wear the same clothes. i gained a few pounds but that's no big deal. maybe the biggest difference is i don't smile as much. maybe i don't carry my body quite the same. i guess i slouch a little more, have a more difficult time looking people in the eyes. they see Paige but it's not the Paige they know, not the Paige i know. people have no idea how confusing things are in my head, how difficult it is to focus and pay attention, how frustrated and hurt i am. if they can't see a cast or crutches, nothing seems physically wrong, then things must be o.k. they have no idea what i've been through. how i wish i could scream out to them, "see me for who i am. i am feeling so much pain."
>
> – i feel like telling people the truth: i've been raped and sodomized, went crazy for remembering, then had to be institutionalized in a psychiatric hospital because i was going to thrust myself out a two story window in the hopes my neck snapped. maybe then they'd stop staring, stop wondering whether i'm switching or not, stop wondering why i've been away for so long and seem so different. people who know i'm multiple are afraid of me; people who don't know are uncomfortable with who i've become. all of them push me away without knowing it. i'm so far away as it is. how much farther can i go?

Many people with mental disorders struggle with competing desires: the need to be heard yet needing to maintain silence. Our shame and fear keep us from sharing. But even when we do open up with others, the backlash can be worse than the isolation. We struggle, at times unsuccessfully, with negotiating who, when, and how to tell.

Speaking the truth may diminish individual isolation, but it can also cause a backlash, be unsafe, or even dangerous. Survivors can put themselves at risk of greater harm by telling people who react negatively or even violently. Some people are abandoned by their friends and families who deny the abuse happened; some have boyfriends and husbands who exploit alters sexually and in other despicable ways;[63] others are completely disregarded and ignored because they are considered crazy. Out of fear of possible repercussions, many of us are silenced further and withdraw even deeper inside ourselves. Jane Phillips explains why she remained silent:

> In its most obvious form, there seems to be the simple fact that human beings somehow feel better, their troubles eased, their burdens lighter, when someone else has sat and listened. The problem, though, with multiplicity is that what one has to tell is far too much, too horrifying for the ordinary, untrained listener. Listeners react in all too human ways: they minimize, they disbelieve, they laugh, they deny.[64]

We become deeply disconnected from our families, friends, neighbors, and communities. Scores of people are holed up in their homes, in some cases wanting to die, because there aren't enough people or resources to help. Collectively, individual isolation is an enormous social problem.

Social isolation can be viewed as a symptom of societal neglect. In other words, if denial, secrecy, and shame weren't the prevailing social norms in regard to child abuse and violence, the victims of such devastating abuse wouldn't become so isolated. They could more easily come forward with their stories of abuse, resources would be abundant, and more social service and mental health providers would be educated about how to detect and treat abuse. Like many, I spent two years not being able to hold my head up, being completely ashamed of having a mental disorder. I thought for certain people would notice. How I felt is a reflection of not only me, but of a culture that allows an individual to feel so ashamed for being how she is. Shame, denial, and secrecy force people into isolation. Social norms influence the degree to which anyone can become and remain severely isolated within society. For some, the effects of societal rejection can be catastrophic. Isolation keeps people from getting better sooner; the societal costs become exponential.

The intergenerational costs of abuse to society are also alarming, since a significant amount of child abuse and violence is passed down through generations. Lisa Poupart in "Daddy I'm Sorry" writes about her abusive father, a man filled with rage from his own abusive past and experiences with racism as an American Indian:[65]

When he was a small boy he tried
to summon the spirits with a flute
That his father threw out the window
while promptly beating his face in

On the bus to the big school
the white kids called him
timber nigger
and the only good indian is a dead one
unless he plays ball

So he learned to run and tackle
to cheer the onlookers
Til his father stabbed a hole in the pigskin
while promptly breaking the foot that he kicked with

Then starts to drink his Blue Ribbon
smashes his head through the windshields
numbing the pain of an existence
too aching to bear

And
somewhere between two and nineteen
he turned hollow and dried up inside
his spirit flew off to the West

His body a shell left behind
to carry out revenge
for five hundred years of genocide
that he ate from an empty government hand-out can

When he put a rifle to his wife's head
and raped his two babies

he never even felt it
because he was already dead

The legacy of family violence is insidious and far-reaching. Abused children who do not receive intervention, counseling, or treatment increase the likelihood of being abusive toward others or of becoming abused again in later life. Experts across many disciplines agree that an abused child is more at risk for behavioral, psychological, and developmental problems than a nonabused child.[66] The long-term effects of child abuse are also clear. Adult revictimization is particularly pronounced for females who are sexually abused as children. The adult survivor frequently lacks the tools necessary to develop healthy relationships. She may "become involved with dangerous people without realizing it. Perpetrators may, in fact, search out people with these vulnerabilities."[67] This also translates into a more difficult time getting out of abusive situations because self-esteem, confidence, and a sense of control over one's body is diminished or absent. Adult males physically abused in childhood are more likely to be aggressive and physically abusive toward others. Incarcerated adults and youth have higher rates of reported child abuse and victimization than the general public.[68] Children who have been physically, emotionally, and/or sexually abused are predisposed to violence and abuse in adulthood. This does not mean they will inevitably become abusive or victimized, but they are much more prone to such behaviors as they grow up. The cycle of violence remains an insidious aspect of this culture.

So why is it that boys who are abused are more likely to become abusive toward females, whereas girls who are sexually abused are more likely to be revictimized in later life? Male-owned institutions affect all spheres of life, including where our ideas come from and how we think. The very traits that many regard as biological, such as males being strong, rational, independent, and aggressive, and females being emotional, nurturing, dependent, and passive, are actually *learned.*[69] In other words, in general, boys are taught to be masculine, whereas girls are taught to be feminine. While I am simplifying a very complex, multifaceted process, the results are profound. Masculine traits, i.e., those ascribed to males, are considered more significant and better than feminine traits, i.e., those considered female. We can understand adult violence and revictimization better by analyzing how feminine and masculine traits affect each of us. The following is an everyday example of how feminine and masculine traits influence daily life for most males and females.

Men are paid more money to do physical labor, e.g., construction work, than women to do more administrative labor, e.g., secretarial work,[70] even though administrative labor often requires more education and training than physical labor. Arguments are made by my students in women's studies courses that construction work is "harder" than secretarial work. The value of the work, that is, whether it is truly more difficult or not, is based on a particular ideology or belief. In this case, physical labor is perceived as more difficult than the administrative and organizational labor required for most secretarial positions. Administrative labor is devalued, while physical labor is valued. This is simply a cultural ideology and practice, not anything based in "fact." It is not the fact that construction work is easier or harder than secretarial work because, clearly, not all construction workers can perform administrative work. The fact is, these modes of work are valued differently. The valuation of certain types of work, as well as the ways we eat, walk, dress, and behave, has enormous consequences for both females and males. The examples of how feminine and masculine traits affect the lives of females and males are endless.

How does all of this relate to abused boys becoming abusive adults? Boys learn through every institution that they are the dominant and more able-bodied sex. Boys are taught and learn that physical strength, toughness, and even violence are attributes that make boys men. Physically, economically, and mentally, one way they learn to dominate females is by frightening them. Ultimately, many females learn through personal experience and institutional practices that they are the weaker, less deserving sex; they learn how to be afraid and victimized by males, to be passive and subservient, and to internalize any anger they might feel into more fear, guilt, and shame. Even though much has been accomplished in the past several decades, especially, to teach girls that it is worthwhile to be independent and strong, culturally and unconsciously we still expect females to be passive and demurring. It is no wonder that many abused boys grow up and become abusive in later life and even more girls find themselves in abusive relationships as adults. The cycle of abuse continues because of the beliefs and practices ingrained in our collective minds. Abuse continues because it has not been stopped and because these archaic and hurtful practices have not been sufficiently challenged.

Of course, not all boys and girls follow these social norms. Females, including grandmothers, mothers, and sisters, also abuse children. Abused children can grow up and never become abusive themselves. And many women learn to hang on to their anger and rage, never demurring for anyone. Sylvia Fraser writes about her own experience:

> Little boys are taught to convert fear into rage or bravado. Little girls, to convert anger into fear. I was a hostile little girl, a furious teenager and a frequently bad-tempered adult. Anger was my salvation, the way I survived in my father's house, but it became my prison, blocking softer emotions. Now, as that tough shell cracks, a more vulnerable self is released.[71]

The pain and suffering of severe abuse can be devastating. There can be immense conflict in the experience of abuse and how one feels about and reacts to it, both in the present and long term. For most of us, it means stuffing intensely profound emotions deep inside our very beings. Despite the more systematic nature of violence by males against females, every sort of childhood violence is deplorable.

The personal, political, and social consequences of childhood traumatization are unfathomable. Billions of dollars are spent each year to treat and punish abused and abusive people. Millions of people are isolated and alone, terrorized by their pasts and fearful of their futures. Every day scores of children are beaten and harmed, violated in despicable ways, learning to do the same to others when they get older. When we fail to respond adequately as a nation, we perpetuate the cycle of abuse and the effects are exponential.

Violence against women and children is systematic and profound; it is akin to being at war.[72] Yet how often do we think of political warfare when another child has been hospitalized in intensive care from being beaten by her stepfather or another woman has escaped a deadly domestic violence dispute with her husband? As a collective society, we have failed to recognize the insidious nature of violence and abuse directed at women and children. What would happen if we began to treat survivors of child abuse and domestic violence as veterans of war? They would have special hospitals to go to, monthly assistance and aid, and medical care until they were better. Although Veterans Administration hospitals may be inadequate and understaffed, there is a place for veterans to go for help. If such hospitals existed for survivors of severe abuse and trauma, perhaps we could finally witness how many millions of people in this country are terrorized daily by violence and horrific conditions. Instead, child abuse is regarded as an individual problem where a person might spend thousands of dollars, and in some cases hundreds of thousands of dollars, in a lifetime getting help: in the form of therapy; lost wages from post-traumatic stress reactions; medications for anxiety, sleep problems, and depression; physician and hospital bills for chronic medical conditions; and chiropractors and massage therapists because our bodies are so sore and tired. The collective resources and money spent on child abuse is astronomical. Mostly the costs fall on individuals, survivors forced to pay for their own victimization.

Dissociative identity disorder is the direct manifestation of a culture that allows horrendous violence and abuse to take place against innocent children. Yet individual suffering happens in a societal context. I am not only angered by the many individuals within my own family who caused or perpetuated the abuse, I find deplorable the many social, political, and legal institutions that enable child abuse to occur and remain silent and shameful. Child abuse and multiplicity are the result of societal neglect:

– I WALKED ALONE in the darkness, tripping over the path that led far away from all the vileness and cruelty. further and further along, deeper and deeper within. i found a little place that was quiet and safe, barely large enough to hold me. cuddled in the dark, my head resting on my knees, i went to sleep. i did not move and barely even breathed. i went to sleep for years.

– i was hit by a two-by-four and my little place rattled. the hole started caving in and i fought to free myself. struggling for days, months, years, i finally found my way out of the darkness, into this all-too magnificent light. the brightness is painful, almost unbearable. everything is loud, people screaming to be heard. i find i am

starving—for food, for touch, for understanding. where have i been? how long have i been there? why was i there? the memories start flooding back—the bondage, the cats, blood, and screams. children waiting for their turns. burned arms, twisted legs. nowhere to go. so i run, run deep, deep within. i find the path and keep running, never looking back, hoping to escape forever.
– too many children running for safety . . . go deep inside so no one can touch you, hurt you, or even love you. far, far away where you'll never get out. sad, tormented creatures, unloved, unworthy. we strike out, hurt others like we were hurt. hit me again, she cries, i hate myself, i deserve it anyway. our lives and bodies mutilated and destroyed. so much sadness, desperately alone, gripping pain, we are the survivors, the ones who got out. but to what, i ask?

Many of us eventually find a way out of ourselves, but only to discover more abuse and suffering. Sadly, it is all many of us know. People who have been traumatized by severe child abuse know all too well the effects of the cycle of abuse. We bear witness to it each and every day.

I used to think my soul had been raped, that it was, and would forever remain, violated. Now I believe it stayed protected. I found a way to escape, and with every violation I ran further and further inside myself. But there came a point several years ago when it was necessary to come out. Through incredible good fortune, pure determination, and support from a number of caring people, my soul has remained intact—I am strong and healthy, and I know who I am. But lots of kids never get out; they stay gone forever, completely lost in themselves, or mentally, physically, and spiritually mutilated in the process. Those living with multiple personalities symbolize the lengths people can go to torture and harm others, as well as the amazing capacity to cope in the face of it. We may have learned to cope, but far too many of us remain lost and suffering. Though the personal consequences of child sexual abuse are somewhat predictable, the damage done to our communities is immeasurable. Child abuse, and the resulting psychological and physical problems that develop, leaves a devastating wake in our collective souls. As a society we have neglected individual suffering far too long. It is vital that we make public the private voices of those crying out to be heard.

Each institution must take responsibility for the devastating effects of abuse and find concrete ways to eradicate it. Leadership within every institution is needed. When the Roman Catholic Church calls a "no tolerance" policy on child molestation by clergy, they are acting in the best interests of children; they are teaching their congregations and the public that child abuse is intolerable and wrong. When the government funds the mental health profession for research on trauma-related psychiatric problems and early childhood traumatization, they are working to understand and eradicate abuse. When national mental health organizations begin to recognize dissociative identity disorder as a severe psychiatric illness, they are helping the public as well in supporting those who suffer. When young girls are supported in their efforts to participate in "rough" sports and the martial arts, they are being taught how to protect themselves both physically and mentally. When children in foster homes and foster care are adopted into loving homes, we teach all children that young people matter. Child abuse will end when personal suffering and violence are not tolerated.

5 Supporting the Survivors

> I learned, after countless lessons, that no matter how scary life seems the only really scary part is facing the fear down, and taking another step.
>
> —Sarah Olson, *Becoming One: A Story of Triumph over Multiple Personality Disorder*

Without consistent practices and services in place to assist survivors of abuse, most of us are left to our own devices to piecemeal treatment and care. One of the ways this happens is by connecting with and receiving help from concerned individuals, including loved ones, health care workers, social service providers, and the religious community. Concerned individuals can provide support to survivors of severe childhood abuse in a myriad of ways. Some of the most basic ways involve adjusting personal attitudes and getting more informed about child abuse and traumatic stress. This chapter is devoted to survivors, loved ones, and those working in the helping professions to assist with greater education, treatment decisions, and alternative means of healing for those suffering from trauma-related conditions. Frequently, people experiencing severe traumatic symptoms need a great deal of help. Involvement by loved ones and concerned therapists can literally mean the difference between wellness and despair, and even life and death.

In the midst of trauma, it is difficult to care for oneself. But having conscious intentions to love and respect ourselves is the most powerful tool we have to heal. In this chapter I provide a discussion of the ways we can take care of ourselves to develop a more healthy way of being in the world. Learning to love ourselves means replacing old, toxic body memory with good ones. It does not matter what we do, nor even how we do it. *What matters is that we commit ourselves fully to healing our entire being and having the patience to trust it will happen.* "Healing comes when we 'shine the light' on what is, what was, and what needs to be."[1]

Get Informed

Education is what will change perceptions, attitudes, and behaviors about traumatic stress, recovered memories, and conditions caused by abuse. When we acknowledge our own culpability in perpetuating abuse, we can then fathom the role of society in helping to create and sustain conditions that create it. So while institutions are certainly responsible for creating and maintaining conditions of abuse, individuals also share a responsibility in its elimination. A fundamental way to understand what I mean is examining the role of language in society and how this affects perceptions of childhood trauma and dissociation.

The general public may have no idea how certain language is offensive to those experiencing multiplicity and other mental illnesses. There are references made regularly, on television shows, movies, and in public, about multiple personalities. Sybil Isabel Dorsett survived horrific cruelty as a child and developed extreme multiple personalities as a result.[2] Decades later, Sybil remains a regular household name, even among those who never read the book or saw the movie. Her name continues to be used inappropriately and offensively by mainstream television media especially. The name Sybil is used to stereotype a myriad of outlandish, hysterical, and extreme behaviors: demonic possession, hearing voices, violence, psychotic behavior, and witchcraft. References to Sybil, along with Jekyll and Hyde, are made in ignorance and reinforce false stereotypes of the experience of multiplicity. It allows people to make fun of a very serious and potentially debilitating psychiatric condition. While the impulse to make a joke of mental illness may be a way to handle fear or ignorance, these words hurt. Scores of people living with multiplicity already feel alienated, ashamed, and harshly judged, and such comments only intensify this experience. The first way to show support and understanding to people living with multiplicity is to recognize our own inappropriate attitudes and language.

Using words like *multiple* and *multiple personalities* affects the way multiplicity is perceived. Recently I was talking with a representative of an Internet server to close an account. With one Internet server I have two separate accounts, under two different names, using the same phone number. Certainly I am not the only one who does this. The representative asked if there were two separate people living in my home, since he saw two different names. I told him no. He then asked jokingly, "Do you have multiple personalities?" I replied in a serious tone, "As a matter of fact, yes, I do." He apologized, stumbled along, and obviously felt embarrassed by what he had said. When I told a couple of friends about this incident, they were surprised by his comment. But what my friends and therapists don't realize is these ignorant and sometimes hurtful comments *happen all the time*. All one has to do is pay attention and listen. I think it is vitally important that individuals begin to recognize when and how such terms are utilized, and educate those who use them incorrectly and hurtfully. I am sure this Internet representative by no means wanted to insult me; in fact, he was trying to be funny. But his comment wasn't funny; it was ignorant and insulting. Education about certain words and expressions is vitally important to spreading knowledge and understanding about DID and other mental health conditions.

When we are afraid and ignorant of the mentally ill, we intensify their suffering. When we flippantly make references to multiple personalities and other mental illnesses, we inadvertently exacerbate negative stereotypes. Through recognizing our attitudes and behaviors, including the language we use, we join in solidarity with abuse survivors. Education is a necessity if we, as a society, want to stop abuse and discrimination. By educating ourselves about the role of trauma in people's lives, we learn to recognize abusive conditions. We then become more able to intervene and stop it.

We can also educate ourselves through research, reading, and discussion. The subject of childhood abuse may not be as taboo as it was twenty years ago, but multiple personality and ritualistic abuse certainly are. The more secret anything is, the more taboo it is. Knowledge, and talking freely about it, can have an enormous impact on how traumatic stress and dissociative disorders are researched, supported, and treated. As survivors especially, one of the most empowering things we can do for ourselves is to get informed.

Writings on traumatic stress abound, including memoirs, self-help books, academic writings, Internet websites, pamphlets published by national and international organizations, books geared toward clinical treatment, and scientific writings addressing the brain and psychobiological aspects of trauma. For the person first seeking information, this literature can be overwhelming and confusing. Moreover, not everyone finds relief from getting informed through books. In fact, certain aspects of knowledge can be extremely troubling and anxiety provoking. Sometimes we may feel better by remaining ignorant and uninformed. Perhaps this is what denial is all about: protecting ourselves from that which we do not want to know. I believe survivors can receive better treatment and care, and feel less victimized overall, by getting more informed. Information can allow people to be more committed to and involved with the healing process.

Reading is essential for anyone trying to understand or assist survivors of severe childhood trauma (see Appendix A). Books and self-help guides gave me peace of mind, and even companionship, during gut-wrenching times. Many inspirational memoirs and autobiographies written by child abuse survivors, those living with multiple alter personalities, and survivors of cult abuse helped me feel less crazy and alone. While reading certainly has been beneficial to me, at the same time, books on abuse can be heart wrenching and difficult to read. I recommend survivors especially read memoirs with caution and care, since they may be triggering and upsetting.

For those, such as myself, interested in clinical and scientific perspectives on trauma, dissociation, and multiplicity, there are many excellent works (see Appendix A). Clinical books may be too overwhelming and detailed for a person having a difficult time. However, these resource books should definitely be in every provider's office that deals with abuse victims. A therapist once said to me that she didn't have contemporary psychiatric books on multiple personality because she didn't agree with the treatment approaches. I knew immediately this therapist's comment had more to do with her lack of knowledge than her disagreement with treatment perspectives. Clinical books frequently contain an abundance of information about the etiology (i.e., the cause) and long-term effects of childhood trauma. They offer perspectives on the ways multiplicity manifests physically, psychologically, and biologically. Particularly for the mental health professional, reading or even focusing on one of these books alone is insufficient. Each perspective adds an enormous amount of information to the overall understanding of trauma and dissociation. When I began seeing one therapist, she had little experience working with DID. Yet she had been treating clients with sexual abuse backgrounds for years. She began reading books on multiplicity, and I know her research helped me and our working relationship tremendously. Gaining such knowledge can only help therapists and doctors to assist their clients better.

It can be thoroughly exhausting to teach others, including therapists, about traumatic stress and the experience of multiplicity; survivors are tired enough as it is. One of the best things that happened early on was that a close friend, after learning about my multiplicity, spent the next several days in the library researching and reading about multiplicity, dissociation, and traumatic stress. She came back asking excellent questions, letting me know when she didn't understand something. I read such and such, she'd say, but does it apply to you? The interest she showed in wanting to understand what was happening to me—not out of weird curiosity but because she cared—was truly remarkable. It is what I wanted every friend to do who wasn't familiar with multiple personalities. The fact that my friend read, and then prepared questions for us to discuss, was what mattered. She continued reading until she became more comfortable with me and DID. What is striking to me is how much more of an expert she became in dissociation and childhood trauma than many of the therapists and doctors I have seen.

My advice to those seeking information is, first, don't just read and sit on the information. Process it and ask questions. If your friend, family member, or client is unable or unwilling to talk with you about it, ask a trained and experienced mental health professional. Second, as you read, begin to ask yourself what stereotypes and judgments you have about abused children and multiple personality. These judgments can directly affect your response to, and your ability to help, someone living with DID. What beliefs do you have about the recovery of repressed memory? Do you believe ritualistic and cult abuse really happen? I had a close friend who, I am certain, thought I was possessed. We were on the phone talking when another caller, a woman with a deep, loud voice, interrupted the line. My friend let out a little shriek. The interruption happened at the same time I was telling my friend about the difficulty I still had switching from one personality to another. The line went dead, so I called her back right away. "I was so scared, Paige," she said. We both laughed uncomfortably, but I was also very sad. It had been over two years since first learning of my multiplicity, and she, a bright, educated woman, was still afraid of me and this disorder.

It is not just the untrained, uninformed public who holds stereotypes and fears about multiplicity and mental illness. Mental health professionals can remain only partially trained and unable to recognize their own prejudices and fears. Joan Frances Casey in her autobiography of multiple personality explains how therapists' judgments cloud their ability to help clients:

> Somehow this disorder hooks into all kinds of fears and insecurities in many clinicians. The flamboyance of the multiple, her intelligence and ability to conceptualize the disorder, coupled with suicidal impulses of various orders of seriousness, all seem to mask for many therapists the underlying pain, dependency, and need that are very much part of the process.[3]

The only way to move beyond our own fears and judgments is to challenge ourselves through education, discussion, and introspection. Physicians and health care providers must be able to detect trauma-related disorders and dissociative symptoms. It is the only way people living with these conditions will get quality health care. Knowledge, coupled with action, can influence everyone around us. Self-knowledge also contributes to the number of people who are fully informed and comfortable about the condition of multiplicity. Social change begins by individual awareness and action.

The Internet can be another excellent resource to find information about trauma and dissociation. There are hundreds, if not thousands, of Internet sites to get information about childhood abuse and trauma-related illness. (Just about all public libraries now have computers where anyone can access the Internet. Librarians can assist you in how to use the computer as well.) My sister once asked me how she should know what is good and bad over the Internet. I didn't know at the time, so I started asking my therapist and other survivors. I began by looking up the resources at the back of clinical books and those suggested by prominent organizations (see Appendix A). I gained a tremendous amount of knowledge and perspective by spending time on known Internet websites and was able to pass this information on to others.

Treatment Issues for Survivors

People suffering from severe trauma seek the services of all different sorts of professionals in all types of settings. Determining what you want and need is vitally important, especially when it comes to your own treatment. A multitude of issues must be faced regarding any psychiatric diagnosis and in making informed decisions about treatment and care, including the following:

- Dealing with a diagnosis of DID
- Selecting appropriate treatment and care
- Medication issues
- Support groups and connecting with others
- The pros and cons of government aid

Many more issues and decisions should be considered, but because of space limitations, I have chosen to cover those that can be most critical to recovery.

Dealing with the Diagnosis

A diagnosis of dissociative identity disorder, and learning you have multiple personalities, can be overwhelming. In the midst of considerable chaos and confusion, at some point one must deal with the diagnosis itself. Joan Frances Casey reacted strongly when told by her therapist she might have multiple personality disorder:

> She might as well have told me that I was possessed by demons. I was more worried about *her* mental state than my own when she said that, but I refrained from expressing my derision. . . . People called me compulsive, a workaholic, overenergized, an over-achiever, too intense, but no one would call me crazy.[4]

Casey's response is common: we think the diagnosis signifies we are crazy.[5] However one might feel initially, perhaps the most important aspect to consider is whether the diagnosis is helpful and how it might be harmful.

Because of the seriousness of the condition, one must be very cautious in accepting blindly a DID diagnosis. To protect yourself from a possible misdiagnosis, I suggest that if possible, try to get a second opinion by an experienced psychiatrist or clinical psychologist who is trained in psychiatric testing. I had been in a psychiatric hospital just two days when I wrote the following:

> – THE PSYCHIATRIST IS TELLING ME i could have one of three things: severe depression with anxiety something; psychotic behavior which includes anxiety, paranoia, and hallucinations; or dissociative identity disorder (multiple personalities). theoretically, post-traumatic stress can look like any of these, which i already know i have. personally, i think i can rule out the first two. i'm pretty sure i'm not psychotic. wouldn't you suspect you are? and wouldn't you show signs of this earlier on in life? i don't think it's severe depression because i've been clinically depressed before and that's not how i feel right now. I'm pretty sure I'm multiple. . . . heck, i even told my therapist two weeks ago i might be. but shouldn't i consider the

other two possibilities? the shrink wants me to stay through the weekend and have a bunch of psych tests done just to make sure. . . . i still can't believe i've actually cracked and had to be hospitalized in a psych ward.

A close friend was furious by this early diagnosis and found it absurd that anyone in two days could confirm I was psychotic or multiple. Dissociative identity disorder is a serious psychiatric diagnosis that should not be taken lightly. If at all possible, try to get a second or even a third opinion.

There are significant reasons why a clinical diagnosis of DID might be helpful, and even necessary, despite all the diagnostic problems that can occur. The diagnosis might enable a person to receive particular health care benefits or support from social service agencies. More important, the diagnosis might help explain and validate the way we are, such as odd and unexplainable behavior and lapses in memory. In her memoir of multiplicity, Jane Phillips recalls her initial feelings about the diagnosis of multiple personality:

> Privately, I found the idea of multiplicity both terrifying and appealing. Terrifying because evidence seemed to be mounting on a daily basis: journal entries I didn't quite recall making, mysterious items on grocery lists, people on the street who knew me well whom I only vaguely recognized. But multiplicity was appealing, too. It seemed to *fit.* It explained a hundred inexplicable episodes from the past; it offered to order the chaos of my mind, to shed light on all my dark urges and my mysteries.[6]

A diagnosis can help to explain and clarify a lot of confusing things. Like Phillips, the label of DID helped to validate unexplainable events and behaviors, serious lapses in memory, constant noise in my head, and severe migraines throughout my life. As much as the diagnosis made sense to me, I was also terrified of what a label of having multiple personalities would mean.

For some, a diagnosis of DID can be hurtful, detrimental, and even nonsensical. Many feel stigmatized and judged, while others are treated differently by family, friends, and even health care providers. I met another patient who told people she was schizophrenic because she thought it was less stigmatizing than saying she was multiple. Her thinking was that at least with schizophrenia, there is medication to take and a person won't be told they're fabricating their illness. Others feel that the label of multiple personality is a terrible reflection of personal failure. Beverly R. in *Multiple Personality Disorder from the Inside Out* states:

> Through all of my mental illness trials and tribulations I never felt crazy or out of control. Now that I have been diagnosed as a multiple I feel like a freak. I am having a hard time believing that I can have a healthy relationship with anyone, especially a man. I am feeling very lonely and empty. Now that I know what is wrong with me I am terrified that my people will come out inappropriately. I do not have control over them right now. My therapist says as I become more integrated I will have control and everyone will work as one.[7]

It can be completely terrifying and shameful to be unable to control the internal system. The fear and shame, along with the sense of personal failure, kept me from making contact with others. I, too, felt like a freak. I was afraid of being judged as crazy and for acting inappropriately. Acceptance of the label "multiple," and the experience of multiplicity itself, can be an enormous struggle for the survivor. Most of the general public cannot even fathom what it feels like to be living and diagnosed with a stigmatized mental disorder. Being labeled as someone with multiple personalities can hurt like hell.

A diagnosis of any mental illness might cause family and friends to react harshly or flat-out deny it; out of fear and ignorance, many just cannot handle it. A person might even be abandoned altogether by their loved ones. Referring to her closest friend, Jane Phillips shares her experience:

> But when I told her I was a multiple, she reacted with a fury that wounded and astonished me. . . . But now I am careful, in a way I never was before, about what I say about my life, my feelings, and my thoughts, because it is clear my disorder distorts our

> equilibrium: what we need from, and what we offer to, one another no longer works out in the old, easy way.[8]

Loved ones might have a difficult time accepting the actual diagnosis, let alone support you in the day-to-day experience of multiplicity. However well-intentioned a person might be, she may not be ready or able to deal with the news:

> – WITHOUT THESE PEOPLE and their feelings and words, i have no existence, no identity, and i would die. so i soak in everything, unable to decipher, unable to stay protected. yet i continue to trust. and trust means disappointment, betrayal, even shame. over and over again i have tried so hard to make friendships work, to make relationships happen, to carry the load. and now, in my time of crisis and great need, i rely on my friends to carry me. it has been hard to let them help. it has been even harder to watch them fail. as my weaknesses become more exposed, so do theirs. they just can't handle what has happened to me. and neither can i.

For me, my diagnosis coincided with a mental breakdown. It was not only the diagnosis that people were reacting to but my shattered life as well. Negative and unsupportive reactions from family and friends make us more cautious in letting our current and past experiences be known. We might stop sharing with others or close ourselves off from the outside world. We can intensify, unwittingly, our own isolation.

A smaller percentage of people experiencing multiplicity cannot grasp the condition because they are unaware of their alters. Nora, a psychiatric patient at Sheppard-Pratt Hospital, explains:

> I struggle with hate and despair; I hated what people did to me; but there was no rescue, no comfort . . . just pain. . . . When the little girl in me comes out, she brings pain. . . . I guess that's true with my other personalities . . . at least that's what Dr. V. [her therapist] tells me. . . . I don't know if I'm multiple or not. I think I am; I have periods where I don't remember anything, and people tell me I'm being nasty and angry; or I may sit in the

corner and whimper for hours and not remember anything. I may, every once in awhile, hear a voice in my head; but I don't have long conversations with my other personalities like Molly or Beth [other patients in the hospital] . . . I'm not like them . . . I find myself in the past a lot . . . it tires me . . . look at me . . . do you like what you see? . . . I just want to die and disappear from the earth.[9]

I can only imagine what it must feel like not to be conscious of my alters. While I was not fully conscious for many years, I am now. I am one of the fortunate ones.

It is not surprising that people diagnosed with DID frequently alternate between finding the diagnosis beneficial and at other times detrimental or surreal. Dealing with the diagnosis may be as challenging as living with the experience of multiplicity itself. And, in the midst of struggling with the diagnosis, one must still find appropriate treatment and support.

Selecting Treatment Providers

Decisions regarding treatment providers, such as selecting therapists and psychiatrists, can be overwhelming. One must evaluate the costs, determine preferences for particular therapists and treatment approaches, evaluate the efficacy of inpatient versus outpatient treatment, locate service providers, and attempt to understand health insurance plans and options. Saying I was overwhelmed by all of the decisions to be made is an understatement! For those newly in crisis, vital matters need to be researched and decided right away. The first involves mental health insurance.

Health Insurance

Different issues arise for those who have mental health insurance coverage and for those who don't. For those who have at least some form of health insurance, with the help of a friend or colleague, figure out your health insurance coverage right away. Many policies do not have coverage for mental health treatment while others may be very limited. Health insurance companies have much to say regarding how, when, where, and by whom a person is diagnosed and treated. For example, most insurance companies require you to see a specified doctor or therapist. Some companies require that a particular diagnosis be made in order to treat a client. Other insurance companies limit the number of therapy sessions depending on the diagnosis and issues being addressed. Plans might require that your therapist have a particular degree or certification. Companies can also limit the number of days for inpatient mental health hospitalization, fail to cover certain treatments, or charge exorbitant co-pays. This makes it *essential* that each person know the details of the mental health section of her health insurance plan.

Medical insurance companies frequently require clients to see a particular doctor, and it is extremely difficult to transfer to another, more capable, person. The only psychiatrist on my health insurance plan was incompetent, or so I thought. But rather than continue to see him, I petitioned the insurance company and requested a more qualified doctor to deal with my condition (see Appendix C for draft letter). My therapist wrote a letter as well and made the case that she and another psychiatrist worked closely together and could monitor my progress better. Fortunately, the letters worked and I was approved to see someone else. Despite roadblocks to adequate treatment, I recommend, however possible, to stay persistent in your efforts to get quality care. If possible, find a therapist or friend to help you.

For those who are uninsured, as soon as possible, I recommend you seek out assistance to cover medical costs immediately, including prescription drug coverage. Here are some ideas for places to seek help:

1) Unless you live in a very small community, most cities now have community health centers or mental health treatment centers that can provide lower cost care. Check in the phone book, but if this doesn't work, you can also find out about these services through a local hospital, especially a psychiatric ward. Call a couple of therapists' offices to ask about resources for the uninsured and places known for sliding-scale fees for low income clients. Oftentimes offices have referral lists of their own.
2) Look into state and county funded programs for the uninsured. Medicaid is state-sponsored medical insurance and care, and in some cases offers help for prescription medications. Each state has different qualifications for Medicaid, and in some cases one must

qualify as seriously mentally ill (SMI) in order to get help. Programs are based on income, need, and net worth, so not everyone qualifies for aid.

3) In many states there are organizations to assist with disability law in support of the Americans with Disabilities Act. These offices can provide information on resources available in your area. However, some offices are more responsive than others to those with psychiatric disabilities. In the least, they may be able to provide leads and ideas of how to get help.
4) I also encourage you to find out through your local Social Security Administration office the requirements for filing for disability. To qualify for disability, one must not have been able to work for six months due to a psychiatric or medical problem. If you qualify for disability, you are also entitled to Medicare, federal health insurance.

Learning about insurance issues can be extremely stressful. But unless you fully understand your insurance policy or are completely uninsured, your ability to receive quality care may diminish without proper information. Try not to get discouraged; sometimes you might have to make several calls before you find a helpful resource. When possible, ask a therapist, friend, or family member to assist you through this process.

The other decision needing to be made immediately is selecting a therapist. In some cases particular therapists are assigned to you under insurance plans and there is little chance of seeing someone else. But if you actually have to *find* one, here are some helpful hints. While many of the recommendations pertain specifically to multiplicity, they can be used by anyone trying to find quality therapists.

First, refer to an already prepared list of questions to ask therapists. The Sidran Foundation and HealingHopes (see Appendix A) have put together thorough lists of questions to ask potential therapists. It is a good idea to have these lists in hand when calling offices. Perhaps the most important criteria are that you find someone who believes your history of abuse. Despite all the evidence that shows otherwise, some mental health practitioners remain skeptical about the extent of violence, childhood abuse, and incest in our lives. I met with a psychiatrist when I first starting dealing with childhood incest. I remember telling him shyly and shamefully that I thought I had been molested by my father. He proceeded to ask me about the rest of the family and abuse, and I told him what I knew: my father molested my sister and me, my father was physically abusive, my mother's partner assaulted my brothers, my uncle molested me and my sisters and probably my mother, my oldest brother molested my little sister, and the same brother recently had an affair with her boyfriend. That's all I knew at the time. He had the audacity to tell me he had never heard of so much incest and abuse in one family. Imagine my shock at his statement. I knew my family was bad, but surely it couldn't be the *worst.* What amazed me the most, however, was his focus on something in the present. He kept asking how I knew for sure my sister's boyfriend and our oldest brother had an affair. "Are you sure?" he kept asking. "Yes, I'm positive," I kept telling him. He didn't believe me. I left his office feeling even more humiliated than when I first arrived.

Far too many mental health service providers continue to downplay, and in some cases disbelieve outright, the preponderance of childhood abuse in our lives. Others continue to maintain negative and false stereotypes about severe dissociative problems, especially related to DID. My sister, a trained and certified social worker, asked me once, "You don't talk to yourself, do you? I have a client who's multiple who talks to herself and scares people." My sister was afraid I would scare my nieces, perhaps herself as well. While I thoroughly appreciate parents' attempts to protect their children, her comment illustrated her ignorance about multiplicity. Insecurities can prompt therapists to develop false fears and denial strategies about severe abuse and dissociation. Clearly, if a therapist doubts your experiences or is unable to assist you adequately, move on to someone else who is more understanding and open to hearing your truth. It is not that a therapist needs to believe everything or needs to acquiesce to your every whim. Therapists should *at least* recognize that despicable childhood violence occurs and severe trauma-related disorders can result.

Once you have questions in hand, and an idea of what you want in a therapist, the next thing is to find someone experienced and qualified. I recommend you try to find a therapist who *at least* has experience treating severe childhood trauma and post-traumatic stress disorder. Preferably, for those experiencing multiplicity, find someone who has both experience *and* specialized training in DID. Mental health professionals might say that if you have a good therapist whom you can trust, then experience with DID isn't necessary. Clearly, if there are no other options, then working with a trusted therapist is important. But I can't imagine my first year of treatment had I not found a well-trained clinical psychologist with extensive experience treating multiplicity. So much is unknown and terrifying, it really does help to have therapists who know what they are doing. I asked my therapist numerous times, "Is this normal? Is this what it is like for other people like me?" She always responded by telling me everyone is different, but she was also able to say that what I was experiencing was common. She validated my experience with known research and practice, and that was really comforting to me. She was also readily familiar with physiological aspects of trauma, medication issues, and crisis treatment related to multiplicity.

There are a number of places to look for help. Perhaps the first place to start is the professional organizations that maintain membership listings of therapists who treat trauma-related and dissociative disorders (see Appendix A). If these organizations do not work out (the reason may be simply that you live in a small town and there are no members in your area), there are other sources to try. For example, the Yellow Pages of your phone book list counselors and psychologists (often under separate headings). Try to find a community mental health center or counseling center. These places can often make referrals if they don't treat trauma clients themselves. You can also call a couple of therapists' offices (and this is where you might try clinical psychologists) in the Yellow Pages and ask who in the area specializes in dissociative disorders or sexual trauma. Even if you haven't been sexually abused, therapists who work with sex abuse clients are often familiar with PTSD and childhood traumatization. I know others who found therapists by calling nurses' stations in psychiatric units of local hospitals. Psychiatric nurse practitioners learn about good therapists through their patients and doctors. Another place to inquire about referrals is your family physician. Physicians frequently keep referral lists for clients needing counseling. The search for possible therapists can be tedious and grueling, but hopefully well worth the effort.

Since so many good books and resources now provide suggestions for interviewing potential therapists, I want only to mention how very important it is to trust your intuition and listen to other survivors. I was referred to a psychologist, the "expert" on dissociative disorders in my city, by two other psychologists. She was also on the Sidran Foundation membership list. I was so happy she had agreed to see me. She was obviously busy and had lots of other DID clients already. But after I met with her, I had an uneasy feeling and something didn't seem right. I wrote the following after our session:

> – WAS IT THE STUFFED ANIMALS all lined up like a military regimen? or all the baby animal posters that i knew she put up cuz she thought she was supposed to. was it that she sees clients from 8 in the morning till 8 at night, always once a week, always for an hour and a half? how does she ever help anyone in crisis? what would happen if i was in crisis? when i asked her about it, she didn't even answer me. she just kept looking at me and asking more questions. or was it that she already started talking about me having even more personalities? like she said so casually that j. could be different ages. she just met us. how could she say that?

It wasn't that I didn't like her. She clearly had a lot of training and experience with multiplicity. But something just didn't *feel* right. This was the expert in my city and I had psychologists, one a prominent member of the local APA, telling me so. What was the problem then? Here I was, just some disordered, fragmented woman, scared to death of her own shadow, but feeling terribly uncomfortable about this first meeting. I really struggled with my own reactions: am I just avoiding therapy, or is there something really troubling about her? After much deliberation, I decided not to go back.

As it turned out, two friends and former clients of this therapist let me know they felt similarly about her. One friend described the therapist as "exploitive" and "evil." Lynn used these words purposefully, she said, because of things that happened during their sessions together. The therapist used what Lynn thought were persistent and manipulative tactics to videotape each of her alters. Lynn described the process as extremely invasive and exploitive, and came away from the sessions sometimes feeling victimized all over again. Like most good patients, Lynn followed along and did what she was told. She was too afraid to tell anyone about her experience, mostly because she perceived this doctor as the expert. I was really happy she shared her experience with me because it helped to validate my own feelings.

What I have found is that people with DID and severe PTSD might be the most reliable source when it comes to finding a good therapist. Yet, sadly, people with multiple personalities, and mental illness in general, lack credibility, even with professionals in the mental health field who should know better. The fact that my friend, another multiple, claimed this supposed expert was evil and exploitive may be dismissed as the ravings of an unstable, crazy person. My friend is integrated now, and I can't help but think this would help add credibility to her story. From my experience, people who live with, or used to live with, multiplicity tend to be highly intuitive people. For many of us it became a much-needed coping strategy throughout years of abuse. Abuse survivors can be very credible and insightful, particularly with anything related to mental health treatment issues.

Support Groups and Connecting with Others

When available, groups can often provide a safe setting to meet, listen to, and interact with others who are going through a similar experience. People suffering with trauma-related problems may have much in common despite individual differences in life histories and backgrounds. For people experiencing multiplicity especially, we have a lifetime of experiences with the condition itself. Very few support or therapy groups exist for those with dissociative disorders for several reasons.[10] First, people with DID frequently go in and out of crises regularly, sometimes unexpectedly. Many of us are at risk for hospitalization because of possible suicide or self-mutilation. Outpatient therapy groups are difficult to conduct because much concentration and control is needed to keep clients from switching between alter personalities or abreacting (i.e., the physical reliving of a past trauma in current time). Even when sexual abuse survivor groups are available, they aren't necessarily the type of group that is most needed or wanted for other trauma survivors. Especially for those who are newly diagnosed with dissociative disorders, our day-to-day struggles may have more to do with severe dissociation and an inability to function in daily life rather than the horrifying abuse that caused it.

Therapists decline to offer DID groups also because they can be extremely difficult to run. Since clients are frequently at different stages of recovery, which can mean an enormous range between coping abilities and ability to function, group work is less advantageous. Others believe DID clients should not be combined with non-DID clients. Because of the stigma attached to having multiple personalities, groups are not often advertised or are inaccessible. One of the communities in which I lived had one support group for people with DID that met once a month. It was full for the ten months I was interested. In another city of over one million people, I found two groups for DID. One was a support group for people first diagnosed with DID, but I was further along in the healing process. The other required you to be a regular client of the therapist, yet this was the same "expert" therapist I mentioned previously. From the research I have conducted and the many women with whom I have spoken, my experience with trying to find a DID support or therapy group is common: resources are scant.

For anyone with a mental illness or disorder, choosing to associate with others like yourself may be a difficult and conflicting decision. One might be thrilled with the idea of someone to talk to who understands your life. But however isolating mental illness or multiplicity may be, connection with others may be even more risky, as Jane Phillips points out:

> Another multiple, I felt, might understand me in some way he [her therapist] never would. I was suddenly desperate to meet a kindred spirit and to compare notes and perhaps have a few laughs about living with such an odd disorder. On the other hand, another multiple might understand me *too* well. I feared feeling vulnerable and exposed.[11]

I wondered, like Phillips, how much I wanted someone to really *know* me. But I also wondered how much I really wanted to know someone else. I was afraid, especially, of how severe another person's condition might be:

— I MET THREE OTHER WOMEN in this community diagnosed with DID. but i'm scared of two of them. they self-mutilate a lot, and one has hundreds of scars all over her arms. both are in and out of the hospital all the time. it scares me i could end up like this, too, like somehow i could catch it. i called the third one but she won't call me back. maybe she's afraid of me.

If support groups are limited or unavailable, one option is to create your own group with the help of your therapist. Many times therapists know of other trauma survivors, including those with serious dissociative conditions, who can help bring people together. Calling other therapists known to treat PTSD and dissociative disorders to ask if they have potential clients for the group is another option. Informing therapists of your desire to start a group can help it come to fruition. For the first couple of sessions, you might ask your therapist to sit in to help establish the rules and boundaries of the group. Although I never participated in a group myself, I finally met two other people with similar experiences whom I could call or meet with on occasion. The connections I made with these women became an important aspect to my healing. Finding support and validation from others can be lifesaving.

Internet chat rooms may also provide support and connection with others. I have friends who swear by chat rooms; that is, they appreciate being able to communicate with others like themselves. But I think one must be extremely cautious with how, when, and under what circumstances chat rooms, especially, are utilized. I suggest that all Internet exploration be done very carefully, since links can send you immediately to pornography, cult organizations, and disturbing information. For this reason alone, it is advisable, especially in the beginning, to stick with well-known, established sites. For those who have suffered ritualistic abuse, I strongly advise getting help from a friend or therapist to do any Internet exploration. If necessary, ask them to look up information for you. Maintaining healthy boundaries is frequently difficult or even impossible for those who have suffered severe childhood abuse. With the Internet, especially, a false sense of intimacy can develop whereby people can lie about who they are and what they really want. Some intentionally prey on the vulnerable. Internet communications can lead to possible exploitation by sharing private information you have told no one else; by giving out personal information, such as your real name, address, or phone number; or by being harassed. For those who experience multiplicity, if one is not co-conscious with all of her alters, the Internet can put one in a highly vulnerable situation, as she might not even remember being online. Child parts might act in ways that may be inappropriate with older people.

Everyone has to come up with their own rules for using the Internet that make sense. Here are a few rules I have established for myself:

1) Don't write or imply anything that you wouldn't say to a person's face. It is a good reminder, anyway, that I am not necessarily protected by the Internet even though I cannot be seen physically.
2) Never surf while looking up information on ritual abuse, even if a site looks promising.
3) Never spend more than an hour at a time looking up information. I get too tired, and it is then that I start feeling vulnerable.
4) If I start getting bothered, upset, or anxious by *anything,* I stop immediately, no matter what.

Establishing and maintaining healthy boundaries is critical. The greatest concern must be taking care of yourself.

Medication Decisions

Those trained in Western psychiatry and psychology tend to be proponents of medications to help alleviate traumatic stress symptoms. At times, medication may be necessary in order to function. An eight-year-old alter wrote the following one night about how badly we hurt sometimes:

— THE WORST THING is when the big people inside get upset, because then everybody gets upset. like when j. comes out he paces up and down the house and he is so mad. sometimes he even starts yanking our hair. and then every time he hears something it is like our fingers are in a light socket. it hurts real bad. then sometimes she gets loud and says bad words and gets all excited. we can't say who "she" is but we know. then the little ones don't want to sleep because they're so scared. our head will hurt real bad and it will get real loud inside. it is really hard sometimes. i try to help everybody be calm but sometimes i just can't. then i get tired too and i just want to go away and go to sleep.

– like right now our stomach hurts. sometimes it does this. we think about things and then it hurts. sometimes it is our head, like the top of our head especially. it will feel like someone is smashing it with a shovel. our shoulders and neck hurt all the time. it's because we still get worried waiting for something bad to happen. but it's lots better then it used to be and that is good. i wish we didn't hurt so bad all the time.

There were so many times when prescription medications were the only thing that kept me sleeping and even functioning. Fortunately, not everyone dealing with severe child abuse issues needs to be medicated. But when it is necessary, it is important to be part of the process to determine what is needed.

People with serious post-traumatic stress disorder and DID are notorious for their inability to sleep, and it is for this reason alone that a skilled psychiatrist or other professional certified to prescribe medications is critical. Sleep is vital to our mental and physical well-being, and without it we can only deteriorate. Prior to a psychiatric hospitalization at a trauma clinic, I had gone several months with sleeping very poorly and was completely sleep deprived. Sleep was my nemesis:

– WE ALL FEARED NIGHTTIME. we'd close our eyes but could never sleep. the little ones couldn't sleep because they were so afraid; the older ones were anxious and hostile; we had bad nightmares and horribly drenching night sweats. we'd wake up startled every hour on the hour. it was a hellish experience. and it was definitely a miracle the first time we finally slept soundly through an entire night. it had been about six months and all we wanted to do was sleep after that.

Typically, one sees a psychiatrist for medication management, but in some states psychiatric nurse practitioners have a license to prescribe medication. Whatever their professional license, the main consideration is that they *know their medications well.* In other words, going to someone who is unfamiliar or lacks up-to-date knowledge with the most current research and information on the treatment of traumatic stress symptoms is probably not the best person for you, even if that person is friendly and compassionate. I went to one psychiatrist who could not remember the names of medications, let alone their side effects. Literally, he would flip through pages on his unorganized desk to try to find brochures from pharmaceutical companies. Anyone with a psychiatric disability will become more disabled with a person who is unfamiliar with current medications and their effects.

The first two times I met with one particular psychiatrist, he kept wanting to talk to my alters. I could tell he was utterly fascinated with multiple personalities and had very little experience with it. His behavior was extremely invasive and voyeuristic, but I feared that if I did not acquiesce to his requests, I would not get the medications I needed. What I have learned since is that if a medications person keeps asking about your alters, even encouraging you to switch in the office, and has little information about your day-to-day needs, then something is wrong. It is my experience that when therapists and psychiatrists begin asking very detailed and personal questions about the internal system early on in treatment, they may be overcompensating for their own inexperience and incompetence. In some cases, it is unnecessary for professionals managing medications to know details about the internal system at all. Unless there is a problem with the medication itself, including the taking of it, then specifics regarding your abuse history or your internal system may be irrelevant. Guaranteed, your daily struggles will be less difficult when you find a skilled medication prescriber.

During my first psychiatric hospitalization, I was afraid to take the medication being prescribed to me by the admitting psychiatrist whom I had just met. My previous experience with psychiatrists was marginal, and I had a limited reference about psych wards in general. What came to mind, especially, was the movie, *One Flew Over the Cuckoo's Nest.* I had fears of being overmedicated and becoming zombie-like. So for the first two days of my admittance, I refused all medication. The admittance form was clear: I could deny any treatment. Because I did not feel properly informed about what was going on with me, nor how the medication would help, I refused to take it. But on the third day I was threatened by my psychiatrist: either take the medication or be released from the hospital. Fearing what I would do to myself if released, I took the medicine. After release, I eventually found better psychiatric care and learned that *patients have choices regarding medications.* I learned to negotiate with my doctors about how, what, and when I was medicated.

As I will say again, the best recommendations come from clients themselves. On the recommendation of another woman diagnosed with DID, I finally found a psychiatrist who was both highly skilled and compassionate. He helped me to understand what was going on in my brain in terms of the hyperarousal and sleep deprivation. Within three weeks I was finally able to sleep soundly again without feeling drugged. During my second psychiatric hospitalization, I was prescribed myriad medications to deal with severe dissociation, horrible post-traumatic stress symptoms, sleep deprivation, and depression. Fortunately, I had an excellent psychiatrist who appreciated my concern about being overmedicated. I was put on what seemed like a lot of medication at the time: Serzone, an antidepressant frequently used to treat PTSD; Depakote, a mood stabilizer often used to help those with severe PTSD and DID; a very low dose of Seroquel, a neuroleptic used for treating PTSD symptoms and has a sedative and relaxing effect; Ambien, a sleeping pill to be taken until the antidepressant was fully effective; and Ativan, an antianxiety medication to be taken as needed during a flashback or panic attack.[12] But these medications helped me get through a very rough time. I believe medications are needed sometimes to help stabilize a person in crisis. Having a voice in what is prescribed, and in my case the dosage prescribed, makes a huge difference. It is your right to ask whether you have choices in medications and what other options might be available. Finding a doctor who accepts your opinions and needs, and can help you manage your day-to-day life, is critical.

Medication decisions so much of the time involve the ability to pay. Many providers have samples of prescription medications that are free to clients, but the only way to receive this medication is to ask. Although it may feel uncomfortable, you should inform your doctor you are unable to afford the medication. Many pharmaceutical companies provide free samples or have discount programs for patients unable to pay. Most of the time you must inquire about such programs from your health care provider. Medicare has an Internet website that offers information on statewide, county, and local prescription drug discount programs.[13] I moved again and after much searching, I found an excellent psychiatric nurse practitioner for my medications. Although she was not a Medicare provider, she charged a sliding-scale fee and gave me free samples of the medications I needed. Her fee with the free samples made it less expensive to see her than someone else who accepts Medicare but had few free samples. Sometimes you have to be a little creative with the resources available in your area.

Like many, however, I have had both valuable and hurtful experiences with medications. Side effects for me have included lethargy, metabolism changes, weight gain, constant dry mouth, stomach problems, a decrease in sexual functioning, and increased headaches and migraines. Because of the side effects of some medicines, along with a myriad of other medical problems, I began to pursue nontraditional approaches to healing. For example, there are excellent Chinese medicine doctors skilled with acupuncture and herbs, as well as naturopathic physicians and nutritionists who can assist in diet and herbal supplements. At one point, I was able to eliminate all prescription medications by accepting the treatments of a Chinese herbalist. I drank prepared herbal teas twice a day for over a year and eventually started having acupuncture. Some of my symptoms diminished or went away immediately. Within three months of treatment, I was able to sleep through the night without medications. Within four months, I was off all medications altogether. My primary care physician and psychiatrist both were shocked by the rapid changes. These herbal treatments were lifesaving for me.

Such treatments may be too expensive for some to even consider. Many insurance companies, including federal Medicare, refuse to regard acupuncture, massage, and other nontraditional healing approaches as viable treatment options. In my experience, nontraditional healers tend to be more flexible with costs, so it is worth the effort to try to negotiate an affordable fee. I continue to be very persistent with negotiating fees with everyone now, including doctors with fixed

Medicare fees. Remember, doctors and other healers will not drop their fees if you don't ask.

Just as one should be cautious with all potential doctors and therapists, one must also be cautious about suggested treatments, including fees and time frames of when you can expect results. Because certain treatments may be unfamiliar to you, I recommend that you bring a trusted friend with you to the first few appointments. That way, the friend can act as eyes and ears in case you are nervous, scared, or too dissociated to pay attention or ask important questions. The most essential thing to keep in mind is your ability to make choices about your treatment, and this includes how, when, and under what circumstances to accept aid from people.

Government Aid: The Pros and Cons

People unable to work because of psychiatric disabilities can apply for federal Social Security disability, state welfare, and other state aid for the seriously mentally ill (SMI). Accepting governmental assistance may be necessary in order to meet your basic living needs and to receive necessary medical care. Social Security Disability (SSD) helps people when they are unable to work. Federal law says you must be unable to work for a full six months to qualify for disability. If you think you may be eligible for SSD, or are just not sure, the first thing you want to do is call (or have a friend call) the Social Security Disability Office (1-800-772-1213). They will send you a packet of information about qualifications and applying for benefits, including a pamphlet entitled *Social Security: Disability Benefits.*

There is an enormous amount of information to learn about Social Security Disability before one can even make an informed decision about whether to apply. The process of applying can be enormously tedious and exhausting. There are lengthy and confusing forms to be filled out that ask for detailed personal information. Letters and forms are sent by the disability office to your doctors, therapists, hospitals, and former employers to confirm your inability to work. Once your application is filled out, you are required to meet with a disability representative to discuss your case. In some cases, you may be required to meet once with a psychiatrist designated by the SSD office to evaluate your mental health and your ability to work. Once all of the information and evidence is submitted, a special office reviews your application to determine eligibility. It can take several months from the time you first submit your application to when the final decision is made.

If determined eligible, the amount of your disability check is dependent on your previous years' earnings. All workers pay into Social Security, and it is this money you've already paid that determines your aid. The more income you have earned in the past several years, the greater your disability check each month. Conversely, for those who have been unemployed or worked part-time prior to applying, the checks will be smaller. Many of us are unable to live on this monthly check. This is why it is very important to be as accurate as possible in determining the date when your illness or disorder first affected your ability to work.

In some cases, disability decisions can be made retroactively up to twelve months. That is, the SSD office can determine that your disability started a year before the date they received your application. This is what happened in my case. I submitted my application one and a half years after I first became unable to work. (It took me that long to figure out I *could* apply. I had been receiving a fellowship through my university and assumed I couldn't qualify as disabled. I was wrong. If you are working part-time or are in school, do not assume that you cannot qualify for SSD.) The disability office paid me retroactively for each month I was considered disabled but hadn't collected disability—it equated to one year of disability payments totaling thousands of dollars. I was extremely fortunate. Without this money, I would have ended up in poverty.

I believe that part of the reason I was found eligible is because of all the support I had. For example, I had a wonderful therapist familiar with SSD procedures who helped me tremendously. She let me know the process and was completely supportive when I became overwhelmed or frustrated. She wrote a letter on my behalf and submitted a form from an interview we had done together. I also had a dear friend help me fill out the long application, a form that took me two weeks to fill out. Another close friend came with me to the meeting with the disability representative. She asked great questions and held my hand when I started having a hard time. If at all possible, try to find support through this process, as it can be extremely frustrating and even upsetting. The SSD office has people who can help if other help is not available.

Many people with psychiatric disorders apply for Social Security Disability but do not qualify, even if they have lost their jobs and are unable to work. Others are unaware they can apply, and even more cannot fill out the lengthy and confusing forms. The Social Security Disability application process can be time-consuming, frustrating, and anxiety provoking. In addition, it can take several months to receive a final decision. One must be prepared for how grueling the process can be. For certain, an enormous amount of personal commitment and determination is needed to get through this process.

For me, one of the most difficult aspects of the application process was dealing with the new label "disabled." I remember it being really difficult to admit to myself, let alone to anyone else, how bad things had gotten for me. On some days, I was unable to care for myself, let alone go to work. Many people suffering with trauma and dissociative disorders are great at hiding how bad things are from friends and family, even from therapists and doctors. I was demoralized about my condition and was terribly ashamed of myself for losing the ability to function and work. It was devastating because I had been in the workforce since I was eleven years old, and this was something I was proud of. A myriad of feelings can emerge with admitting to yourself and others you are disabled and unable to work.

Another very difficult aspect of the process was how the forms were not written for someone dealing with multiplicity or severe PTSD (perhaps the same could be said about most mental illnesses). My experience with multiplicity, especially, was utterly inconsistent from moment to moment. I could vacillate between being completely dysfunctional one minute, crying on the floor uncontrollably like a three-year-old, to being able to work on my doctoral dissertation the next. The only thing I could expect was that everything—my moods, behaviors, ability to eat or dress myself, read or work—changed on a constant basis. The unpredictability of our lives can make it difficult to fill out the disability forms because there are no easy answers to such questions as "What kind of activities do you do in your day?" (see Appendix B).

If you are approved for SSD, you also qualify for Medicare, or federal health insurance. Although Medicare may be lifesaving, there are definite problems for those with serious psychiatric disabilities. For example, Original Medicare, one of two options available to those eligible, does not currently pay for prescription medications. Those diagnosed with DID and PTSD can be medicated for all sorts of problems. Medication costs can be prohibitive. Medicare co-payments on therapy and psychiatric sessions are 50 percent. In other words, the disabled client, usually unemployed or at least on a fixed income, is expected to come up with the remaining 50 percent of the fees on her own. Hourly rates for psychiatric care can be as high as $175 an hour. I was charged $75 for an initial visit with a psychologist (her charge was $150 per hour), someone I never saw again. While there are fixed Medicare costs, out-of-pocket expenses can still be outrageously high. Fortunately, you may be able to negotiate fees with a provider. But many people stop seeing therapists regularly because they cannot afford it. In addition, not all medical services are covered, and frequently the co-pays become cost prohibitive as well.

With the second Medicare plan offered, you are required to select a certified HMO (health maintenance organization) who might have more affordable co-pays and additional services, such as prescription medication coverage. But by selecting this option, one loses choices in treatment and care. One is typically limited by specified therapists and physicians, treatment options, and basic medical care. It is possible that a selected HMO does not have a qualified therapist knowledgeable about severe childhood traumatization, let alone experience in treating post-traumatic stress or multiple personalities. In too many cases, quality and choices in care must be sacrificed for affordability.

Keep in mind there may be other health insurance options available. For example, if you are forced to leave your job because of your inability to work, you might qualify for COBRA, an extension of health care provided by your company. COBRA is federally mandated; that is, employers who have over fifty employees are legally required to offer COBRA to anyone leaving the company. It means you are covered for health insurance up to eighteen months, sometimes longer for people with disabilities. The downside is that COBRA can be expensive. Most companies do not tell you about COBRA because it costs them more money for you to be on it. But by law they have to make health insurance available to people who leave the company. Of course, you remain unemployed, but at least you have health insurance. Also, once you apply for disability, it might take several months for a decision to be made on your application. It is definitely preferable to have health insurance, and therefore necessary care, while you are waiting for the disability decision.

State welfare, county, and local assistance programs are also available to those with serious psychiatric disorders. State welfare is determined by economic need, rather than federal disability based on inability to work. Many people receiving federal SSD require additional assistance, including state welfare, housing assistance, and additional health insurance. State welfare can be an option, especially to help cover prescription drugs and exorbitant co-pays. Each state's program is different, however, and you must research what the benefits and limitations are for receiving the aid. In order to receive welfare in some states, you are required to go to specific doctors and therapists, having virtually no, or very little, choice in the matter. By accepting state assistance, many times you give up flexibility and options in treatment and care in exchange for affordable care.

However overwhelming all of these health care decisions can be, know that with every little step taken, you empower yourself further by becoming informed, responsible, and intolerant of revictimization. The healing process can be very slow. I remember when I first got hospitalized and met a woman diagnosed with both DID and PTSD who had been going through this a few years already. She had solid, practical advice and information for me. But when I started reading the books she suggested, I was overwhelmed. Everything I read said it was going to take a long time to heal (like five to seven years), and I did not want to hear it. I was certain I would be on the fast track—the way I live my life normally. My own healing started out that way, but that's not how it ended up. So I understand when you read something and think, "That's not going to be me!" However long it takes for you to feel better about things, know that it will still feel like too long. No one wants to live with a serious psychiatric disorder, and certainly no one wants to become debilitated by it. Healing from all the abuse, confusion, and pain may seem foreign and unrealistic. I remember just two months after my breakdown, a psychologist in an inpatient trauma clinic asked me, "What long-term goals do you have for yourself?" The question seemed both bizarre and ludicrous. I never thought at that moment of time that there would ever be a "long term" for me. But here I am now, writing this book and envisioning a future for myself. Perseverance, hope, and a will to matter can make an enormous difference in one's everyday life.

Perhaps the most valuable advice is to keep believing that no matter how bad it gets, no matter how much you want to hurt yourself or run away from it all, things will slowly get better. It is only in retrospect sometimes when I recognize and appreciate my own progress. Clara wrote one day:

> – WE USED TO BE AFRAID of everybody and big people scared us. d. didn't even know what she was eating one time because she didn't get to eat very much. the little ones used to be real scared at night so we had to leave the lights on. sometimes we would hide under the covers. we wouldn't even open the drapes during the day. and one time we bought black shower curtains to cover our windows. we would stay inside our bedroom and not go anywhere. it's like we were living in a cave.
>
> – one time we couldn't drive because d. came out and put her leg on the seat when we were driving so we had to stop. she was scared and tired. sometimes she can't talk because she's so afraid something bad will happen to her. she tries real hard to talk but she just can't. she listens to everything though. and c. was in a basement for a really long time and it's so bright and loud now for him and it hurts his eyes and ears. he used to be jumpy all the time and scared at sounds. he would just want to curl up like a baby. i didn't blame him one bit.
>
> – but things are tons better now cuz the little ones come out more and they even like to play. they have favorite foods and favorite places to go and favorite people to be with. like they made friends with Skye, Lisa's son who is really cool. things used to be real bad before, but they're lots better now. i hope this helps other people know that things really will get better.

Five years ago I wanted to die. I was afraid of my own shadow and so ashamed of who I was. Three years ago I was afraid to sit on a porch because the world seemed too expansive and cruel. The progress I have made is truly remarkable.

Progress may be very slow, but you have to trust yourself and, if possible, trust in the universe to help get you through it. Besides living through the abuse itself, a commitment to heal may be one of the most difficult and courageous things you will ever face in your life. Each day you may have to remind yourself that things will get better even when they seem like they are getting worse. I know what it feels like when every day, every minute and hour of the day, is a consuming, painful struggle. And I know what it feels like to want to give up. But I also know with complete certainty there is life after death, there is beauty in the midst of ugliness, and there is hope and love in the midst of utter despair.

Survivor Self-Care and Personal Empowerment

There are many ways we can heal ourselves from the damage caused by years of abuse. I am convinced that in order to heal fully from severe childhood trauma, we need to build a surplus of positive, loving bodily experiences to recondition our traumatic stress reactions. A dear friend reminded me in the following passage how important it is to have unconditional love for ourselves:

> the baby has become a child, has become an adult. the stages of life have been successful, even with all the obstacles. all was not fun, but every one of these stepping stones have brought development. there is much ahead, and with the unconditional relationship she has with herself and her true friends, all will make the passage much more peaceful.[14]

We lighten our heart and our very being when we learn to love ourselves.

Body therapies can help restore the damage caused by abuse. Therapies include simple acts we do for ourselves, such as massaging our hands or sinking our feet into sand, as well as more elaborate practices, such as participating in a yoga class or having a professional massage. I have been fortunate to be able to try and participate in several professional body therapies. Whatever one's financial or physical means, the most important aspect is to be committed to healing your body, and this means you may have to be creative and open-minded about your selected therapies.

Underneath all of the ugly, twisted memories in my body are long-forgotten pleasurable experiences. I am reminded of this each time I go to the ocean. As I sink my feet into the warm, grainy sand, I come alive inside. My body remembers what it was like at three years old to toddle around the beach with a bucket in hand, playing in the sand and sticking my feet in the ice cold ocean water. My body remembers the smell of salty water, the sound of seagulls flying overhead, and the feel of the ocean breeze against my face. I sing in delight at how happy I feel, about how happy I once was. The ocean is a healing place for me now because it brings back positive and loving memories of my childhood, a brief time when I felt free and safe. By retraining each of our senses, we are learning how to love ourselves unconditionally.

Self-Help Techniques

One of the most profound ways we can love ourselves is through self-care. What I mean by this is learning to treat yourself like you would your very best friend or your own child. It means learning to parent yourself wisely and wholeheartedly. One way we can do this is to devise plans for when times are rough. The plan can be for a specific period of time or more general for whenever one feels vulnerable or out of sorts. A good friend recently was interviewed about her experiences as an incest survivor for a PBS special. We talked that evening, and I asked her what her plan was to take care of herself. She didn't have a plan yet, so we worked out one together. After she hung up the phone, her plan was as follows:

- Get into her pajamas and make some hot chocolate.
- Get the beds ready so she and her son would be ready to sleep when he got home.
- Screen all phone calls and only talk with her closest friends.
- Decide a quiet activity for her son before bedtime.
- Put on quiet, soothing music to fall asleep to.

- Say a prayer to the Grandmothers to ask for their protection and love.

As wonderful a parent as my friend is to her son, she forgets sometimes to parent and nurture herself. When we come up with healthy ways to nurture and love ourselves, and then follow through with them, we are parenting ourselves in very symbolic and meaningful ways. Many abuse survivors never learn what it means to care for the self. But without it, we will never be whole.

It is common for those who have suffered extreme abuse to loathe their bodies, so disconnection is often a way of life. When we act consciously in positive ways to heal ourselves, the effects can be enormous on our psychological, physical, and emotional health. The following are simple self-help practices to help awaken and enliven bodily sensation:

- Buy fresh fruit or a favorite food and savor each bite of it.
- Feel the sensuousness and enjoyment of soaking your feet in warm water.
- Massage your hands or feet with pleasant smelling lotion.
- Buy a beautiful flower.
- Listen to the soft sounds of nature, such as birds singing, trees blowing in the wind, or a water fountain. Buy or borrow a CD of nature music if you are unable to leave your home.
- Teach yourself a craft, such as knitting or woodworking, to use your hands against pleasurable fabrics or materials.
- Add some of your favorite colors to each room by using cards, ribbons, drawings, or pictures.

Having conscious intentions about caring for oneself will undoubtedly make a significant difference in one's overall health and well-being.

I know in my most depressed, despairing state, I had an extremely difficult time feeling positive about anything, let alone about myself or any of my senses. But I desperately wanted to get better. So I began by doing one consciously soothing thing each day. What I found is that I was already doing things—brushing my hair, eating an avocado and tomato sandwich, and sitting in the sun—but just wasn't aware of it. These practices helped me to recondition my body to feel and accept pleasure. Each time we stay conscious during a positive experience, and can recall it later, we help to heal our entire being from the brutality of abuse.

We can soothe our bodies, minds, and spirits in other ways. Light exercise, stretching, yoga, and the martial arts can be extremely helpful in healing the body from trauma. Though I fully understood its importance, I often struggled to make movement a part of my daily routine. At times even breathing felt overwhelming, and leaving my home was out of the question. With encouragement from my therapist, I began by doing little things in my home: sitting in a chair and breathing deeply five times in a row; stretching my arms and legs when I was watching television. These practices helped me build up to other ones. I found it definitely helps to participate in practices you enjoy doing. Eventually I became able and willing to walk and do light gardening. I bought a yoga videotape at a thrift store and started practicing it in the living room. I also bought a five-pound weight and starting doing exercises for my arms. All of these practices, from deep breathing to yoga, can help us become more connected to our bodies. This connection is fundamentally crucial for our spiritual, mental, and physical well-being.

Depending on one's ability, more strenuous exercise can be extremely valuable in helping to work through intense emotions. I have always been involved in organized sports, and later in the martial arts, but as time went on, it became more difficult for me to participate in such activities—I would dissociate too much, and it was difficult being around other people. But I missed the physicality and intensity of sports. A friend taught me how to garden, and now gardening has become my sport of choice. I cannot tell you how many holes I dug in the backyard while gardening! Sometimes it takes a little creativity to come up with ways to get exercise and physical stimulation. Most of us need to be nurtured considering all the emotional scars and mental chaos in our lives. I like to think of exercising, stretching, and moving my body as deliberate techniques to nurture and love myself. When one is able, attempting to engage in more intensive body therapies can be a powerful outlet for deeply embedded emotions.

Professional Body Therapies

Trauma victims frequently have a precarious relationship with their bodies. That is, we can simultaneously loathe ourselves yet desperately desire contact with another. Conflict about intimacy can create apprehension about trying professional body therapies. Others are scared of how it may affect them. The act of touch by another can produce profound physical, emotional, and even spiritual reactions. I bawled the first time I let a massage therapist touch me because of how intense the feelings were. Touch by another can symbolize great courage and the determination it takes to heal ourselves from child abuse. Contact can also produce a strong sense of community and solidarity between people who would otherwise be alone.

There are a number of professionals who work to heal the body and eliminate pain: massage therapists, chiropractors, reflexologists, acupuncturists, and many others. Therapeutic massage became a necessary respite for me during intensive and difficult periods. I met my massage therapist six months after my mental breakdown. I felt like Sue became a significant part of my struggle: we were involved in a collective effort to heal not just me and my body but *all* battered and abused women. I wrote the following after a session with Sue:

– I WENT IN FEELING HEAVY, so much pressure in my head, fatigue throughout my body. But now I feel light, pressure gone. And my writer is here looking at the world in a whole new light. Light isn't just metaphorical, it's physical, symbolic, too, of the ebb and flow of my life right now.

– I'm moved, literally, by touches on my head, "cranial work" as Sue calls it. A real transgression of space and place. My body right now feels more like my own, not someone else's or another person's to occupy. Her office is a place I go to feel safe, a place to let go. And what happens is I wake up from whatever fog I may have been in, displace or dislodge those beings and thoughts that seem foreign. My mind and body join together. Through this uniting there is joy—joy because for the first time in a long time I can feel myself

> and I don't feel split apart. I'm not confused by who or what I am. I become rejuvenated. So I try to hold on to these feelings of lightness and wholeness for as long as I can, however many minutes it may last.
>
> – Sue has become a bright spot in my long and grueling week. Her healing, magic touch inspires me, consoles me, and validates my pain. She helps me keep fighting because I know there will be relief and support, a sister who understands the struggle and the difficult work I'm facing. She has struggled herself and recognizes the work that women need to do in order to heal society. The cause right now is survival, and this is solidarity.

The sharing of trauma through touch and physical contact can be an immeasurable act of solidarity and support to people who find themselves isolated and hurting.

Martial Arts and Self-Defense Training

Too many females learn through experience that sexual abuse, assault, and harassment are inevitable. We are taught, usually at a very young age, to submit to aggression.[15] For example, females learn through socialization to freeze and become numb during abusive and threatening situations. The body and mind store through memory freezing and numbing responses, with the effect of creating passive females during fearful attacks. Yet these responses are simply learned and part of the way most females are conditioned and trained to act. Self-defense training and the martial arts challenge female passivity by giving women and girls tools to act more assertively. Scores of women have turned to self-defense classes and martial arts to combat their fear of violent attack but also as a way to regain some dignity. Self-defense and the martial arts can provide an arena to train the body in new, more empowering ways.

I found Shotokan karate, a Japanese form of karate focusing on the mind/body/spirit connection, to be an important space to reexperience and relearn the limits of my mental and physical body. I learned how to get and remain focused and (mostly) present during an intense, sometimes frightening, experience. The longer I practiced, the more I was able to recognize the point at which I began to dissociate. Such training had a significant impact on my daily life, helping me to be strong and courageous in the face of terrorizing childhood memories. It even had a positive effect on my ability to sleep. By engaging in such self-defense practices, females, especially, can develop a more confident physical and emotional disposition; for many, such as myself, it becomes a brand new way of being in the world.

Part of what will transform the mentality and experience of victimization is recognizing one's capacity to overpower, or even harm, another. This does not mean, however, that a person who practices self-defense becomes, nor should become, aggressive or violent. I believe we must be able to picture ourselves harming another in order to fully trust our confidence in the face of an attack. In doing this we begin to see ourselves as warriors rather than victims. I realize this point might be controversial, and I even have close friends who would vehemently disagree that a woman needs to think of herself as potentially violent before she can defend herself during a brutal attack. But this perspective has been enormously beneficial to me given my own history of childhood violence and the social and personal expectations to submit. In believing I can defend myself, I take on a formidable presence; I possess and exude strength, courage, and the will to matter. It is imperative that female survivors, especially, transform the learned behavior of "frozen watchfulness"[16] to allow for a female strength, a strength found and maintained in the body and mind. We must retrain ourselves to act assertively rather than to freeze. Self-defense and martial arts practices can allow for a new type of activism and solidarity to emerge when survivors work together and encourage each other in very physically and emotionally challenging ways. We empower ourselves when we challenge the forces and circumstances in our lives that have made us passive, submissive, and vulnerable to male violence.

Trying new body therapies can feel overwhelming. When it is a struggle to eat or shower, going to a class to practice yoga or karate may seem completely unrealistic. So take small steps. Begin to notice your body movement at home and recognize, for example, when you walk into the kitchen and stretch for a can of soup in the cupboard. Then add movement to your daily schedule. Eventually you may want to try massage or other professional therapies. Then one day, you may find a beginning class in yoga, the martial arts, or dance. However you choose to build body therapies into your life, remember that it takes time and patience. It also helps to have support.

I offer the following recommendations for the person who needs help and support in trying new body therapies:

1) Bring a close friend with you to sessions, especially the first couple of times. Friends can help gauge the situation for safety and also ask questions to make sure you are comfortable. I was fortunate to have friends who would drive me to sessions and even participate with me in yoga and karate training.
2) Make sure the body therapist or instructor is someone reputable and known by a friend or therapist.
3) Tell the provider that you are nervous. You can do this without necessarily getting into details of why. Sometimes it is important to keep your experiences private, especially in the beginning. There may be times, after you get to know and trust someone, that you share your psychiatric or child abuse history; it may assist the provider to help you better. Always check in with yourself to make sure you are doing what feels most comfortable.
4) Massage or other treatments may suggest taking off your clothes, but you can leave them on if you need to. There have been plenty of times with my massage therapist that I left my sweats and T-shirt on. I certainly felt more safe and relaxed doing it this way. The most important thing is to commit yourself to doing whatever you need to do to make yourself feel comfortable and safe.
5) There may be days when it is necessary to stop a session early, or bad days when you are unable to attend the therapy or practice at all. Give yourself permission to cancel or leave the sessions early. There were days when I would just watch a karate class to feel like I was doing something. Watching other people move their bodies was helpful to me. Discuss with your provider early on that you may have days when you are unable to attend.
6) Let your therapist and close friends know anytime you are starting a new body therapy. Remember, any body work might stir up intense emotions and body memory. Think about it this way: as our bodies respond to healthy touch and movement, we release the negative

toxins created during abuse. Friends and therapists can give you support while you begin new therapies.

7) Do not try to force yourself to participate in practices you are not ready for. It is essential that you be patient with yourself and that you learn your own tolerance level for each new method you try.

What is most important about body therapies is that you trust and respect your own sense of safety and well-being and recognize these may change. I began to prioritize body therapy as just as important as my psychotherapy sessions. I am certain that as my body has healed, so too has my mind and vice versa. Body therapies significantly add to our mental, physical, and spiritual well-being. There has to be a balance between encouraging yourself to try new body therapies and having flashbacks while doing so. If there are certain sensations, e.g., smells, tastes, or fabrics, you have an aversion to or get flashbacks from, find other pleasurable sensations. Being loving to yourself also means accepting and honoring your own limits. It may be that as you heal, certain sensations or behaviors won't be triggering anymore, while others will remain so. *These changes are all part of the healing process.*

Our bodies continue to be violated in adulthood until we make the conscious, deliberate decision to stop it. This can be an enormous task, but it is definitely possible. The many memoirs of abuse victims are testimony to the power of healing and hope. Joan Frances Casey writes eloquently of her own healing:

> Who was I now? I was still aware of internal separation, but the external voice, expression, decision, action, was single, reflective of all of me. I was the Flock, with all the personalities, flying in formation in some tightly woven instinct to be one. A group mind with a single thought, moving toward a shared destiny. I was the thought, the voice of all who were, of all that I could be. Evolving, growing. A person.[17]

I have thought for many years that friends are better than therapists. I envision friends working together as a community to support, love, and care for each other. Maintaining this vision throughout my healing was extremely difficult because I had to accept that individuals have very different limitations, expectations, and definitions for what it means to provide support. I learned early on that I could not count on my biological family for assistance, so I desperately needed help from my friends. While I received a great deal of support, it did not come easy. A close friend reminded me recently that in order to maintain some friendships, I had to significantly lower my expectations of them and what the friendship entailed. I had to teach people how to care for me, and in some cases, this was a monumental task. Loved ones may be ill equipped and unskilled, and sometimes lack the same enthusiasm and dedication to another person's healing. This was evident for me. Friendships became one-sided, for sure, where I needed much more attention than I could return. I had to develop "committees" of friends, create networks of who could help with what. It meant great loss and disappointment along the way because every friendship changed dramatically. I had to learn rather quickly to accept whatever a person was able to give, whenever the person could give it, then not hold judgments about what should have been given or even what I really wanted. I had to accept people where they were on any given day, at any given moment, and that people's abilities to give could be as sporadic and inconsistent as my own. Perhaps this is why learning to love yourself is so vitally important; it is what we can control and ultimately what we can be the best at. So while I had a great deal of support from friends, there was an enormous emotional cost for me and for them. It took hard work, determination, and many hurt feelings to make it happen. In the end, however, individual support is hardly adequate. Many more social tools and remedies are needed on a broad basis to alleviate the devastation caused by abuse.

6 Working Together to Ease the Suffering

"What do you feel there is left for you to do?"
"Heal the earth. My mission in life is to heal the earth and all living things."
"Yeah, but is there anything left for you to do for your own healing?"
"That *is* for myself. I don't see my healing as separate from that."
—Kyos Featherdancing, quoted in Bass and Davis, *The Courage to Heal*

Advocacy on behalf of children and child abuse survivors is needed on all sorts of levels. Only when we, as a society, start asking the right questions and begin to notice otherwise able people become disabled and mentally absent will we begin to understand the damaging effects of traumatic abuse. Our communities, like individuals, must learn to listen and act:

– NOBODY WANTS TO KNOW what really happened to me. nobody asks. nobody hears the gory details: that bottles were shoved inside me, that big, dirty hands touched every part of my body, that i was forced to have a penis shoved repeatedly into my seven year-old little throat. nobody asks why my hips hurt all the time or why my lips blister, bleed and crack so often. nobody wants to know about me being pinned down to the cold, linoleum floor, about cleaning the bloody sheets, about how my great uncle, the priest, made me sit on his lap and fondle him, and how he stuck his grimy hands inside me. nobody asks what i remember, nor why it continues to haunt me today. but someone needs to ask. someone needs to answer.

Severe child abuse, violence, and sexual assault are not problems that can be eradicated by individual healing and advocacy alone. Children, especially, cannot be expected to stop abusive conditions in their lives when they do not have the resources, maturity, or power to do so. Teaching children to be alert and knowledgeable about potential violence and abuse is obviously important. But unless we address the role of institutions in the perpetuation of abusive conditions, individuals will continue to be held responsible for their own abuse.

Far too many people are suffering in silence, desperately waiting for someone to help. Peggy J. in "Silent Screams" writes:[1]

we tried to tell you
in so many ways,
the pain, fear, despair, shame;
yet what came forth were
the silent screams.

it's not that we haven't tried —
you and us — to speak,
to hear, to understand,
to listen to these
silent screams.

there's no dramatics, no drama
no hysterics, no acting
yet we plead for help through
the silent screams.
we're screaming now;
please hear us, please hold us,

please reach out even though we look so calm;
please don't let these be more of
those silent screams.

These silent screams need to be heard by everyone, particularly those in positions of authority who can make significant changes in people's lives.

Child abuse is not only, or even primarily, a family problem. Severe child abuse occurs within a societal context, that is, a society replete with cultural attitudes and practices in which abuse, violence, and inequality are promoted and maintained. Parents and caretakers abuse children because they are part of a larger society that allows it. When the government, religious institutions, schools, and the media cease to perpetuate violence and abuse, parents will follow, whether by social pressure, through consistent laws, or through massive education. Predominant political and social institutions must engender principles that disallow for abuse and inequality.

We have a social obligation to address a serious health problem: the devastating consequences of child abuse. In the previous chapter, I provided examples of how individuals can respond to the suffering of survivors. Individual support matters greatly to the survivor, but it is not enough. Because institutions within society are so powerful, it is a monumental task for a few individuals to make significant long-term changes within any institution. In this chapter I discuss the many ways in which nonprofit organizations, communities, businesses, and major institutions, particularly the government, can intervene and assist those who continue to be affected by severe childhood abuse. *The best thing we can do to support survivors and to eradicate child abuse is to work together to stop it.*

The Role of Institutions

Long-term social change cannot happen without support and action by the government and other major institutions. This means addressing the practices, structures, and systematic ways in which institutions perpetuate abuse.

The institution of religion plays an enormous role in the everyday lives of millions of people. The Roman Catholic Church, Southern and National Baptist Conventions, United Methodist Church, Evangelical Lutheran Church, and the Church of Jesus Christ of Latter-day Saints together have over 104 million members in the U.S. alone.[2] Whether or not people attend church services or participate regularly in church activities, religion remains a significant social and moral force in people's lives. Religious institutions have a tremendous amount of authority over how people think, behave, and feel. This authority can be utilized to empower and enrich our lives. The United Methodist Bishops marched on Washington, D.C., in 2002 to lobby Congress on behalf of children's rights and child welfare. Methodist leaders utilized their influence and power to effect social change through public policy. Religious authority can also be utilized and abused in egregious ways (see chapter 4).

The sexual abuse scandals in the Roman Catholic Church illustrate how *any* powerful institution can control the lives of those in its authority. Structurally, the Catholic Church in particular is in need of an overhaul. Policies need to be implemented, practiced, and monitored to reflect an absolute no-tolerance policy on child molestation and other abuses of power. The National Alliance to End Sexual Violence released an eight-point plan addressing the sexual abuse problems of the Catholic Church. They recommend that abusing priests be dismissed, the acts reported to police, and restitution, therapeutic interventions, and support provided to families. When silence about pedophilia is no longer the norm, child welfare becomes a priority. Never again should a family be forced by a powerful organization to sign a statement waiving their right to speak. When lay Catholics, including psychologists, business leaders, and parents, meet to try to deal with these problems, enormous steps are being taken to protect children. When the Roman Catholic Church calls a no-tolerance policy on clergy pedophilia and abuse, they are changing the structure of their organization to address their limitations in child protection. The Catholic Church scandal should serve to remind everyone that abuse of power happens within every denomination and major institution. Direct action, in the form of public policy, institutional changes, mass education, and restitution to victims and their families, is needed to address and combat abusive conditions.

School boards and district offices are also in a position to end abusive practices in schools by making all forms of corporal punishment illegal. Corporal punishment in schools reinforces to everyone the mentality that children must be hit in order for them to behave and learn. Physicians, psychologists, and child advocates have found corporal punishment traumatizing, inhumane, and unconstitutional. Many diverse organizations support the abolition of corporal punishment, including the American Medical Association, the American Bar Association, the American Psychiatric Association, and the National Association for the Advancement of Colored People (NAACP). School boards and trustees must take a more active role in its elimination by doing the following:

1) Actively listing and admonishing those school districts that continue to hit children
2) Developing and then utilizing alternative methods of discipline that are more effective and humane
3) Seeking out available resources by organizations opposed to corporal punishment, including the Center for Effective Discipline and the National Coalition to Abolish Corporal Punishment in Schools
4) Letting teachers, parents, and children know that violence against children, including all forms of hitting and spanking, is wrong.

Schools can also play a role in the elimination of child abuse by utilizing the services of existing organizations trained in the detection and prevention of abuse, such as the Southern Arizona Center Against Sexual Assault (SACASA).[3] SACASA has been active in schools teaching children of all ages about sexual abuse, harassment, and assault, and they also provide support to those children who come forward with abuse experiences. They have been active in the policy arena working on local and national levels to eradicate abuse. In addition to these services, however, schools must begin to address the conditions that lead so many children to be abused in the first place. "Good touch/bad touch" instruction is certainly a start. Since most abuse happens in the context of the family or with others known to the child, such programs are not enough however. A focus on stranger abuse can be interpreted by young people to mean that stranger abuse is much more serious than abuse happening in the home. Programs need to address more directly family violence and other abuses perpetrated by loved ones.

Children learn in every institution that inequality and the subordination of children are the norm. Most children learn through experience to expect to be treated poorly by anyone older or bigger. Schools can take an active stance against this by addressing directly in the curriculum, in age-appropriate ways, all forms of inequality in school, including sexual harassment, bullying, the belittling of students (by students and teachers alike), and the abuse of power by teachers. Telling children they have a right to their bodies in one situation, then hitting or belittling them in another, demonstrates the many contradictions in society. When authoritative control is the predominant teaching method, children learn they are weaker and subservient to adults. All of these practices reinforce to children that they have no rights, especially rights to their bodies. Teachers must also begin to address the issue of sexual inequality in developmentally suitable ways to help children learn what happens when certain groups of people have power over others.

Of every institution, the federal government has the most authority to eradicate abuse. Foremost, the U.S. Congress can take a more aggressive stance against institutional violence by enacting laws that prohibit all forms of corporal punishment in the home, schools, churches, and other establishments that care for children. While most states prohibit corporal punishment in day care centers, the federal government must go further to make abuse illegal in every institution. Most egregious is the legality and social acceptability of physical violence in homes. Statutory and common law give parents the legal right to hit their children so long as it is "reasonable" for the welfare or safeguard of the child.[4] This same force used against another person, in many cases, *could be criminally prosecuted.*

Another major step to eradicate abusive conditions is to create laws and policies that do not discriminate. The Temporary Assistance for Needy Families (TANF) program has been found to be discriminatory against single mothers and same-sex couples. Several million children under the TANF program lack decent child care. The government could eradicate abusive conditions, particularly those caused by poverty, through the reauthorization of TANF, which takes these problems into account.[5] The TANF program, as well as its reauthorization, highlights the government's overall disrespect and disregard for single mothers, children, and anyone in poverty. Abuse is exacerbated under these conditions: single mothers are forced to stay in abusive relationships, young children are left alone at home or in horribly inadequate day care centers because their mothers cannot afford to pay for decent child care, and traumatic stress becomes a way of life for these families, with potential catastrophic effects. "Welfare as we know it" may have ended, but child poverty and abuse is alive and well because of the inability and unwillingness of the federal government to recognize or stop it.

Federal agencies, under the authority of the presidency, also have an enormous influence on the welfare of children and the mentally ill. Under the U.S. Department of Health and Human Services, several agencies address specifically violence, mental health, and children, including the Administration for Children and Families, the Centers for Disease Control, and the National Institutes of Health (NIH). Hundreds of millions of dollars are allocated to the National Institute of Mental Health (NIMH), an institute of NIH, for research on the prevention and treatment of traumatic stress, child abuse, and female battery. Yet only 25 percent of this funding goes to experts outside the fields of psychiatry and psychology, such as those in the social sciences, education, or law. Increased funding to public policy experts and other social scientists could provide more in-depth critical analysis of social structures and practices that contribute to violence against women and children. Greater funding could be allocated to qualitative studies that focus on children's and adult survivors' accounts of abuse. Real-life stories are desperately needed to educate others of the political, economic, and social contexts of abuse. I have made my life story political through the research and writing of this book to help create awareness of the terrorism experienced in the everyday lives of millions of women and children. Similar research needs to be conducted on a larger scale to address more adequately the social and political conditions in our lives that exacerbate personal suffering.

Increased resources are also needed in the area of trauma-based disorders, including post-traumatic stress and dissociative disorders. With the aftermath of the attacks in New York City on September 11, 2001, and the help of NIH, post-traumatic stress disorder has become more nationally recognized. In my own life, most of the people around me, including my therapists and close friends, were having post-traumatic stress reactions to the attacks. Nationally, the effects were enormous. Many people were reacting to the attack itself, but it caused a ripple effect on past traumas experienced in their lives. Federal agency directors, educators, and mental health experts are in a better position to help make the necessary link between international violence and the violence experienced in everyday life. DID must also become a funding priority and recognized as a major mental illness caused by severe childhood trauma. Resources allocated to PTSD and DID not only will help those suffering with these disorders but also will help to increase strategies to detect and prevent child abuse.

Nonprofit and Professional Organizations

Many national and international organizations support the research, treatment, and prevention of child abuse, severe traumatization, and the mentally ill. The Children's Defense Fund, Child Welfare League of America, and Childhelp, USA, have been very active in public advocacy, education, and lobbying on behalf of children and families in poverty. Numerous professional organizations are responding directly to the current mental health crisis of child abuse survivors, including the International Society for the Study of Dissociation, the International Society for Traumatic Stress Studies, and the Sidran Foundation. The National Alliance for the Mentally Ill (NAMI) is a leader in providing support, education, and public policy advocacy on behalf of the mentally ill. The American Psychiatric Association, with over thirty-seven thousand members, has also been influential in legislative lobbying. The issues they addressed in 2002 alone included the following:[6]

1) Support of mental health parity legislation, which seeks to abolish Medicare mental health discrimination with the 50 percent co-pay for therapy. The legislation would require the federally mandated 20 percent co-pay comparable to general health care co-payments.[7]
2) Support of a comprehensive prescription drug benefit under Medicare, which would aid the mentally ill in receiving necessary medication.

3) New federal investments in psychiatric research, particularly to increase the U.S. Department of Health and Human Services, National Institutes of Health budget to reflect the needs of the American people.
4) The enactment of patient protections against abusive managed care practices.
5) Inclusion of nondiscriminatory coverage of treatment of mental illness and substance abuse in any children's health care legislation.

The American Medical Association and American Psychological Association have also provided significant resources for lobbying Congress and federal agencies on behalf of children and the mentally ill. Through massive lobbying and education, professional organizations have had a significant impact on social policy.

Professional organizations play a significant role in the education and training of mental health service providers on trauma-related issues. However, there remain thousands of therapists and primary care physicians across the country treating people of all ages for trauma-based and dissociative disorders who are acting independently of national resources. While the responsibility ultimately rests with the individual therapist to access resources and acquire training, professional organizations must also be responsible for providing affordable and accessible services to everyone. While many organizations mentioned previously already provide extensive outreach and training services, more can be done. With collaboration across organizations and interests, a greater number of providers can be trained to provide the best care possible to their clients.

The following are examples of what professional organizations can do to aid in the education and training of mental health and social service providers:

1) Provide low-cost training materials and free on-line resources.
2) Sponsor a greater number of workshops in poor and minority communities where costs and access to travel may limit participation.
3) Base membership fees on income and ability to pay (i.e., sliding scale).
4) Reduce workshop and conference fees so no one is excluded by

costs alone. Provide materials that can be disseminated at low cost to mental health practitioners.

5) Work more closely with other professional organizations, such as NASW (National Association of Social Workers) and NAMI, to reach a greater number of individuals treating psychiatric disorders based in traumatization.
6) Allow nonmembers to access this information as well, since it is through clients that therapists often learn of available resources.

This last suggestion may be controversial, since some mental health practitioners consider clients and patients less credible and able to handle such information. I firmly believe resources on treatment and prevention should be made available to survivors and others committed to the eradication of abuse.

Community and Local Government Support

Our communities can better address, prevent, and treat violence and the long-term effects of abuse in many ways. Even though the circumstances and effects of trauma are more readily discussed and understood today, our local communities and governments, for the most part, remain silent on the issue. Community leaders need courage to become more publicly active against interpersonal violence and child abuse. Many local nonprofit organizations are able to operate because of public support, private foundation dollars, and local governmental funding. The Survivors Healing Center in Santa Cruz, California, is one of these places.[8] The center was cofounded in the 1980s by Ellen Bass, a coauthor of the book *The Courage to Heal,* a pathbreaking book dealing with child sexual abuse and healing. The center provides extensive information, education, therapy, and support specifically to survivors of child sexual abuse. Because of its success and mission, the center receives funding from their city and county governments and local businesses. When communities, local governments, businesses, and nonprofit foundations publicly support such efforts, they are taking a necessary stand against the eradication of child abuse and violence against women.

Drop-in centers, legal aid programs, support centers for the abused, and child abuse prevention programs must continue to be funded and, in many cases, expanded. Although state and local governmental resources are available for some people, they are frequently inadequate. Severely traumatized people need a great deal of help and support, not just in terms of mental health treatment, but for everyday needs and dealing with bureaucracies. Jenny, an eight-year-old alter, tried to explain it to our therapist one day:

> – PEOPLE NEED HELP for even little things like calling a doctor when you've been charged too much or calling Medicare to see if they got all the forms. it's like the lawyer in [John Grisham's] "The Street Lawyer" who makes calls for old people and poor people and helps them with all their problems. people with mental problems need help, too, and not always from social workers. because sometimes they're too busy and not so friendly anyway. it's really good when your friends and therapists help with these things. but i think there should be more places to go for people like us to get help.

Many cities have programs that assist disabled individuals in their homes, and others provide walk-in legal, social, and economic support to needy people. Publicly funded drop-in centers could be effective at helping people deal with all sorts of issues, such as homelessness, employment, child care, and health insurance. Ultimately, by getting people functioning better and back in the workforce, everyone benefits. But in order to work well, greater collaboration is needed across many service sectors and funding agencies.

Coalition Building: A Necessary Response

Building coalitions across issues is the most promising way to achieve social change. I was struck by the number of organizations and interests involved in whether and how the TANF program should be reauthorized in 2002. Dozens of diverse organizations lobbied Congress, including the Child Welfare League of America, Children's Defense Fund, the League of Women Voters, and the National Council of Churches. From making children central to the TANF program to addressing discrimination against single mothers and same-sex couples, tremendous resources were being utilized by these and other organizations to influence congressional policymaking. Although in some cases competing issues were being lobbied for, these organizations agreed that fundamentally, child poverty should be given a major priority. Economic and social conditions are much more likely to be addressed through coalition building.

All over the country, coalitions are working together to fight for such issues as children's rights, workers' rights, women's equality, racial equality, unemployment, and fair housing. The Children's Defense Fund is nationally recognized for working closely with supportive members of Congress and other national organizations and interests to bring children's issues to the national forefront. These coalitions have successfully influenced social policies regarding foster care, adoption, and child welfare rights. The Duluth Abuse Intervention Project (DAIP), for example, provides an innovative approach to dealing with wife battery by closely coordinating the efforts of police, prosecutors, medical professionals, intervention programs, and services to victims.[9] Considered a "coordinated community response," this program recognizes the need to coordinate services across many organizations and agencies to address the repercussions of wife battery while focusing on victim safety. These projects demonstrate the need for greater coalition building across many diverse services and issues.

Considering the myriad of agencies involved in child protection and welfare, developing coordinated community efforts seems the most hopeful response. Childhelp, USA, is successfully providing coordinated services to abused children and their families. The Childhelp Children's Center of Arizona houses fifty-eight full-time professionals in the areas of law enforcement, child protective services, medicine, and crisis intervention to provide a multidisciplinary team approach to dealing with child abuse. The center has been able to reduce the trauma experienced by children and their families by decreasing the time it takes to review and decide cases. Children are spending less time in custody and are in a more supportive environment when there. Such programs make it possible for children and families to recover from abuse and receive treatment much more quickly and efficiently than with traditional criminal justice approaches.[10] Comprehensive approaches to dealing with serious social problems, such as wife battery, child abuse, and homelessness, can help to empower groups of people who traditionally are revictimized by the agencies established to help them.

I frequently think about how dramatically different things could be for survivors if there was greater collaboration of efforts. For the last four years I have been conceptualizing what it would take to have special houses for people working through severe trauma-related issues. I wrote the following a few months after my third and last psychiatric hospitalization:

– MAYBE IF PEOPLE had somewhere safe and supportive to go, they could heal better, maybe even heal quicker. some day i am going to open a center for people like me. it will be a large house, or maybe cabins, and a quiet, safe place for people to rest and heal. maybe ten people could live there at any given time. they can stay for as little as a month or up to a year if needed. there will be regular house visits by doctors, therapists and social workers, a van with a driver for shopping, errands, and appointments. there will be regular support groups and healing circles. maybe there could be a massage therapist, yoga instructor, and herbalists as well. it would be great to have contact with educators at a university or community college. students might want to intern for the house to help make it run smoothly. maybe some of the residents would even be able to take classes or go to lectures at the college.

– i imagine people would read, write, or even paint, maybe learn small crafts. there could be a study room with books and a computer hooked up to the Internet. there could be an exercise room with a treadmill and weights and whatever else would help for body treatment. maybe people would go for walks together or alone. the house will be in the forest near the ocean. damaged and hurt people need to be surrounded by nature. there could be a garden for those who want to tend it, with fresh vegetables and herbs. maybe we could sell produce at the farmer's market during the spring and summer to help support the center.

– what would be really different about this house is that there will be house-helpers, caring individuals, perhaps therapists, educators, and others, who would volunteer their time, maybe from one to four weeks per year, to help operate the house. they would help cook meals, clean, and just offer a loving, supportive presence to the house. maybe as residents get better, they can return in later years as house helpers themselves.

What drives me now is this vision I have for developing houses for trauma survivors, people who need more support than what they currently receive at home, or people who need a break from their life in order to heal from the psychological traumas of abuse. Staffed by committed professionals, these nonprofit treatment centers would offer a homelike setting for survivors to receive what they often desperately need to heal: unconditional love and support. In order for such programs to exist, ample financial assistance is needed from private foundations, large corporations, supportive organizations, and the public. Collaboration and commitment are what will make this happen.

A Call to Action

Getting involved in the lives of people living with multiplicity will help to expose the many dimensions and complexities of child abuse, including why it occurs, how it is experienced, and how to stop it. As much as child protective services, treatment centers, pediatricians, and mental health professionals are able to identify abused children, most incest still goes undetected. The vast majority of people living with multiplicity have childhoods filled with inexplicable physical pains and somatic symptoms. Understanding how these pains were masked, silenced, and denied can help us to detect children experiencing abuse today. Greater recognition and education will help us to develop more effective tools to prevent future abuses. Learning about multiplicity goes well beyond helping individual survivors living with serious psychiatric disorders; it provides a unique opportunity for greater detection, prevention, and treatment of child abuse.

Research in the area of child abuse, women's mental health, and multiple personality, specifically, has brought to light something as terrifying to me as war or international terrorism: the terrorism that goes on in the everyday lives of millions of women and children living in the U.S. It is reprehensible that thousands of women and children are murdered each year from battery, abuse, and neglect. Children are susceptible to violence and abuse in their homes, schools, places of worship, counselors' offices, gymnasiums, and doctors' offices. Culturally, we are blind and numb to these heinous offenses. *Multiplicity is the direct result of a society that chooses denial over truth and ignorance over humanity.* At times throughout my healing process, I was incredulous that life went on for everyone else while people with serious debilitating mental problems were suffering in silence and all alone. I believe, fundamentally, that people are fearful and unable or unwilling to get involved for fear the real truth will be exposed: no child is really safe from abuse because we cannot even acknowledge how brutally pervasive and systematic it is, and once we recognize this, we are, without any doubt, obliged to act.

It is a fallacy to think negligent parents alone are to blame for the millions of children who are abused each year. Child abuse is not simply a problem originating and exercised in the family. If this were the case, treatment, incarceration of abusers, and massive parental education about the repercussions of childhood violence would solve the problem. Child abuse is much more insidious and far-reaching than the family. Every major social and political institution is responsible for the preponderance of violence directed at women and children. We must teach our children they have the absolute right to be respected and treated fairly—not through empty words but through concrete, visible action. When children learn they are deserving and respected within every major institution and organization, they can act this way themselves. It is only then that the cycle of violence will be broken. To eradicate abuse, we must, as a collective society, address the social, political, and economic conditions that lay the foundation for widespread abuse to occur.

Children will be safe when there is public awareness and full acknowledgment of *all* forms of abuse in young people's lives. Child abuse is a national epidemic reaching catastrophic proportions. It is real, common, and potentially fatal. We take a stand against child abuse when we respond proactively to the large numbers of people who develop severe dissociative disorders, anxiety disorders, eating disorders, alcoholism, drug addictions, and clinical depression because of sexual, physical, and emotional trauma experienced in childhood. Greater recognition, prevention, and treatment of child abuse and its devastating effects will undoubtedly reduce the numbers of people, such as me, who continue to have serious long-term medical and psychiatric problems in adulthood. As much as most of us wish it weren't so, thousands more children are being abused each day in graphic and terrifying ways. Every year more women and men find themselves in mental health centers and psychiatric hospitals seeking treatment for abuse they sustained in childhood. Public acknowledgment of the repercussions of abuse is desperately needed. It is up to all of us to end the devastation caused by violence and abuse:

1) For survivors it may mean a total commitment to healing.
2) For concerned individuals it may mean greater involvement in organizations working on behalf of children, those in poverty, and the mentally ill, or changing the personal ways we contribute to the suffering of others.
3) Mental health practitioners and social service providers can spend more time reading about and researching the latest information on dissociation and trauma, and have lists of important resources and subscriptions to helpful newsletters readily available in their offices.
4) Pediatricians and other medical doctors can take advantage of existing educational and training programs specifically developed to detect, assess, and treat child abuse.[11]
5) For professional organizations it may mean recognizing the value of providing free training materials to mental health professionals and survivors unable to pay the fees, or increasing collaboration between organizations and agencies concerned about abuse.
6) Business leaders can take a more active stance, through greater education, funding, and community involvement, against all forms of violence, including that which goes on in the workplace.
7) Activists and organizers can continue to strive to advocate for coalition building whenever possible, and become active in the education and dissemination of real-life experiences of the abused.
8) For all of us it means supporting responsible political candidates

who support equality and non-violence, and are committed to making necessary policy changes through every branch of government.

9) Most important, for government, religious, and other political leaders, it means stopping the ignorance and denial about violence against women and children through significant public policy changes, interventions, and massive public education.

Action is needed now! Thousands more women and children are brutally assaulted each day that we fail to act. We have the power to eradicate the viciousness of abuse by working together to confront the conditions that create and perpetuate it. We are all responsible and we are obliged to act.

Postscript

Over two years have passed since I first began writing this book. My life, in every conceivable way, is much more enriched and fulfilling than ever before. What has helped me to heal the most is learning how to take care of myself, and this includes breathing deep, loving thoughts into my very essence. Loving myself has become a top priority. What I have learned is that personal, conscious intentions to be well and healthy are just as important as the need for more adequate medical care and greater societal supports for the suffering. I have also discovered the power of prayer. For me, prayer is hope; it is the realization that every being, every star and planet, every tree and river, is connected; we are all one. This perspective is particularly symbolic for those whose minds become completely shattered. It is a belief I take to heart now.

Since my initial diagnosis with multiplicity, my internal system has changed dramatically. I still think of everyone inside as "we," because their voices and spirits remain an enormous part of who I am today. No longer am I far outside myself, though, and I believe I no longer lose time. A few months ago, the little ones began running on the beach, but soon after I felt the older ones join in. It was beautiful; we were all running together, happy and free, delighting in the day, altogether as one. In that moment something magical happened: I knew I was better. That's not to say I don't have rough patches every now and then. My PTSD still bothers me sometimes and under heavy stress I still find myself dissociating. But I now know the worst is over and I can face anything.

My dear eighty-eight-year-old neighbor said to me recently, "Each time I see you, you're different. I don't mean you just look different, but you *are* different." She was smiling oh-so-big when she said it, and I realized for the first time someone who didn't know me as "sick" or troubled loved me the way I am. We laughed and hugged, and I knew this was how it was supposed to be, for me and for everyone else, always. In that moment I was profoundly proud of who I was.

I have been through what felt like hell, but I made it out. I have hope in a way that I dared not even conceive before. More than anything, I want every person suffering from the terror of abuse to have hope for themselves and a better world. When every fiber of your being wants to curl up and die, may you summon the strength to continue to fight. And most of all, may you find the will to matter and the courage to speak.

Appendix A

Resources on Traumatic Stress and Dissociation

The following are my recommendations for finding treatment and researching issues. Many excellent resources are not listed here. My hope is that the few I present will be meaningful and helpful to those needing assistance. For full citations, please refer to the references.

Where to Begin

So many books have been helpful to me over the last several years. I highly recommend *Trauma and Recovery* by Judith Herman. This is an excellent resource for understanding, treating, and recovering from severe trauma, and it is accessibly written for everyone. Here are three of my favorite books that address directly adult survivors of child sexual abuse:

The Courage to Heal: A Guide for Women Survivors of Child Sexual Abuse by Ellen Bass and Laura Davis

Recollections of Sexual Abuse: Treatment Principles and Guidelines by Christine Courtois

Reach for the Rainbow: Advanced Healing for Survivors of Sexual Abuse by Lynne D. Finney

So much of the time I felt like I was having a spiritual crisis in the midst of a psychological breakdown. *Anatomy of the Spirit: Seven Stages of Power and Healing* by Carolyn Myss provides a more holistic perspective on mental, physical, and spiritual health. Her perspective helped me to remember that no matter how dissociative I was, I was still one. It also helped to reinforce the belief that we, in the most universal sense, are all connected. *Shine the Light: Sexual Abuse and Healing in the Jewish Community* by Rachel Lev is another great book that provides much hope and spiritual healing through testimonies of women sexual abuse survivors in the Jewish community.

Books about Multiplicity

The following books deal with multiplicity specifically and are helpful for survivors and their loved ones:

Amongst Ourselves: A Self-Help Guide to Living with Dissociative Identity Disorder by Tracy Alderman and Karen Marshall

Multiple Personality Disorder from the Inside Out by Barry Cohen, Esther Giller, and Lynn W. is an excellent work containing hundreds of poems and writings by people with multiple alter personalities. In addition, it has an excellent resource and referral list in the back of the book.

United We Stand: A Book for People with Multiple Personalities by Eliana Gil is a very simple yet helpful book about dissociation and multiplicity for people first learning about these conditions.

The Dissociative Identity Disorder Sourcebook by Deborah Bray Haddock is a wonderful resource guide. The first chapter is particularly helpful for survivors first learning of their multiplicity. There is also an excellent resource list at the back of the book.

The following clinical assessment and treatment books on multiplicity should be in the office of every mental health provider who deals with trauma and dissociation:

Rebuilding Shattered Lives: The Responsible Treatment of Complex Post-Traumatic Stress and Dissociative Disorders by James Chu

Diagnosis and Treatment of Multiple Personality Disorder by Frank Putnam

Dissociative Identity Disorder: Diagnosis, Clinical Features, and Treatment of Multiple Personality Disorder by Colin Ross

Treating Dissociative Identity Disorder by James Spira and Irvin Yalom

Scores of memoirs have been written about abuse and multiplicity. Some of the most compelling and well-known memoirs on multiplicity include the following:

The Flock: The Autobiography of a Multiple Personality by Joan Frances Casey

When Rabbit Howls by Truddi Chase

Becoming One: A Story of Triumph over Multiple Personality Disorder by Sarah Olson

The Magic Daughter: A Memoir of Living with Multiple Personality by Jane Phillips

First Person Plural: My Life as a Multiple by Cameron West

Helpful Internet Websites

There are hundreds, if not thousands, of listings for the treatment, support, and research of dissociative disorders, traumatic stress, and child abuse. The following websites are reputable and informative, and can help you get started. Please note that some website addresses change over time.

HealingHopes (http://www.healinghopes.org)

is a nonprofit organization providing interactive support via the Internet and information to abuse survivors diagnosed with dissociative disorders including DID. By far, this is one of the best resources for survivors. Their library is extensive and easy to use, and moderated forums and chat rooms are available. For those who have suffered ritual abuse, information is provided in a straightforward, nonthreatening way. They also provide an extensive list of questions to ask potential therapists.

The Sidran Foundation (http://www.sidran.org)

is another excellent source of information for multiplicity and traumatic stress, providing information to survivors and mental health professionals alike. Sidran is a national nonprofit organization dedicated to the training, support, and treatment of dissociation and trauma. Sidran also compiles a list of therapists by city and state who treat or are interested in treating DID and PTSD. They've also devised a helpful list of questions to interview potential new therapists. They post articles by experts in the field, provide links to other organizations and resources, and act as a clearinghouse for the most updated information on dissociation and trauma.

Many Voices (http://www.manyvoicespress.com)

is a bimonthly newsletter with articles written by and for survivors and therapists. Included is an extensive resource guide of services, including supportive organizations, Internet websites, helpful books, conferences, inpatient treatment centers, and hospitals specializing in traumatic stress. This is an excellent resource for survivors and their loved ones, and every mental health professional treating dissociative disorders should have a copy in the waiting room.

Selected Organizations to Locate Therapists

The following organizations provide membership lists of mental health professionals but do not necessarily endorse the therapists themselves. Remember, just because a member may be listed as treating traumatic stress and dissociative disorders does not necessarily mean they are good or experienced. The first three organizations are most helpful and specifically geared toward trauma and dissociation. The rest are listed alphabetically.

Sidran Foundation
410-825-8888
www.sidran.org

Sidran members are dedicated to understanding dissociation and trauma. You can request a membership list via their website or by calling the office directly.

International Society for the Study of Dissociation
847-480-0899
www.issd.org

ISSD is an international nonprofit organization dedicated to the research, training, and treatment of dissociative disorders. You can obtain a list of members in your area that treat dissociative disorders by contacting their office or by making an e-mail request.

International Society for Traumatic Stress Studies
847-480-9282
www.istss.org

ISTSS is another organization dedicated to the research and treatment of traumatic stress. Membership lists can be obtained through their website.

American Psychiatric Association
202-682-6060
www.psych.org

This is a medical specialty society, mostly made up of psychiatrists and physicians, working to provide humane care and treatment for all people with mental disorders. Their website contains a list of questions to ask potential psychiatrists, and you can get a listing of members in your area by phoning their main office.

American Psychological Association
1-800-964-2000
www.apa.org

The APA website locates therapists in your area, however, state and local APA chapters (which can be found in the local phone book) have lists of therapists *and* their treatment preferences.

National Alliance for the Mentally Ill
1-800-950-NAMI
www.nami.org

NAMI is a leader in providing support, education, and public advocacy on behalf of the mentally ill. Their website is very informative on mental illness in general, though information on DID specifically needs developing. You can obtain a list of members in your area through their website.

National Association of Social Workers
202-408-8600
www.socialworkers.org

The NASW directory of members is only partially included in the website, though very useful since it lists therapists' credentials and work histories. A book can be purchased that lists all members and their specialties, though it may be unnecessary.

Appendix B

Applying for Social Security Disability

The Social Security Disability application process can be very cumbersome, and much time and effort is needed to fill out the forms. Most especially, it is important to stay as active as possible in the process. Mental health service providers and loved ones can help enormously. The following suggestions will help with the application process.

Asking for Help

Ask a close friend, family member, or therapist to help you through the process. If this is not possible, find a helpful clerk in the SSD office. To do this, call the main number (1-800-772-1213) or find where the closest office is in your area (look under Social Security Administration in the U.S. Government listings of the phone book). My therapist and friends were wonderfully supportive in helping me apply for SSD. I talked with my therapist regularly about updates and things I needed to do. One friend helped me fill out the forms. Another friend came with me to meet with the SSD officer to turn in my application. I am convinced that having this support made a significant difference in how the final decision turned out and how I coped through the process.

You can list a trusted friend on your original application who can help make inquires for you and discuss your application with SSD officers. This was extremely useful for me!

Filling Out the Forms

As soon as you receive the forms, make a copy of the blank forms *before you fill them out.* This way, you will be able to be messy and write notes to yourself before you turn in the final version. I spent a few weeks taking notes and talking with a close friend and my therapist about what I was writing. You will have better success if the forms are legible and coherent.

I found the forms very difficult to fill out because they asked very personal questions about myself and my daily living. Many of us who are living with trauma-related and dissociative disorders experience a continuum of moderate days to truly horrible days. I was given excellent advice by both my therapist and a kind woman at the SSD office: Fill out the forms as honestly and as accurately as you can. People reviewing the forms understand that our days are inconsistent. In addition, they can probably tell if you are exaggerating. The "Daily Activities" form was particularly difficult for me to fill out. The following are examples of how I responded to a few of the questions:

Q: Do you prepare your own meals? If yes, which meals do you usually prepare?

A: "Yes and No. I can prepare breakfast, lunch, or dinner. On good days I can prepare small meals for myself. On bad days I can't. It really just depends."

Q: What kind of food do you usually cook? Explain.

A: "I cook easy things when I can like things out of a box. I'll make cereal in the morning, make a sandwich for lunch, then make noodles with vegetables or just noodles for dinner."

Q: Does anyone help you in the preparation of meals? If yes, explain.

A: "There are days that I can't cook or make myself anything and then my friends help or a friend calls to remind me to eat or helps me eat over the phone."

I just filled out the form truthfully, even though it seemed redundant to keep saying things change all the time.

After you turn in your application, the SSD office sends separate forms to your providers, including therapists, psychiatrists, social workers, and hospitals, to fill out. Much of the time, waiting for a decision from disability has to do with waiting for these forms to be returned. When possible, call these providers regularly (or have a friend call) to make sure the forms have been submitted by the respective offices. Your persistence will help providers fill out the forms more quickly.

Bringing an Advocate

In some cases you are required to meet with a psychiatrist or other mental health professional chosen by the disability office. The *idea* of meeting with yet another psychiatrist can be very stressful. If the meeting is required, remember to be yourself and answer the questions as truthfully as you can. If possible, try to bring an advocate with you, possibly your therapist or a friend. You may not be able to have loved ones in the room with you, but they can be there to support you in the process. I do not know why I did not have to meet with an appointed psychiatrist. It may be that the more thorough your own therapist and/or psychiatrist is with the letters and forms submitted, the less likely you will be required to see someone from the SSD office. In this instance, it really helps to have supportive mental health providers in your corner.

When You Move

If you move to another city or state while your disability eligibility is being determined, it may delay the process. In the middle of my application process, I moved out of state two times. The moves required several calls on my part to the SSD office to make sure all of my paperwork and letters from providers were transferred correctly. Some of the paperwork was lost in the transfers, and I was able to get the new paperwork submitted more quickly.

Dealing with the Process and Outcome

Getting disability and the subsequent health insurance through Medicare was lifesaving for me. But the process felt demoralizing, tedious, very stressful, and difficult. I weighed the pros and cons with my therapist and closest friends, and decided it was what I should do. Not everyone will come to this decision. Moreover, many who go through this grueling process are denied. There are appeals processes, though how effective they are I do not know. For those who make the decision to apply, having a backup plan in case you are denied is worthwhile. I think the most important thing is to have realistic expectations about the process and outcome.

Appendix C

Letter Requesting Change of Doctor

January 1, 2003
Health National
1000 Main Street
Industry Central, NY 10000

Dear Insurance Representative:

I am currently insured under plan #12345. According to the plan, I am required to see the psychiatrist on staff, Dr. John Smith. I have met with Dr. Smith on two different occasions, and it is my belief that he is not fully skilled to treat my particular psychiatric illness, dissociative identity disorder (DID). I came to this conclusion after he made several inappropriate comments to me. He also told me he was not sure which medications to prescribe to treat my symptoms.

For the last few months I have been treated by a psychologist, Dr. Jane Brown, who has recommended I see another psychiatrist, Dr. Lisa Shankwan, whom she works with closely. Dr. Shankwan has extensive experience and knowledge treating patients with DID. I request that I be covered under this insurance plan to begin working with Dr. Shankwan as soon as possible. The sooner I heal properly, the sooner I can get back to my normal life. Ultimately, this will be much more cost-effective for your company.

Thank you very much for your consideration in this matter. I can be reached at the address and phone number below should you have any questions about this matter.

Sincerely,

Full Name
Street Address
City, State, Zip
Phone

Notes

Preface

1. Davidson 2002; NCACPS 2002.

2. AACAP 2002.

3. JIE 2001.

4. Although corporal punishment in schools is banned in twenty-seven states, the remaining states allow for the spanking, paddling, and/or hitting of children by teachers and principals in public schools. In Mississippi one in ten students are paddled each year, and teachers in Texas account for more than one-fourth of all school paddlings in the country (NCACPS 2002). The Center for Effective Discipline (CED 2002) is a nonprofit organization providing information to the public about corporal punishment and alternatives to its use. The CED also coordinates the National Coalition to Abolish Corporal Punishment in Schools. For more general readings related to corporal punishment and the physical abuse of children, see Davidson 2002; I. Hyman 1990; R. Hyman and Rathbone 1993; and Winton and Mara 2001.

5. See NCACPS 2002 for data on the 1997–1998 school year.

6. HHS 2001a, 10.

7. NCCA 2001.

8. CAA 2002; and NCHE 2002.

9. Many discuss the importance and necessity of writing about and recovering lost trauma narratives; see Bass and Davis 1994; Coffey 1998; Henke 1998; Herman 1997; hooks 1989; Lev 2003; and Poupart 1997, 2001.

10. For an excellent resource on gender differences regarding PTSD, see Kimerling, Oimette, and Wolfe 2002.

11. Gilbertson in "How do I speak."

Chapter One

1. For national statistics on mental disorders, see Brannon 1999; HHS 2001c, 2002; NAMI 2001; NMHA 2002a; and Sidran 2002a.

2. The *Diagnostic and Statistical Manual for Mental Disorders* (DSM-IV-TR) is the primary diagnostic guide used by psychiatrists and other mental health professionals to define, describe, and evaluate psychological and psychosocial disorders (APA 2000). According to the *DSM-IV-TR,* people diagnosed with borderline personality disorder have a "pervasive pattern of instability of interpersonal relationships, self-image, and affects, and marked impulsivity beginning by early adulthood and present in a variety of contexts," including franticness to avoid abandonment, difficulty controlling anger, unstable and intense relationships, or recurrent suicidal behavior (APA 2000, 710).

3. Various explanations have been given for the overrepresentation of women diagnosed with DID, including biased research samples (Putnam 1989), gender differences in behavioral responses (Courtois 1999; Glass 1993; Herman 1997; Putnam 1989; Ross 1997; and Steinberg and Schnall 2000), the women's movement and feminism (Acocella 1999), and the gendered nature of violence and victimization (Acocella 1999; Courtois 1999; Glass 1993; Herman 1997; Putnam 1989; Ross 1997; and Steinberg and Schnall 2000). It is also speculated that more women than men are diagnosed with DID because males react to childhood abuse in aggressive and antisocial ways, e.g., alcoholism and fighting, that mask dissociative symptoms, and many of these men may be in prison (Putnam 1989; Ross 1997; and Steinberg and Schnall 2000). However, the total numbers of men and women in U.S. prisons diagnosed with DID (or other mental illnesses) are unknown.

4. HHS 2001c.

5. See Cohen, Giller, and W. 1991; Keyes 1981; and West 1999 for narratives written by and about males. For a discussion of abuse against males, PTSD, and dissociative disorders, see Kimerling, Oimette, and Wolfe 2002; and Steinberg and Schnall 2000, chapter 10.

6. National statistics on sexual abuse and assault vary across sources, particularly differences between female and male victimization. Mostly because of differences in ways data are collected and analyzed, most agree that violence perpetrated against females occurs much more frequently and systematically than violence against males. For national statistics, see HHS 1996, 4, 2000, 2001a; OJJDP 2001; SACASA 2002; and V-Day 2002. For readings on the relationship between gender and violence, see Ferraro 2000; Kivel 1999; O'Toole and Schiffman 1997; Rickel and Becker 1997; and Tjaden and Thoennes 2000.

7. Dissociative identity disorder is one of five dissociative disorders included in the *DSM-IV-TR*. The others include dissociative amnesia, fugue states, depersonalization disorder, and dissociative disorder not otherwise specified (APA 2000, 526–29). See also Steinberg and Schnall (2000) for a complete discussion of each of these disorders.

8. See Herman 1997; ISSD 2001; and Kimerling, Oimette, and Wolfe 2002. According to the "National Vietnam Veterans Readjustment Study," more service people in Vietnam developed PTSD than any other war in our history, with combat veterans being most at risk. Over two million American men and women served in Vietnam, and an estimated three hundred thousand veterans, or 30 percent, experienced PTSD sometime after returning home, while an estimated 15 percent continue to suffer today. The National Center for Post-Traumatic Stress Disorder has found that as many as 50 percent of the men and women who served in Vietnam have developed serious traumatic stress symptoms after returning home (NCPTSD 2002, 1).

9. HHS 2001c.

10. The U.S. population in 2000 was 281.4 million people according to the U.S. Census Bureau.

11. Sidran 2002a, 1.

12. Putnam 1989; Ross 1997; and Sidran 2002a.

13. Studies of the numbers of patients residing in hospitals who fit the diagnostic criteria for dissociative identity disorder vary somewhat due to lack of accurate testing and research. Most experts agree that the numbers of patients living with multiplicity, whether diagnosed or not, is significant; see Ross 1997; and Sidran 2002a.

14. It has been universally found that dissociative identity disorder is as prevalent in other countries as it is in North America. The countries in which prevalence studies of DID have been conducted include Australia, Belgium, Bolivia, Canada, Colombia, Czech Republic, England, Germany, Guatemala, Hungary, India, Israel, Japan, Mexico, the Netherlands, New Zealand, Norway, Puerto Rico, Scotland, Sweden, and Turkey (see Sidran 2002b for a full list of citations). Also see Martínez-Taboas (1995) for a discussion of multiple personality in Puerto Rico.

15. According to the DSM-IV-TR, the following four criteria must be met in order for someone to be diagnosed with dissociative identity disorder: "The presence of two or more distinct identities or personalities (Criterion A) that recurrently take control of behavior (Criterion B). There is an inability to recall important personal information, the extent of which is too great to be explained by ordinary forgetfulness (Criterion C). The disturbance is not due to the direct physiological effects of a substance or a general medical condition (Criterion D). In children, the symptoms cannot be attributed to imaginary playmates or other fantasy play" (APA 2000, 526).

16. Silverman 1996, 25–26.

17. Glass 1993, 33.

18. Sidran 2002a, 3.

19. Putnam 1989, 47–48.

20. For example, Barbara Walters conducted an interview with Anne Hecht, an actress who acknowledged having multiple personalities and supernatural experiences. I am not sure of Walter's intentions, but later, on another talk show, she joked about Hecht's personalities and alien encounters. Sally Jesse Rafael had three people on her talk show diagnosed with multiple personality that had, collectively, hundreds of alters (the average number of alters for an individual diagnosed with DID is ten).

21. One of the most vocal groups who deny the existence of repressed memory and multiple personalities is the False Memory Syndrome Foundation, founded in 1992. Several authors challenge us to reconceive what it means to label a person mentally ill or disordered. Showalter (1997) analyzes what she calls "hysterical epidemics," such as recovered memory of child abuse and multiple personalities. Szasz (1987) challenges mental illness as "fact" and argues that it is primarily a social construction designed to alienate certain individuals who fail to fit into prescribed social and cultural norms. For other readings that critique the condition of multiplicity, and false memories more generally, see Acocella 1999; Hacking 1995; and Loftus and Ketcham 1996.

22. See Hebald (2001) for a personal account of a woman's shocking journey

through the mental health institution being misdiagnosed and overmedicated by zealous and incompetent doctors.

23. There are many historical reviews and analyses of the validity of multiple personalities as an experience of childhood traumatization. Courtois (1999) has been most helpful to me in understanding the history and politics of the repressed memory/false memory debate. Others address the validity of multiplicity directly; see Allen 1995; Glass 1993; Kluft 1985, 1996; Martínez-Taboas 1995; Putnam 1989; Ross 1997; Spira and Yalom 1996; and Stout 2001. Collectively, these writings offer historical, social, and political perspectives about dissociative disorders, childhood trauma, and repressed memory.

24. Phillips 1995, 9.

25. Stout 2001, xi–xii.

Chapter Two

1. 42 U.S.C. §5102 (1974).

2. Child abuse statistics are taken from Childhelp 2002; HHS 2000, 2001a; NACC 2002a; and Steinberg and Schnall 2000.

3. According to the *Third National Incidence Study of Child Abuse and Neglect,* the actual incidence of abuse and neglect is estimated to be three times greater than the number reported to authorities (HHS 1996). Most experts in the area of child abuse and sexual violence agree that government statistics on abuse are grossly underestimated; see Courtois 1999; Ferraro 2000; Harvey and Herman 1992; and Sheffield 1997.

4. According to expert Kathleen Ferraro (1998), family violence is based on male power and dominance, principles and practices found in a sexist society. She argues that laws cannot protect women and children from sexism.

5. For various readings in the area of family law and perspectives on the status of children, see Bortner and Williams 1997; de Hahn 2000; Garbarino, Stott, and Faculty 1989; Hodgson 1997; Humm et al. 1994; Jacobs and Davies 1994; NACC 2002b; Rickel and Becker 1997; Schwartz and Fishman 1999; Straus and Kantor 1994; and Weisz 1995.

6. Sources for this information came from HHS 1996; NACC 2002a; Widom and Maxfield 2001; and OJJDP 2001. For characteristics and dynamics of perpetrators of family violence, see also Chu 1998; Coffey 1998; Ferraro 2000; Gil 1986; Gil and Cavanaugh-Johnson 1992; Herman 1997; and Ross 1997.

7. For readings in the area of sibling abuse, see Caffaro and Conn-Caffaro 1998; Frazier and Hayes 1994; Wallace 2002, chapter 5; and Wiehe 1997.

8. There are a number of social theories crossing many disciplines on perpetrator characteristics and behavior, particularly why some individuals become intensively violent; see Dobash and Dobash 1998; Pagelow 1984; and Wallace 2002.

9. Putnam 1989; and Ross 1997, 120.

10. Putnam 1989, 49.

11. NACC 2002a; and Oates 1996.

12. Alleged child abuse cases are reported primarily to state child protective service agencies. But not all states gather standardized information, nor do all states report statistics to the federal government. Moreover, leading experts agree that most incidents of child abuse are never reported. An excellent resource for information regarding these issues is the National Association of Counsel for Children (NACC 2002a).

13. Allen 1995.

14. There is wide agreement among experts that witnessing domestic violence has a negative lasting impact on children; see Ferraro 2000; Herman 1997; Kolbo, Blakely, and Engleman 1996; NIH 2001b; OJJDP 2001; Rickel and Becker 1997; and Winton and Mara 2001.

15. Finney 1992, 24.

16. Fatalities in the home due to abuse are most notably caused by neglect and physical violence; see Childhelp 2002; and Winton and Mara 2001.

17. The percentage of cases that become this extreme is unknown, since child abuse is estimated to be three times as high as what is reported and studies tend not to differentiate severity of abuse. However, it has been found that when the perpetrator is a biological parent, the child is more at risk of sustaining serious physical injury (HHS 1996).

18. See Courtois 1999; HHS 1996; Rush 1980; Sgroi 1982; and Wallace 2002 for definitions and discussions of child sexual abuse and incest. Louise Armstrong (1994) provides a provocative analysis of the politics involved in women coming forward with accounts of childhood incest. Rachel Lev (2003) captures the unique experiences of sexual abuse survivors within the context of the Jewish community.

19. One-fourth of the sex abuse offenders were parents, about one-half were known to the child (relatives, neighbors, etc.), and less than one-fourth were strangers; see HHS 1996.

20. The exact reasons why stepfather abuse is common is unknown. However, it is speculated that abusive men, particularly pedophiles, prey on single mothers with children; see Herman 2000.

21. The child's feeling of betrayal from a sexually abusive parent or caretaker is profound; see Courtois 1999; Freyd 1996; and Herman 1997.

22. Courtois 1999, 118.

23. Poupart 2001, 15.

24. HHS 1996.

25. Herman 1997, 100.

26. Putnam 1989.

27. Silverman 1996, 22.

28. Research and actual cases abound as to the validity of sadistic ritual and cult abuse. See Gould 1992; Healing 2002; Newton 1993; Noblitt and Perskin 2000; Oksana 1994; Ryder 1996; and Wallace 2002.

29. There are many perspectives about ritual, cult, and satanic abuse, whether it actually happens, and how widespread it is; see Brick 2001; Holmes 2000; Hudson 1991; Noblitt and Perskin 2000; Oksana 1994; Ross 1997, 2000; Ryder 1992, 1996; Showalter 1997; and Wallace 2002.

30. For research on the commonalities across ritual abuse accounts, see Adams 2000; Hudson 1991; Noblitt and Perskin 2000; Ryder 1992, 1996; and Wallace 2002. In the 1980s Sandi Gallant was one of the pioneers in investigative research on ritual abuse who found commonalities across people's experience (see Bass and Davis 1994, 419–21).

31. Glass 1993, 118.

32. More sophisticated cults understand the process of dissociation and can program alter personalities to come under the complete control of the cult. Cult-created alters might be programmed to return to the cult, act as messengers or prostitutes, or commit suicide if information about the cult gets out. Ryder (1996) provides several cases where such tactics have been utilized. See also Ross (2000), who suggests that Manchurian candidates have been programmed by psychiatrists to commit various crimes; the programming involves the creation of alter personalities such that the person is unaware of the alters.

33. Ryder 1996, 54.

34. Glass 1993, 102.

35. Gould (1992) provides an extensive list of symptoms that develop for children who have experienced ritualistic abuse, including strange and unusual sexual beliefs and practices, beliefs in the supernatural and occult symbols, and fear or preoccupation with death and dying. See also Noblitt and Perskin 2000; and Wallace 2002.

36. For more on this, see Allen 1995.

37. For readings in this area, see Garbarino, Stott, and Faculty 1989; Herman 1997; HHS 2001b; and Vermilyea 2001.

38. Not all of these behaviors listed mean that a child has been traumatized, and of course there are times when a child has experienced a traumatizing event but does not exhibit any of these reactions. These are the *likely* symptoms and reactions according to extensive research conducted by Herman 1997; HHS 2001b; March and Jackson 1993; Oates 1996; and Vermilyea 2001. Moreover, a child who has been battered, or is battered on a regular basis, may show other more visible signs of abuse, such as bruising, lacerations, or broken bones, to name a few.

39. Olson 1997, 10.

40. Lisa M. Poupart, notes to author, October 2002.

41. Cohen, Giller, and W. 1991, 67.

42. Avery Gordon (1997) does an excellent job at capturing both the illusiveness and authenticity of imagination. People who are threatened in extreme ways can become more terrified of their imaginations than the actual threats or harm done to them. This is one reason why terrorism is so powerfully effective. See also Coffey

(1998) and Herman's (1997) discussion of the effects of totalitarian control on victims.

43. Garbarino, Stott, and Faculty 1989; and Herman 1997.

44. Olson 1997, 11.

45. Kathleen Ferraro (2000) provides a compelling analysis of power relations in the family, woman battering, and its effects on victims.

46. Several leading experts in the area of trauma and abuse discuss trauma-bonding, or "traumatic bonding," and the complex relationships that develop between perpetrator and victim. See Chu 1998; Coffey 1998; Courtois 1999; Ferraro 2000; Gil 1986; Gil and Cavanaugh-Johnson 1992; Herman 1997; and Ross 1997.

47. There are excellent readings about survivor shame and guilt; see Bass and Davis 1994; Courtois 1999; Haines 1999; Herman 1997; Lev 2003; and Poupart 1997, 2001.

48. Shame, particularly its relationship to sexuality, is a significant part of the female experience, whether abused or not. Shame is a tool frequently utilized socially, culturally, and politically to dominate females especially. Refer to Haines (1999) for a wonderful guide to assist those dealing with issues related to sexuality and a healthy sex life; see also Bass and Davis 1994.

49. Scores of writings discuss the various ways children speak about abuses in their lives; see Courtois 1999; Garbarino, Stott, and Faculty 1989; Hodgson 1997; and Winton and Mara 2001. Michelle Comstock (2001) has conducted extensive research on how traumatized female youth articulate their abuse experiences, including the relationships they have with their bodies. For international perspectives on children's testimony of abuse, see Bottoms and Goodman 1996.

50. Hodgson 1997, 95.

51. There are several prominent reasons why the abuse in the McMartin preschool was not substantiated. The children's testimony became discounted as "less credible" than adults, partly because many of the children's testimony changed over time. It is difficult enough for young children to explain any experience, let alone one that is so traumatic. The kids were unable to continue repeating verbally the same experience over and over again; their testimony was inconsistent. Also, when legal processes operate so slowly, most adults, let alone children, forget the details of what happened a year or two prior; many of the children were unable to remember fully what had happened when it came time for trial. Although courts and judges today generally have a better understanding of child psychology and testimony, small children, especially, remain regarded as unreliable witnesses.

52. Olson 1997, 7.

53. Sylvia was an alter personality of Lynda Seeley; see Seeley in "Within and Without."

Chapter Three

1. For example, see Chu and Dill 1990; Courtois 1999; Fredrickson 1992; Freyd 1996; Marmar 1997; Ross 1997; and Steinberg and Schnall 2000. For biological

perspectives on trauma, see Bremner and Marmar 1998; and van der Kolk, McFarlane, and Weisaeth 1996.

2. I use Renee Fredrickson's (1992) perspective to help explain the relationship between trauma, dissociative strategies, and memory loss.

3. For scientific perspectives on the brain and memory, see Marmar 1997; and van der Kolk, McFarlane, and Weisaeth 1996.

4. Phillips 1995, 58.

5. Experts in the area of dissociation agree that there is always a host or original personality, a fundamental core of a person that precedes and withstands extreme abuse. It becomes a task in therapy to identify the host personality and integrate it with created alters. For a clinical discussion of host personalities and the newly created alters, see Chu 1998; Haddock 2001; Putnam 1989; and Ross 1997.

6. Steinberg and Schnall 2000, 17.

7. APA 2000.

8. NAMI 2001; and Ross 1997.

9. Ross 1997, 145.

10. Coffey 1998, 153–54.

11. See Allen 1995; Herman 1997; Putnam 1989; Ross 1997; Steinberg and Schnall 2000; and van der Kolk, McFarlane, and Weisaeth 1996. As more research is conducted in the area of dissociation and traumatic stress, we will begin to understand why certain people are affected by multiple personalities while others are not.

12. Chase 1987, 9–10.

13. Sizemore 1989, 41.

14. A few weeks before her death in 1998, Shirley Ardell Mason made public she was the person on whom the book and movie *Sybil* were based.

15. Schreiber 1973, 23–31.

16. For various clinical perspectives regarding therapy and memory recovery, see Chu 1998; Courtois 1999; Haddock 2001; Herman 1997; Putnam 1989; Ross 1997; and Spira and Yalom 1996.

17. Francine Shapiro has been a leader in the development and training of EMDR both nationally and internationally. For a basic description of EMDR, see Shapiro and Forrest 1997.

18. Sizemore 1989, 40.

19. Phillips 1995, 31.

20. See Friedman 1994; Herman 1997; and van der Kolk, McFarlane, and Weisaeth 1996.

21. West 1999, 48–49.

22. Carolyn Myss (1996), a pioneer in the field of energy medicine, has a useful model for understanding how body memory relates to our state of mind and how medical problems can develop when we are not healthy emotionally and spiritually.

23. Ross 1997.

24. Bass and Davis 1994, 436.

25. Keyes 1981, 26.

26. People are disembodied during dissociative states. What differentiates people with DID from others who have out-of-body experiences is the extent of the dissociation and the literal feeling that another body lives inside you. People can be so dissociative, especially during acts of self-mutilation, that they no longer feel themselves. In my friend's case, as she was pulling out her teeth, they did not feel like her own. She does not have multiple personalities. Multiplicity is an extreme version of this, where the loss of control over the body and mind is a more permanent and lived condition.

27. Olson 1997, 16–17.

28. Olson 1997, 19.

29. There are various perspectives on why females learn to freeze in response to aggression and fear; see Herman 1997; Marcus 1992; McCaughey 1997; and O'Toole and Schiffman 1997.

30. Silverman 1996, 192.

31. For more on eating disorders, see Findlen 2001; Hesse-Biber 1997; Hornbacher 1998; and Wolf 2002. For a compelling perspective on the development of eating disorders as a coping strategy to deal with sexual abuse, poverty, and other social inequalities, see Thompson 1992.

32. Bass and Davis 1994, 437.

33. There are fascinating perspectives on energy medicine and ways to heal our bodies ourselves; see, for example, Eden 1998; and Myss 1996.

34. Hornbacher 1998, 202.

35. Cohen, Giller, and W. 1991, 82–83.

Chapter Four

1. Herman 1997.

2. Poupart 1997, 174–76.

3. Much has been written about gender socialization and differences between how males and females are raised; see Chafe 1991; Coontz 2000; Kivel 1999; and Wolf 2002. One of the most profound consequences of sexual inequality is the sexualization and objectification of the female body. Starting at a young age, females are valued for their attractiveness, while males for their accomplishments (Nilsen 1997). The effects on females can be devastating, including eating disorders, sexual violence, pornography, and prostitution. Women studies is an entire field of study dedicated to the research and eradication of sexism and other forms of oppression. For those new to the area, I recommend Andersen 2000; Anzaldúa 1990; Comstock 2001; hooks 1984; Richardson, Taylor, and Whittier 1997; and Rothenberg 1998.

4. See Bortner 2002; Dobash and Dobash 1998; and Ferraro 2000.

5. People of color and the poor are severely disadvantaged in a patriarchal and racist society. Angela Davis (2000) explains how race affects gender inequality, especially as it relates to violence against women. For readings that address the intersec-

tions between race, gender, and class inequality, see also Collins 1991; Davis 1981; hooks 1989; Mohanty, Russo, and Torres 1991; Poupart 2001; and Zinn 1999.

6. See CFPA 2002; and DOL 2000. For readings related to gender and work, see Amott and Matthaei 1991; Cobble 1993; Goldberg and Kremen 1990; and Zinn 1999.

7. Perhaps the most blatantly obvious place we see the sexualization of females and sex role stereotypes is in the mass media. Television shows, movies, mainstream magazines, and advertisements objectify the female body regularly, and entire industries benefit from this objectification. For readings in this area, see Andersen 2000; Anderson 1997; Dines and Humez 1995; and Wolf 2002.

8. For readings on the socialization of children in schools, see AAUW 1992; Brannon 1999; and Chafe 1991.

9. See Lerner (1986) for a historical perspective on patriarchy and sexual inequality.

10. Bella Moon in Bass and Thornton 1983, 158.

11. Scores of people are currently on death row. Although many organizations are working to abolish the death penalty, and some states have put a moratorium on killings, the death penalty remains a common practice where a disproportionate number of poor inmates and people of color are killed.

12. For readings regarding incarcerated youth and other dependent children, see Bortner 1998; Bortner and Williams 1997; Schwartz and Fishman 1999; and Weisz 1995.

13. I find the historical overviews of child and social welfare policy by Davidson (1994) and Pleck (1987) most helpful and straightforward. A number of readings address the failure of contemporary U.S. social welfare policies, particularly the government's inadequate response to social inequalities; see also Andersen 2000; Gordon 1990; Hodgson 1997; Kessler-Harris 2001; Sidel 1998; and Zinn 1999.

14. Davidson 1994, 67.

15. Davidson 1994, 69.

16. Numerous readings discuss the effects of the Reagan presidency on single mothers and their children. For example, see Abramovitz 1992; Berry 1993; Goldberg and Kremen 1990; Gordon 1990; and Jacobs and Davies 1994.

17. TANF mandates that people work in exchange for temporary economic assistance and puts a five-year cap on aid. Because of the enormous authority each state has been given with TANF funding, state programs and services vary greatly. Although the government has reduced its welfare rolls and saved billions of dollars in welfare spending, single mothers and their children are being adversely affected. Problems with TANF legislation are being addressed by such diverse organizations as the Children's Defense Fund, the League of Women Voters, and the National Council of Churches.

18. The Children's Defense Fund and the Child Welfare League of America have been instrumental in publicizing the effects of TANF on families and single mothers especially. See also Bortner 2002 and Ferraro 2000 for perspectives on the relationship between poverty and wife battery and abuse.

19. The study was conducted by UC Berkeley Child Welfare Research Center. Todd Trumbull, "Alarming Breakdowns in State Foster Care," *San Francisco Chronicle,* December 1, 2002.

20. Information and statistics on foster care and child poverty were obtained from HHS 1996 and the National Clearinghouse on Child Abuse and Neglect Information (NCCA 2001), which collects and disseminates data from national studies and reporting agencies.

21. Olson 1997, 15.

22. There is much controversy regarding the most accurate terminology to describe domestic violence; terms include intimate partner violence, wife battery, and spousal abuse. Consistent terminology has yet to reflect the fact that females are disproportionately the target of assault and abuse by intimate males (see Dobash and Dobash 1992, 1998; Ferraro 2000; Herman 2000; Kurz 1997; and Wallace 2002). Utilizing more accurate terminology, such as female battery, to describe violence against females does not imply that other forms of violence between intimates does not happen, including abuse by same-sex partners (Renzetti 1997; Wallace 2002, chapter 11; and West 1998), women who assault their husbands (Steinmetz and Lucca 1988), and elder abuse (Wallace 2002, chapter 10). In using terms such as "spousal abuse" or even "domestic violence," female battery is downplayed. The term "female battery" recognizes the unequal relationship between males and females, as well as the disproportionate violence directed at females.

23. Information on intimate partner violence was obtained from Ferraro 1998; and Wallace 2002. See also Tjaden and Thoennes (2000) for a presentation of findings from the National Violence against Women Survey on the extent of intimate personal violence nationwide. Various federal agencies collect statistics on victimization and crime, including the Department of Health and Human Services, the National Institute of Justice, and the Office of Juvenile Justice and Delinquency Prevention.

24. Seeley in "For Christine."

25. Ferraro 2000, 142–43.

26. For readings that help explain the multifaceted reasons why women stay in abusive situations, see Dobash and Dobash 1998; Ferraro 1998, 2000; Jones 1994; and Pagelow 1984.

27. As well-intentioned as domestic violence shelters may be, many remain overfilled, some do not allow children, especially boys over eight years old, and others are overly restrictive. Much of these problems are the result of lack of financial support and serious cuts in government aid. However, many shelters are run in a hierarchal and domineering fashion, leaving women feeling more victimized. For these reasons, thousands of women and children are turned away from shelters each year.

28. See Ferraro 1998.

29. Sarah F. in Cohen, Giller, and W. 1991, 83.

30. See Sheffield (1997) for a full discussion of sexual terrorism, what it is, and how it affects females.

31. Read investigative reports in the *Boston Globe* and *New York Times.*

32. Kurkjian 2002.

33. Carroll 2002.

34. Keneally (2002) explains how secrecy within the Roman Catholic Church is embedded in Church indoctrination and law.

35. APA 2000.

36. Freiberg 2002; and Sipe 1995.

37. Sipe (1995) estimates that 6 percent of Roman Catholic Church priests get involved with minors aged seventeen and under. Of these, one in five children molested are girls. This statistic may have more to do with access than anything else. Boys play a much more active role in Church culture than girls, e.g., as altar boys. It is boys who study for the priesthood and are more actively involved with individual clergy than girls. More recently, cases have become public as to clergy sexual abuse against young females studying to be nuns. Sexual orientation may be a factor in the increased ratio of clergy abuse against boys than girls. However, Sipe found that while one-third of Catholic priests in his study had a homosexual orientation, they were just as committed to their vows of celibacy as heterosexually oriented priests.

38. The Child Abuse Prevention and Treatment Act (CAPTA) of 1974 has gone through many reauthorizations and changes, the most recent being the Child Abuse Prevention and Treatment Act amendments of 1996. See Kempe et al. 1962 for the original research, "The Battered Child Syndrome."

39. For perspectives on gender inequity in the medical field, see Andersen 2000; Brannon 1999; Courtois 1999; Gilligan 1982; Richardson, Taylor, and Whittier 1997; Showalter 1997; and Tong 1989, chapter 5.

40. Andersen 2000; and Brannon 1999.

41. There are many perspectives on the historical roots and contemporary development of female hysteria; see Cixous and Clément 1975; Courtois 1999; Herman 1997; and Showalter 1997.

42. Herman 1997, 15.

43. Sigmund Freud and Pierre Janet were two of the leading investigators during this time.

44. Andersen 2000; and Brannon 1999.

45. Phillips 1995, 78.

46. Phillips 1995, 78–79.

47. Bass and Thornton 1983, 108–9.

48. NACC 2002a, 1. In this 1996 study, educators were the most likely to report suspected child abuse, followed by law enforcement officials and social service providers. It is unknown which abuses, e.g., physical or sexual, were reported within each profession.

49. Most experts agree that the rate of reporting abuse is significantly lower than the actual cases of abuse. In a Chicago-based study, primary care physicians had "some suspicion" of abuse in 21 percent of the cases they had seen for childhood

injuries, yet most of these cases went unreported to authorities (Flaherty et al. 2002). One cannot help but be disturbed by these findings and what it potentially signifies nationally.

50. The critique of state CPS agencies may be well-founded. Inundated by new allegations of child abuse every day, dealing with backlogs of unprocessed cases and attempting to aid families who have been reported, severely understaffed and underpaid, and lacking the resources to carry out their jobs adequately, CPS workers nationwide are ill-equipped and lack the resources to handle the workload.

51. HHS 1999. The report can be ordered by contacting the Office of the Surgeon General or by visiting their website at http://www.surgeongeneral.gov/library/mentalhealth/home.html.

52. HHS 1999, 5.

53. Cohen, Giller, and W. 1991, 78–79.

54. These data come from HHS 1999, 411–17; and NAMI 2001. The Agency for Health Care Research and Quality, a program of the U.S. Department of Health and Human Services, conducts extensive research on health care costs and financing. Refer to their website at http://www.ahrq.gov/research.

55. Calculating direct and indirect health care costs is difficult, since data are not compiled similarly across health care plans nor between organizations or states.

56. Out-of-pocket expenses are derived from co-payments on insurance plans and those who are underinsured or completely uninsured.

57. It is uncertain how many individuals with trauma-related disorders are in psychiatric hospitals because such data have yet to be collected nationally. Because mental illness remains a low priority with prison authorities, it is also unknown how many incarcerated men and women go undiagnosed and untreated. With the data known, however, there are more people with mental illnesses incarcerated in prisons than residing in mental institutions designed to treat them.

58. The research on the length of time DID and PTSD patients spend in the mental health system being misdiagnosed and mistreated is consistent; see Giller and Vermilyea 2002; Putnam 1989; Ross 1997; and Ross and Dua 1993.

59. See Ross and Dua 1993. Although this study took place in Canada, health care costs generally are cheaper there. As the authors explain, what happens in the Canadian system is happening everywhere: misdiagnosis leads to outrageous and unnecessary health care costs.

60. The National Mental Health Association has compiled nationwide data on the direct and indirect costs of mental illness for the purposes of arguing for mental health parity, i.e., having mental health benefits paid similarly as health benefits overall. They report that clinical depression alone costs the U.S. $43.7 billion annually (NMHA 2002b). See also APA 2002a, 2002b.

61. HHS 2002.

62. Scores of clinical research demonstrates the long-term effects of childhood traumatization; see Allen 1995; Chu 1998; Courtois 1999; Gil 1991; Gil and Cavanaugh-Johnson 1992; and Herman 1997.

63. People experiencing multiplicity are often vulnerable, especially to loved ones and those who seek to harm them. Narratives speak poignantly of how child alters can be exploited through sex and how unhealthy relationships can so easily develop.

64. Phillips 1995, 11.

65. Poupart 1997, 143–45.

66. See Gelles and Straus 1987; HHS 1996, 2001b; Loos and Alexander 1997; Straus and Donnelly 2001; Straus and Kantor 1994; and Widom and Maxfield 2001.

67. Vermilyea 2001, 3.

68. Bortner 2002; OJJDP 2001; and Widom and Maxfield 2001.

69. Writings abound on gender socialization, masculinity and femininity, and gender differences in behavior, attitudes, and dispositions. For particularly helpful explanations for those new to this area, see Bartky 1990; Coontz 2000; Gilligan 1982; and Nilsen 1997. Most feminists agree that patriarchy is the root cause of sexism and sexual oppression; for a discussion on this point, see Lerner 1986.

70. Many secretaries will tell you that their work also involves physical labor. My point here is to show the difference between jobs requiring full manual labor and work that is not.

71. Fraser 1987, 224.

72. Compelling evidence illustrates the many similarities between many different survivors of severe trauma and human cruelty, including prisoners of war, victims of street crime, childhood abuse survivors, and military veterans; see Coffey 1998; Henke 1998; and Herman 1997.

Chapter Five

1. Lev 2003, xxvii.

2. There has been controversy about whether some or all of Sybil's alter personalities were caused by iatrogenic effects (physician-created multiple personality) and whether those involved in her care knew this but published the book anyway. A few weeks before her death, Shirley Ardell Mason announced that she was the woman written about in the book *Sybil.* A year after Mason's death in 1998, tape recordings were reportedly found by a psychiatrist who had been given the tapes twenty-five years previously by Schreiber, the author of the book. Before Mason's death, she told her close friend and psychiatrist that everything in the book was true. With Mason, Dr. Cornelia Wilbur (her original psychiatrist), and Schreiber deceased, many wonder why it took twenty-five years to find the tapes, since those involved are unable to respond to these allegations.

3. Casey 1991, 236–37.

4. Casey 1991, 17.

5. See Cohen, Giller, and W. 1991 for personal testimonies of survivors and their thoughts about being crazy.

6. Phillips 1995, 44–45.

7. Cohen, Giller, and W. 1991, 54.

8. Phillips 1995, 13.

9. Glass 1993, 119.

10. Several authors explain why therapeutic groups for dissociative disorders, and dissociative identity disorder in particular, are limited; see Allen 1995; Chu 1998; Herman 1997; and Putnam 1989.

11. Phillips 1995, 191.

12. For an excellent source of information on medication treatment for depression, anxiety, and sleep problems, see Haddock 2001, chapter 7.

13. The website is located at: http://www.medicare.gov/prescription/home.asp.

14. Kim Fitzpatrick Coppola, letter to author, October 20, 1989.

15. Much is written in academia about gender roles and how males and females are raised to act (and react) differently in various situations; see Gilligan 1982; Lerner 1986; Marcus 1992; and McCaughey 1997.

16. "Frozen watchfulness" is an expression used by Herman (1997, 100) to explain what happens to children when repeatedly victimized. Children become frozen with fear and must work diligently to stay watchful in order to protect themselves.

17. Casey 1991, 285.

Chapter Six

1. Cohen, Giller, and W. 1991, 11.

2. Membership in each church is documented differently so that membership roles may not reflect the number of regular church attendees or those who actually practice. Religious scholars believe, however, that millions of Americans are influenced regularly by religious practice, whether they attend weekly services or not. For information on church memberships, visit the following website: http://print.infoplease.com/ipa/A0001481.html.

3. For more information on the Southern Arizona Center Against Sexual Assault, refer to their website at http://www.sacasa.org. SACASA is located in Tucson, Arizona, and has been at the forefront in child advocacy, education, and research on behalf of child abuse victims.

4. Davidson 2002, 1.

5. Legislation often has parameters, including time periods for when particular programs or practices are authorized. TANF is scheduled to come up for another vote in Congress in the year 2002, meaning it is time for its reauthorization.

6. For information on the American Psychiatric Association's positions on each point, refer to their Division of Government Relations in Washington, D.C. See also APA 2002a, 2002b, and their website at http://www.psych.org.

7. As important as parity laws are, research has found that they have had little effect on the mentally ill population. The federal Mental Health Parity Act does not legislate employers to provide mental health benefits, only that when they do, the insurance coverage is equal to other medical conditions. This means that employers can decline to offer mental health benefits or drop the benefits if they had previously

existed. So while it is essential that the federal government be regulated by such laws themselves, e.g., by equalizing Medicare coverage, there would be deleterious effects if current coverage became any worse. For more on this, see APA 2002a; RAND 2000; and Sturm and Wells 2000.

8. Refer to the Survivors Healing Center website at http://www.survivorshealingcenter.org.

9. An independent DAIP evaluation found that 82 percent of the battered women in the program experienced no revictimization, a rate that far surpasses other intervention programs. For a discussion of the DAIP program, see Ferraro 2000. See Pence 1996 for the original study and findings.

10. See Winton and Mara (2001) for their insightful discussion and evaluation of the multidisciplinary approach to dealing with child abuse.

11. CAUSES is one such program and has been active in addressing all aspects of violence against children, including the training and dissemination of information to professionals working with children. CAUSES is based in Chicago. Contact their website for more information: http://www.causesforchildren.org.

References

Abramovitz, Mimi. 1992. "Poor Women in a Bind: Social Reproduction without Social Supports." *Affilia* 7, no. 2:23–43.

Acocella, Joan. 1999. *Creating Hysteria: Women and Multiple Personality Disorder.* San Francisco: Jossey-Bass.

Adams, Jeannie. 2000. *Childhood Ritual Abuse: A Resource Manual for Criminal Justice and Social Service.* Ogden, Utah: Mr. Light & Associates.

Alderman, Tracy, and Karen Marshall. 1998. *Amongst Ourselves: A Self-Help Guide to Living with Dissociative Identity Disorder.* Oakland, Calif.: New Harbinger.

Allen, Jon G. 1995. *Coping with Trauma: A Guide to Self-Understanding.* Washington, D.C.: American Psychiatric Press.

American Academy of Child and Adolescent Psychiatry (AACAP). 2002. "Facts about Gun Violence." http://www.aacap.org/info_families/NationalFacts/coGun Viol.htm. 7/9/2002.

American Association of University Women (AAUW). 1992. "The AAUW Report: How Schools Shortchange Girls." Washington, D.C.: American Association of University Women Education Foundation and National Educational Association.

American Psychiatric Association (APA). 2000. *Diagnostic and Statistical Manual for Mental Disorders.* 4th ed., text rev. Washington, D.C.: American Psychiatric Association.

———. 2002a. "Mental Health Parity—Its Time Has Come." Division of Government Relations. Washington, D.C.: American Psychiatric Association.

———. 2002b. "Research and Services for Mental Illness." http://www.psych.org. 7/15/2002.

Amott, Teresa L., and Julie A. Matthaei. 1991. *Race, Gender, and Work: A Multicultural Economic History of Women in the United States.* Boston: South End Press.

Andersen, Margaret L. 2000. *Thinking about Women: Sociological Perspectives on Sex and Gender.* 5th ed. Boston: Allyn & Bacon.

Anderson, Lisa M. 1997. *Mammies No More: The Changing Image of Black Women on Stage and Screen.* New York: Rowman & Littlefield.

Anzaldúa, Gloria, ed. 1990. *Making Face, Making Soul: Creative and Critical Perspectives by Women of Color.* San Francisco: Aunt Lute Foundation Books.

Armstrong, Louise. 1994. *Rocking the Cradle of Sexual Politics: What Happened When Women Said Incest.* New York: Addison-Wesley.

Bartky, Sandra Lee. 1990. *Femininity and Domination: Studies in the Phenomenology of Oppression.* New York: Routledge.

Bass, Ellen, and Laura Davis. 1994. *The Courage to Heal: A Guide for Women Survivors of Child Sexual Abuse.* 3d ed. New York: Harper & Row.

Bass, Ellen, and Louise Thornton, eds. 1983. *I Never Told Anyone: Writings by Women Survivors of Child Sexual Abuse.* New York: Harper & Row.

Berry, Mary Frances. 1993. *The Politics of Parenthood: Child Care, Women's Rights, and the Myth of the Good Mother.* New York: Penguin Books.

Bonner, Helen. 1995. *The Laid Daughter: A True Story.* Austin: Kairos Center.

Bortner, M. A. 1998. "America's War on Youth." *Colorlines* 1, no. 2 (fall):1–3.

———. 2002. "Controlled and Excluded: Reproduction and Motherhood among Poor and Imprisoned Women." In *Women at the Margins: Neglect, Punishment, and Resistance,* edited by Josefina Figueira-McDonough and Rosemary C. Sarri. New York: Haworth Press.

Bortner, M. A., and Linda M. Williams. 1997. *Youth in Prison: We the People of Unit Four.* New York: Routledge.

Bottoms, Bette L., and Gail S. Goodman, eds. 1996. *International Perspectives on Child Abuse and Children's Testimony: Psychological Research and Law.* Thousand Oaks, Calif.: Sage.

Brannon, Linda. 1999. *Gender: Psychological Perspectives.* 2d ed. Boston: Allyn & Bacon.

Bremner, J. Douglas, and Charles R. Marmar. 1998. *Trauma, Memory, and Dissociation.* Washington, D.C.: American Psychiatric Press.

Brick, Neil. 2001. "Data Providing the Existence of Recovered Memory, Ritual Abuse, MK-Ultra, and Information on the Backlash." Paper presented at the annual meeting of the New Hope Healing Institute, July 7, Athens, Georgia.

Caffaro, John V., and Allison Conn-Caffaro. 1998. *Sibling Abuse Trauma: Assessment and Intervention: Strategies for Children, Families, and Adults.* New York: Haworth Press.

Carroll, Matt. 2002. "$13.5m Settlement in R.I. Clergy Abuse." *Boston Globe,* September 10, sec. A1.

Casey, Joan Frances, with Lynn Wilson. 1991. *The Flock: The Autobiography of a Multiple Personality.* New York: Fawcett Columbine.

Center for Effective Discipline (CED). 2002. "Discipline and the Law." http://www.stophitting.com/laws/legalInformation.php. 7/6/2002.

Center for Policy Alternatives (CFPA). 2002. "State Action—Issues: Equal Pay Overview." http://www.cfpa.org/issues/workcompensation/equalpay/index.cfm.10/2/2002.

Chafe, William H. 1991. *The Paradox of Change: American Women in the 20th Century.* New York: Oxford University Press.

Chase, Truddi. 1987. *When Rabbit Howls.* New York: Jove Books.

Childhelp USA (Childhelp). 2002. "National Child Abuse Statistics." http://www.childhelpusa.org/child/statistics.htm. 7/17/2002.

Children's Action Alliance (CAA). 2002. "Facts about Arizona's Homeless Youth." http://www.azchildren.org/caa/mainpages/FactSheets&Links/Links.asp.7/17/2002.

Chu, James A. 1998. *Rebuilding Shattered Lives: The Responsible Treatment of Complex Post-Traumatic Stress and Dissociative Disorders.* New York: John Wiley and Sons.

Chu, James A., and D. L. Dill. 1990. "Dissociative Symptoms in Relation to Childhood Physical and Sexual Abuse." *American Journal of Psychiatry* 147:887–92.

Cixous, Hélène, and Catherine Clément. 1975. *The Newly Born Woman.* Minneapolis: University of Minnesota Press.

Cobble, Dorothy Sue, ed. 1993. *Women and Unions: Forging a Partnership.* Ithaca, N.Y.: ILR Press.

Coffey, Rebecca. 1998. *Unspeakable Truths and Happy Endings.* Baltimore, Md.: Sidran Press.

Cohen, Barry M., Esther Giller, and Lynn W. 1991. *Multiple Personality Disorder from the Inside Out.* Lutherville, Md.: Sidran Press.

Collins, Patricia Hill. 1991. *Black Feminist Thought: Knowledge, Consciousness, and the Politics of Empowerment.* New York: Routledge.

Comstock, Michelle. 2001. "Grrrl Zine Networks: Re-Composing Spaces of Authority, Gender, and Culture." *Journal of Advanced Composition* 21, no. 2 (spring): 383–409.

Coontz, Stephanie. 2000. *The Way We Never Were: American Families and the Nostalgia Trap.* New York: Basic Books.

Courtois, Christine A. 1999. *Recollections of Sexual Abuse: Treatment Principles and Guidelines.* New York: W. W. Norton.

Davidson, Cherilyn. 1994. "Dependent Children and Their Families: A Historical Survey of U.S. Policies." In *More Than Kissing Babies? Current Child and Family Policy in the United States,* edited by Francine H. Jacobs and Margery W. Davies. Westport, Conn.: Auburn House.

Davidson, Howard. 2002. "When Does Physical Discipline Cross the Line to Become Child Abuse?" Center for Effective Discipline. http://www.stophitting.com/laws/homePunishment.php. 7/6/2002.

Davis, Angela. 1981. *Women, Race, and Class.* New York: Random House.

———. 2000. "The Color of Violence against Women." *Colorlines* 3, no. 3 (fall):1–7.

de Hahn, Tracee. 2000. *Crimes against Children: Child Abuse and Neglect.* Philadelphia: Chelsea House.

Dines, Gail, and Jean M. Humez, eds. 1995. *Gender, Race, and Class in the Media.* Thousand Oaks, Calif.: Sage.

Dobash, R. Emerson, and Russell P. Dobash. 1992. *Women, Violence, and Social Change.* London: Routledge.

———. 1998. *Rethinking Violence against Women.* Thousand Oaks, Calif.: Sage.

Eden, Donna. 1998. *Energy Medicine.* New York: Putnam Books.

Ferraro, Kathleen J. 1998. "Policing Woman Battering." In *Criminology at the Crossroads: Feminist Readings in Crime and Justice,* edited by Kathleen Daly and Lisa Maher. New York: Oxford University Press.

———. 2000. "Woman Battering: More Than a Family Problem." In *Women, Crime, and Criminal Justice: Original Feminist Readings,* edited by Claire M. Renzetti and Lynne Goldstein. Los Angeles: Roxbury.

Findlen, Barbara, ed. 2001. *Listen Up: Voices from the Next Feminist Generation.* 2d ed. Seattle: Seal Press.

Finney, Lynne D. 1992. *Reach for the Rainbow: Advanced Healing for Survivors of Sexual Abuse.* New York: Perigree Books.

Flaherty, Emalee G., Robert Sege, Christine Mattson, and H. J. Binns. 2002. "Assessment of Suspicion of Abuse in the Primary Care Setting." *Ambulatory Pediatrics* 2, no. 2 (March):120–26.

Fraser, Nancy. 1989. *Unruly Practices: Power, Discourse and Gender in Contemporary Social Theory.* Minneapolis: University of Minnesota Press.

Fraser, Sylvia. 1987. *My Father's House: A Memoir of Incest and of Healing.* New York: Harper & Row.

Frazier, Billie, and Kathleen C. Hayes. 1994. *Selected Resources on Sibling Abuse: An Annotated Bibliography for Researchers, Educators, and Counselors.* Beltsville, Md.: National Agriculture Library.

Fredrickson, Renee. 1992. *Repressed Memories: A Journey to Recovery from Sexual Abuse.* New York: Simon & Schuster.

Freiberg, Peter. 2002. "Mass Confusion." *The Advocate* (April):28–31.

Freyd, Jennifer J. 1996. *Betrayal Trauma: The Logic of Forgetting Childhood Abuse.* Cambridge: Harvard University Press.

Friedman, M. J. 1994. "Biological and Pharmacological Aspects of the Treatment of PTSD." In *Handbook of Post-Traumatic Therapy,* edited by M. B. Williams and J. F. Sommer Jr. Westport, Conn.: Greenwood Press.

Garbarino, James, Frances M. Stott, and Faculty of Erikson Institute. 1989. *What Children Can Tell Us.* San Francisco: Jossey-Bass.

Gelles, Richard J., and Murray Straus. 1987. *The Violent Home.* Thousand Oaks, Calif.: Sage.

Gil, Eliana. 1986. *Children Who Molest: A Guide for Parents of Young Sex Offenders.* Rockville, Md.: Launch Press, 1986.

———. 1990. *United We Stand: A Book for People with Multiple Personalities.* Walnut Creek, Calif.: Launch Press.

———. 1991. *The Healing Power of Play: Working with Abused Children.* New York: Guilford Press.

Gil, Eliana, and Toni Cavanaugh-Johnson. 1992. *Sexualized Children: Assessment and Treatment of Sexualized Children and Children Who Molest.* Rockville, Md.: Launch Press.

Gilbertson, Annette. "How do I speak." Unpublished poetry.

Giller, Esther, and Elizabeth Vermilyea. 2002. "FDA Advisory Statement on PTSD." Lutherville, Md.: Sidran Traumatic Stress Foundation.

Gilligan, Carol. 1982. *In a Different Voice: Psychological Theory and Women's Development.* Cambridge: Harvard University Press.

Glass, James M. 1993. *Shattered Selves: Multiple Personality in a Postmodern World.* Ithaca, N.Y.: Cornell University Press.

Goldberg, Gertrude Shaffner, and Eleanor Kremen, eds. 1990. *The Feminization of Poverty: Only in America?* New York: Praeger.

Gordon, Avery F. 1997. *Ghostly Matters: Haunting and the Sociological Imagination.* Minneapolis: University of Minnesota Press.

Gordon, Linda, ed. 1990. *Women, the State, and Welfare.* Madison: University of Wisconsin Press.

Gould, Catherine. 1992. "Diagnosis and Treatment of Ritually Abused Children." In *Out of Darkness,* edited by D. K. Sakheim and S. E. Devine. New York: Lexington.

Hacking, Ian. 1995. *Rewriting the Soul: Multiple Personality and the Sciences of Memory.* Princeton: Princeton University Press.

Haddock, Deborah Bray. 2001. *The Dissociative Identity Disorder Sourcebook.* New York: McGraw-Hill.

Haines, Staci. 1999. *The Survivor's Guide to Sex: How to Have an Empowered Sex Life after Child Sexual Abuse.* San Francisco: Cleis Press.

Harvey, Mary R., and Judith L. Herman. 1992. "The Trauma of Sexual Victimization: Feminist Contributions to Theory, Research, and Practice." *PTSD Research Quarterly* 3, no. 3:1–18.

HealingHopes (Healing). 2002. "Ritual Abuse." http://www.healinghopes.org/library/ra.html. 7/11/2002.

Hebald, Carol. 2001. *The Heart Too Long Suppressed: A Chronicle of Mental Illness.* Boston: Northeastern University Press.

Henke, Suzette A. 1998. *Shattered Subjects: Trauma and Testimony in Women's Life-Writing.* New York: St. Martin's Press.

Herman, Judith Lewis. 1997 [1992]. *Trauma and Recovery.* New York: Basic Books.

———. 2000 [1981]. *Father-Daughter Incest.* Cambridge: Harvard University Press.

Hesse-Biber, Sharlene. 1997. *Am I Thin Enough Yet: The Cult of Thinness and the Commercialization of Identity.* New York: Oxford University Press.

Hocking, Sandra J., and Company. 1992. *Living with Your Selves: A Survival Manual for People with Multiple Personalities.* Rockville, Md.: Launch Press.

Hodgson, Lucia. 1997. *Raised in Captivity: Why Does America Fail Its Children?* Saint Paul, Minn.: Graywolf Press.

Holmes, Leonard. 2000. "What the Hell Is Satanic Ritual Abuse?" Lutherville, Md.: Sidran Traumatic Stress Foundation.

hooks, bell. 1984. *Feminist Theory: from margin to center.* Boston: South End Press.

———. 1989. *Talking Back: thinking feminist, thinking black.* Boston: South End Press.

Hornbacher, Marya. 1998. *Wasted: A Memoir of Anorexia and Bulimia.* New York: HarperCollins.

Hudson, Pamela S. 1991. *Ritual Child Abuse: Discovery, Diagnosis, and Treatment.* Sarasota, Calif.: R & E Publishers.

Humm, S. Randall, Beate Anna Ort, Martin Mazen Anbari, Wendy S. Lader, and William Scott Biel. 1994. *Child, Parent, and State: Law and Policy Reader.* Philadelphia: Temple University Press.

Hyman, Irwin A. 1990. *Reading, Writing, and the Hickory Stick: The Appalling Story of Physical and Psychological Abuse in American Schools.* Lexington, Mass.: Lexington Books.

Hyman, Ronald T., and Charles H. Rathbone. 1993. *Corporal Punishment in Schools: Reading the Law.* Topeka, Kans.: National Organization on Legal Problems of Education.

International Society for the Study of Dissociation (ISSD). 2001. "Guidelines for Treatment." http://www.issd.org/indexpage/isdguide.html. 6/20/2001.

Jacobs, Francine H., and Margery W. Davies, eds. 1994. *More Than Kissing Babies?*

Current Child and Family Policy in the United States. Westport, Conn.: Auburn House.

Jones, Ann. 1994. *Next Time She'll Be Dead.* Boston: Beacon.

Josephson Institute of Ethics (JIE). 2001. "Report Card on the Ethics of American Youth 2000." Reported by the National School Safety Center. http://www.nsscl .org.html. 1/15/2002.

Kempe, C. Henry, Frederic N. Silverman, Brandt F. Steele, William Droegmueller, and Henry K. Silver. 1962. "The Battered Child Syndrome." *Journal of the American Medical Association* 181, no. 17:17–24.

Keneally, Thomas. 2002. "Cold Sanctuary: How the Church Lost its Mission." *New Yorker,* June 17, 58–66.

Kessler-Harris, Alice. 2001. *In Pursuit of Equity: Women, Men, and the Quest for Economic Citizenship in Twentieth-Century America.* New York: Oxford University Press.

Keyes, Daniel. 1981. *The Minds of Billy Milligan.* New York: Bantam Books.

Kimerling, Rachel, Paige Oimette, and Jessica Wolfe. 2002. *Gender and PTSD.* New York: Guilford Press.

Kivel, Paul. 1999. *Boys Will Be Men: Raising Our Sons for Courage, Caring, and Community.* Gabriola Island, B.C.: New Society Publications.

Kluft, Richard P., ed. 1985. *Childhood Antecedents of Multiple Personality Disorder.* Washington, D.C.: American Psychiatric Press.

———. 1996. "Dissociative Identity Disorder." In *Handbook of Dissociation: Theoretical, Empirical, and Clinical Perspectives,* edited by Larry K. Michelson and William J. Ray. New York: Plenum Press.

Kolbo, J. R., E. H. Blakely, and D. Engleman. 1996. "Children Who Witness Domestic Violence: A Review of Empirical Literature." *Journal of Interpersonal Violence* 11:281–93.

Kurkjian, Steven. 2002. "N.H. Diocese Agrees to Pay More Than $5m in Settlements." *Boston Globe,* November 27, sec. B4.

Kurz, Demie. 1997. "Violence against Women or Family Violence? Current Debates and Future Directions." In *Gender Violence: Interdisciplinary Perspectives,* edited by Laura L. O'Toole and Jessica R. Schiffman. New York: New York University Press.

Lerner, Gerder. 1986. *The Creation of Patriarchy.* New York: Oxford University Press.

Lev, Rachel. 2003. *Shine the Light: Sexual Abuse and Healing in the Jewish Community.* Boston: Northeastern University Press.

Loftus, Elizabeth, and Katherine Ketcham. 1996. *The Myth of Repressed Memory: False Memories and Allegations of Sexual Abuse.* New York: St. Martin's Press.

Loos, E., and P. C. Alexander. 1997. "Differential Effects Associated with Self-Reported Histories of Abuse and Neglect in a College Sample." *Journal of Interpersonal Violence* 12, no. 3:340.

March, John S., and Lisa Amaya Jackson. 1993. "Post-Traumatic Stress Disorder in Children and Adolescents." *PTSD Research Quarterly* 4, no. 4:1–7.

Marcus, Sharon. 1992. "Fighting Bodies, Fighting Words: A Theory and Politics of Rape Prevention." In *Feminists Theorize the Political,* edited by Judith Butler and Joan W. Scott. New York: Routledge.

Marmar, Charles R. 1997. "Trauma and Dissociation." *PTSD Research Quarterly* 8, no. 3:1–6.

Martínez-Taboas, Alfonso. 1995. *Multiple Personality: An Hispanic Perspective.* San Juan, P.R.: Puente Publications.

McCaughey, Martha. 1997. *Real Knockouts: The Physical Feminism of Women's Self-Defense.* New York: New York University Press.

Mohanty, Chandra Talpade, Ann Russo, and Lourdes Torres. 1991. *Third World Women and the Politics of Feminism.* Bloomington: Indiana University Press.

Myss, Caroline. 1996. *Anatomy of the Spirit: Seven Stages of Power and Healing.* New York: Three Rivers Press.

National Alliance for the Mentally Ill (NAMI). 2001. "Facts and Figures about Mental Illness." http://www.nami.org/fact.htm. 9/26/2001.

National Association of Counsel for Children (NACC). 2002a. "Children and the Law: Child Maltreatment." http://www.naccchildlaw.org/chldrenlaw/childmal treatment.html. 1/15/2002.

———. 2002b. "Children and the Law: The Legal System." http://www.nacc childlaw.org/chldrenlaw/legalsystem.html. 1/15/2002.

National Center for Homeless Education (NCHE). 2002. "Statistics on Child Poverty and Homelessness." http://www.serve.org.html. 1/3/2002.

National Center for Post-Traumatic Stress Disorder (NCPTSD). 2002. "What Is Post-Traumatic Stress Disorder?" http://www.ncptsd.org/facts/general/fs_what_ is_ptsd.html. 6/20/2002.

National Clearinghouse on Child Abuse and Neglect Information (NCCA). 2001. "Statistics." http://www.calib.com/nccanch/stats/index.cfm. 5/28/2001.

National Coalition to Abolish Corporal Punishment in Schools (NCACPS). 2002. "Facts about Corporal Punishment," Center for Effective Discipline. http://www .stophitting.com/disatschool/facts/php. 7/6/2002.

National Mental Health Association (NMHA). 2002a. "MHIC: Mental Illness and the Family: Mental Health Statistics." Alexandria: National Mental Health Association. http://www.nmha.org/infoctr/factsheets/15.cfm. 3/12/2002.

———. 2002b. "Why Mental Health Parity Makes Economic Sense." Alexandria: National Mental Health Association. http://www.nmha.org/state/parity/parity_ economy.cfm. 10/28/2002.

Newton, Michael. 1993. *Raising Hell: An Encyclopedia of Devil Worship and Satanic Crime.* New York: Avon Books.

Nilsen, Alleen Pace. 1997. "Sexism in English: A 1990s Update." In *Reading Women's Lives: An Introduction to Women's Studies.* Needham Heights, Mass.: Simon & Schuster.

Noblitt, James Randall, and Pamela Sue Perskin. 2000. *Cult and Ritual Abuse: Its History, Anthropology, and Recent Discovery in Contemporary America.* Rev. ed. New York: Praeger.

Oates, R. Kim. 1996. *The Spectrum of Child Abuse: Assessment, Treatment, and Prevention.* New York: Brunner-Routledge.

Office of Juvenile Justice and Delinquency Prevention (OJJDP). 2001. "Action Plan

Update—Addressing Youth Victimization." http://www.ncjrs.org/html/ojjdp/action_plan_update_2001. 1/15/2002.

Oksana, Chrystine. 1994. *Safe Passage to Healing: A Guide for Survivors of Ritual Abuse.* New York: Harper & Row.

Olson, Sarah E. 1997. *Becoming One: A Story of Triumph over Multiple Personality Disorder.* Pasadena: Trilogy Books.

O'Toole, Laura L., and Jessica R. Schiffman. 1997. *Gender Violence: Interdisciplinary Perspectives.* New York: New York University Press.

Pagelow, Mildred Daley. 1984. *Family Violence.* New York: Praeger.

Pence, Ellen L. 1996. "Safety for Battered Women in a Textually Mediated Legal System." Ph.D. diss., University of Toronto.

Phillips, Jane. 1995. *The Magic Daughter: A Memoir of Living with Multiple Personality Disorder.* New York: Penguin Books.

Pleck, Elizabeth. 1987. *Domestic Tyranny: The Making of Social Policy against Family Violence from Colonial Times to the Present.* New York: Oxford University Press.

Poupart, Lisa M. 1997. "Breaking Silence, Telling Truths." Ph.D. diss., Arizona State University.

———. 2001. "Breaking Commands of Silence." *Society of Women Sociologists Network News* 18, no. 2:15–17.

Putnam, Frank W. 1989. *Diagnosis and Treatment of Multiple Personality Disorder.* New York: Guilford Press.

RAND. 2000. "Research Highlights: Are People with Mental Illness Getting Coverage, and Access to Care," RAND Health. http://www.rand.org/publications/RB/RB4533/. 10/28/2002.

Renzetti, Claire M. 1997. "Violence in Lesbian and Gay Relationships." In *Gender Violence: Interdisciplinary Perspectives,* edited by Laura L. O'Toole and Jessica R. Schiffman. New York: New York University Press.

Richardson, Laurel, Verta Taylor, and Nancy Whittier, eds. 1997. *Feminist Frontiers IV.* New York: McGraw-Hill.

Rickel, Annette U., and Evvie Becker. 1997. *Keeping Children from Harm's Way: How National Policy Affects Psychological Development.* Washington, D.C.: American Psychiatric Association.

Ross, Colin A. 1997. *Dissociative Identity Disorder: Diagnosis, Clinical Features, and Treatment of Multiple Personality Disorder.* New York: John Wiley & Sons.

———. 2000. *Bluebird: Deliberate Creation of Multiple Personality by Psychiatrists.* Richardson, Tex.: Manitou Communications.

Ross, Colin A., and V. Dua. 1993. "Psychiatric Health Care Costs of Multiple Personality Disorder." *American Journal of Psychotherapy* 47:103–12.

Rothenberg, Paula S. 1998. *Race, Class, and Gender in the United States: An Integrated Study.* 4th ed. New York: St. Martin's Press.

Rush, Florence. 1980. *The Best Kept Secret: Sexual Abuse of Children.* New York: McGraw-Hill.

Ryder, Daniel. 1992. *Breaking the Circle of Satanic Ritual Abuse: Recognizing and Recovering from the Hidden Trauma.* Minneapolis: Compcare Publications.

———. 1996. *Cover-Up of the Century: Satanic Ritual Crime and World Conspiracy.* Noblesville, Ind.: Ryder Publishing.

Schreiber, Flora Rheta. 1973. *Sybil.* New York: Warner Books.

Schwartz, Ira M., and Gideon Fishman. 1999. *Kids Raised by the Government.* Westport, Conn.: Praeger.

Seeley, Lynda. "For Christine" and "Within and Without." Unpublished poetry.

Sgroi, Suzanne M., ed. 1982. *Handbook of Clinical Intervention in Child Sexual Abuse.* Lexington, Mass.: Lexington Books.

Shapiro, Francine, and Margot Silk Forrest. 1997. *EMDR: The Breakthrough Therapy for Overcoming Anxiety, Stress, and Trauma.* New York: Basic Books.

Sheffield, Carole J. 1997. "Sexual Terrorism." In *Gender Violence: Interdisciplinary Perspectives,* edited by Laura L. O'Toole and Jessica R. Schiffman. New York: New York University Press.

Showalter, Elaine. 1997. *Hystories: Hysterical Epidemics and Modern Culture.* New York: Columbia University Press.

Sidel, Ruth. 1998. *Keeping Women and Children Last: America's War on the Poor.* New York: Penguin Books.

Sidran Foundation (Sidran). 2002a. "What Is Dissociative Identity Disorder?" http://www.sidran.org/didbr.html. 1/12/2002.

———. 2002b. "DID/Trauma/Memory Reference List: Cross Cultural Studies on DID." http://www.sidran.org/refs/ref4.html. 1/12/2002.

Silverman, Sue William. 1996. *Because I Remember Terror, Father, I Remember You.* Athens: University of Georgia Press.

Sipe, A. W. Richard. 1995. *Sex, Priests, and Power: Anatomy of a Crisis.* New York: Brunner-Routledge.

Sizemore, Chris Costner. 1989. *A Mind of My Own.* New York: William Morrow.

Southern Arizona Center Against Sexual Assault (SACASA). 2002. "Statistics on Sexual Assault: National (United States) Statistics." http://www.sacasa.org/nat stat.htm. 7/14/2002.

Spira, James L., and Irvin D. Yalom, eds. 1996. *Treating Dissociative Identity Disorder.* San Francisco: Jossey-Bass.

Steinberg, Marlene, and Maxine Schnall. 2000. *The Stranger in the Mirror: Dissociation—The Hidden Epidemic.* New York: Cliff Street Books.

Steinmetz, Suzanne K., and Joseph S. Lucca. 1988. "Husband Battering." In *Handbook of Family Violence,* edited by Vincent B. Van Hasselt, R. L. Morrison, A. S. Bellack, and M. Hersen. New York: Plenum Press.

Stout, Martha. 2001. *The Myth of Sanity: Divided Consciousness and the Promise of Awareness.* New York: Penguin Books.

Straus, Murray A., and Denise A. Donnelly. 2001. *Beating the Devil Out of Them: Corporal Punishment in American Families and its Effects on Children.* 2d ed. New Brunswick, N.J.: Transaction.

Straus, Murray A., and G. K. Kantor. 1994. "Corporal Punishment of Adolescents by Parents: A Risk Factor in the Epidemiology of Depression, Suicide, Alcohol Abuse, Child Abuse, and Wife Beating." *Adolescence* 29:543–61.

Sturm, Roland, and Kenneth Wells. 2000. "Health Insurance May Be Improving—But Not for Individuals with Mental Illness." *Health Services Research* 35, no. 1:251–60.

Szasz, Thomas. 1987. *Insanity: The Idea and its Consequences.* New York: John Wiley and Sons.

Thompson, Becky Wangsgaard. 1992. "'A Way Outa No Way': Eating Problems among African American, Latina, and White Women." *Gender and Society* 6, no. 4 (December).

Tjaden, Patricia, and Nancy Thoennes. 2000. "Extent, Nature, and Consequences of Intimate Partner Violence: Findings from the National Violence against Women Survey." National Institute of Justice and National Institutes of Health, Centers for Disease Control and Prevention. Washington, D.C.: Government Printing Office, 181867.

Tong, Rosemarie. 1989. *Feminist Thought: A Comprehensive Introduction.* Boulder, Colo.: Westview Press.

U.S. Department of Health and Human Services (HHS). 1996. "Third National Incidence Study of Child Abuse and Neglect." Administration for Children and Families, National Center on Child Abuse and Neglect. Washington, D.C.: Government Printing Office, ACF-105–91–1800.

———. 1999. "Mental Health: A Report of the Surgeon General." Rockville, Md.: U.S. Department of Health and Human Services, Substance Abuse and Mental Health Services Administration, Center for the Mental Health Services, National Institutes of Health, National Institute of Mental Health.

———. 2000. "2000 Trends." Assistant Secretary for Planning and Evaluation. Washington, D.C.: Government Printing Office. http://www.aspe.hhs.gov/hsp/00trends.html. 5/28/2001.

———. 2001a. "Child Health USA 2000: Eleventh Annual Report." Health Resources and Service Administration, Maternal and Child Health Bureau. Washington, D.C.: Government Printing Office.

———. 2001b. "Helping Children and Adolescents Cope with Violence and Disasters." National Institutes of Health, National Institute of Mental Health. Washington, D.C.: Government Printing Office. http://www.nimh.nih.gov/publicat. 5/28/2001.

———. 2001c. "The Numbers Count: Mental Disorders in America." National Institutes of Health, National Institute of Mental Health. Washington, D.C.: Government Printing Office. http://www.nimh.nih.gov/publicat. 5/28/2001.

———. 2002. "Mental Health." Centers for Disease Control, National Center for Health Statistics. Washington, D.C.: Government Printing Office. http://www.cdc.gov/nchs/fastats/mental.htm. 5/10/2002.

U.S. Department of Labor (DOL). 2000. "2000 Annual Earnings: Current Population Reports." Bureau of Labor Statistics. Washington, D.C.: Government Printing Office, Series P60.

van der Kolk, Bessel, Alexander C. McFarlane, and Lars Weisaeth. 1996. *Traumatic Stress: The Effects of Overwhelming Experience on Mind, Body, and Society.* New York: Guilford Press.

V-Day Organization (V-Day). 2002. "Violence: Violence against Women Statistics." http://www.vday.org/content.cfm?/ArticleID = 522. 11/2/2002.

Vermilyea, Elizabeth G. 2001. "Developmental Aspects of Childhood Trauma Contributing to Adult Revictimization." Lutherville, Md.: Sidran Traumatic Stress Foundation.

W., Lynn. 2002. "Growing Older, Divided." *Many Voices* 14, no. 6 (December):8–9.

Wallace, Harvey. 2002. *Family Violence: Legal, Medical, and Social Perspectives.* 3d ed. Boston: Allyn & Bacon.

Weisz, Virginia G. 1995. *Children and Adolescents in Need: A Legal Primer for the Helping Professional.* Thousand Oaks, Calif.: Sage.

West, Cameron. 1999. *First Person Plural: My Life as a Multiple.* New York: Hyperion.

West, Carolyn M. 1998. "Leaving a Second Closet: Outing Partner Violence in Same-Sex Couples." In *Partner Violence: A Comprehensive Review of Twenty Years of Research,* edited by Jane L. Jasinkski and Linda M. Williams. Thousand Oaks, Calif.: Sage.

Widom, Cathy S., and Michael G. Maxfield. 2001. "An Update on the 'Cycle of Violence.'" Washington, D.C.: National Institute of Justice, U.S. Department of Justice, NCJ 184894.

Wiehe, Vernon R. 1997. *Sibling Abuse: Hidden Physical, Emotional, and Sexual Trauma.* Thousand Oaks, Calif.: Sage.

Winton, Mark, and Barbara Mara. 2001. *Child Abuse and Neglect: Multidisciplinary Approaches.* Boston: Allyn & Bacon.

Wolf, Naomi. 2002. *The Beauty Myth: How Images of Beauty Are Used against Women.* New York: HarperPerennial Library.

Zinn, Howard. 1999 [1980]. *A People's History of the United States: 1492–Present.* New York: HarperCollins.

Index

"Abuse: A Trauma That Never Ends" (Nancy G.), 116
abusers. *See* perpetrators
acupuncture, 154
Administration for Children and Families, 177
Adoption Assistance and Child Welfare Act, 95
Aid to Families with Dependent Children, 94, 95
Allen, Jon, 116
almshouses, 93
alters, 68–73 (*see also* co-consciousness; dissociative identity disorder; recall memory): and body recognition, 73; co-consciousness and, 68–71; creation of, 8–12, 53–54; experience of, xii–xiii, 12; exploitation of, 122, 149–50, 208n.32, 216n.63; group therapy and, 147; and host personality, 53–54, 70, 210n.5; and internal system, 54–56, 69–71; and switching, 68–72, 147; Sybil and, 216n.2
American Bar Association, 175
American Medical Association (AMA), 175, 179
American Psychiatric Association, 175, 178, 194
American Psychological Association, 179, 195
Americans with Disabilities Act, 143
amnesia, 34–35, 51, 57, 59 (*see also* flashbacks; recall memory)
Artemis, 67–68
Arthur (Billy Milligan alter), 68–69

backlash, 121–22
Bass, Ellen, 180
Beverly R., 139
biofeedback, 80
bodily resistance, 73–80; freezing and, 74; self-mutilation, 74–78; somatic symptoms and, 65–66; survival strategies and, 50–51, 58
body memory: cellular, 51, 62, 63, 80; DID and, 62–68; illness and, 65; and manifestations of traumatic abuse, 62–63; pain and, 64–67
body therapies, 80–82, 161–62, 164–69 (*see also* healing): martial arts and self-defense, 166–67; professional healers, 165–66; recommendations for, 168–69
books, self-healing and, 133–35, 191–92

California's Department of Social Services, 96
Casey, Joan Frances, 135, 137, 169
Catholic Church. *See* Roman Catholic Church
CAUSES (Child Abuse Unit for Studies), 218n.11
Center for Effective Discipline, 175, 203n.4
Centers for Disease Control, 177
Chase, Truddi, 56, 59
child abuse (*see also* child sexual abuse; incest; physical abuse; ritual abuse; sibling abuse): and children witnessing violence, 27–28, 98, 207n.14; definition of, 19; girls and, 18, 19; patterns of, 18, 83–85; power and, 19–21, 206n.4; severe forms of, 27–28, 207nn. 16, 17; social costs of, 118–29; statistics regarding, 19, 206n.3, 207n.12; types of, 26–35
Child Abuse Prevention and Treatment Act, 19, 95, 110
Child Protective Service, 27, 115, 215n.50
child sexual abuse, 28–30 (*see also* incest): definition of, 28; DID and, 26; and girls, 18; and Roman Catholic Church, 104, 106–9; speaking out by victims, 46–49; treatment of, 180
child welfare, history of, 93–97
Child Welfare League of America, 178, 181
Childhelp, USA, 182
Children's Bureau, 94
Children's Defense Fund, 178, 182
chiropractors and healing, 80, 165
Christine (Seeley alter), 98–99
Chu, James, 116
coalitions, 181–84
COBRA (Consolidated Omnibus Budget Reconciliation Act), 158–59

co-consciousness (*see also* alters; dissociative identity disorder; recall memory): experience of, 68–71; internal communication system and, 56; internet and, 150; switching and, 71
Cohen, Barry, 116
community health centers, 142
community support, 180–81
connecting with others, 130, 133–36, 147–49
consciousness and healing, 163–64
corporal punishment, ix, 92, 175, 176, 203n.4
The Courage to Heal (Bass and Davis), 77–78, 171, 180
Courtois, Christine, 116
cults. *See* ritual abuse
cutting, 75–77 (*see also* self-mutilation)
cycle of abuse/violence (revictimization), 22–23, 25–26, 218n.9; gender and, 124–26; society and, 102–3, 118, 128, 185

"Daddy I'm Sorry" (Poupart), 123–24
death penalty, 92, 212n.11
diagnosis issues, 137–41, 203n.2, 204n.7, 205n.15
diet, 154
disability. *See* Social Security Disability
discipline. *See* corporal punishment
disembodiment, 80, 211n.26
dissociation: as abuse strategy, 50–51; body strategies and, 53, 58; manifestation process of, 53; physical experience of, 51
dissociative identity disorder (DID), 7–11 (*see also* alters; body memory; flashbacks; recall memory): body and, 68–73; causes of, x–xi, 6–7, 8–9, 11, 12, 26–27, 85, 204n.7; characteristics of people with, 10, 54–55; definition of, 7–8, 80, 211n.26; diagnosis of, 119, 137–41, 203n.2, 204n.7, 205n.15; education regarding, 131–36, 184–87; family/friends and, 139–41; gender and, xiv–xv, 204nn 3, 5; prevalence of, 205nn. 13, 14; society and, 127, 205n.21; stereotyping and, 11–13, 131–32, 135, 205n.20
domestic violence. *See* family violence; female battery
domestic violence shelters, 99–100, 213n.27
Duluth Abuse Intervention Project (DAIP), 182, 218n.9

eating disorders: DID and, 14, 66; females and, 5, 6; trauma/child abuse and, xv, 35, 47, 73, 75, 82, 85
economics and mental illness, 118–20, 215n.60
education about traumatic abuse: healing and, 131–36; health care providers and, 122; internet and, 135, 136, 193; organizations and, 178–80; resources for, 191–93
EMDR (eye movement desensitization and reprocessing), 60
Equal Rights Amendment, 90
"Eve" (Chris Costner Sizemore), 59, 61
exercise, 5, 80, 164, 166–68, 183

False Memory Syndrome Foundation, 205n.21
family violence (*see also* female battery; sexism): shelters and, 213n.27; society and, 101–3, 206n.4; terminology and, 213n.22
Featherdancing, Kyos, 171
federal government. *See* government, federal
female battery, 97–103, 213n.22; abuser control and, 98–99, 206n.4; and options against, 100–101; statistics on, 98, 206n.3
Ferraro, Kathleen, 99
Finney, Lynne, 28
flashbacks (*see also* recall memory): adolescents and, 36; experience of, xi, 64, 66, 100; medical visits and, 113; triggers for, 34, 60, 63, 169
foster care, 93–94, 95–97
Fraser, Sylvia, 126
"freezing," 74
Freud, Sigmund, 110
friends and healing, 169–70
"frozen watchfulness," 30, 37, 217n.16

Gayle R., 40
gender. *See* sexism
Geoghan, John J., 106–7
Gilbertson, Annette, xvi
Glass, James, 34–35
"good touch/bad touch" instruction, 175

government aid, 155–61 (*see also* health insurance; Medicare; Social Security Disability; welfare)
government, federal: child welfare and, 93–97; corporal punishment and, 176; female battery and, 97–103; priorities of, 102–3; role of, 176–78
government, local, 181–82
guilt, 36, 38–39

healing (*see also* body therapies): education and, 131–36; and friends, 169–70; holistic approach to, 115–16; nontraditional approaches, 154; resources for, 142–50, 180–81; self-help practices for, 161–64; self-love and, 131, 161
HealingHopes, 143, 193
health insurance (*see also* Medicare; Social Security Disability): changing doctors and, 142, 200; COBRA, 158–59; medication costs and, 153–55; mental illness and, 215n.60; selection of, 141–47; state and local programs for, 159; uninsured assistance and, 142–43
health maintenance organizations (HMO), 158
Hecht, Anne, 205n.20
herbs for healing, 154
Herman, Judith, 30, 36–37, 116, 217n.16
Hogan, Yolla, 57
Hornbacher, Marya, 81–82
host personality, 53–54 (*see also* alters): body images and, 72–73; identification of, 210n.5; recall memory and, 56
houses for trauma survivors, 183–84
hypnosis; and physician-created DID, 13; recall memory and, 60; ritual abuse and, 32
hysteria, 111, 113–14, 131, 214n.41

imagination, terror and, 208–9n.42
incest: definition of, 28; DID and, 9–10, 13, 26, 30; and feelings of betrayal, 29, 207n.21; girls and, 18, 29; and shame/silence, 29–30, 44–45, 83–84; statistics regarding, 207n.19; stepfathers and, 29, 207n.20; traumatic stress and, 29
inequality (*see also* sexism): language and, 131–33, 213n.22
insurance. *See* health insurance; Medicare; Social Security Disability
internal communication system, 54–57, 68–73, 139, 152, 210n.5
International Society for the Study of Dissociation, 178, 194
International Society for Traumatic Stress Studies, 178, 194
internet, as information resource, 136, 150, 193
intimacy conflicts, 165
isolation, 14, 82, 120–22, 140

Kempe, Henry, 110

language bias, 131–33, 213n.22
Laurie, 9
League of Women Voters, 178
Libby K., 82
lobbying efforts, 174, 178–79, 181–82
lost time. *See* recall memory
Lynn, 146–47

McMartin preschool, 46, 209n.51
"Many Voices," 193
martial arts, 80, 166–67
massage therapy, 80, 154, 165–66
Maxine, 20–21, 26, 41–42, 43, 105
media: sexism and, 89, 212n.7; stereotyping by, 11–12, 89, 131, 205n.20; and violence, x, 92
Medicaid, 142–43
medical establishment, 109–18; individual pathology focus by, 110, 117–18; and reporting child abuse, 114–15; sexism and, 12–13, 110–14
medical treatment providers, selection of, 141–47
Medicare (*see also* health insurance; Social Security Disability): mental health benefits and, 157–58, 178, 217–18n.7; nontraditional treatments and, 154–55; and prescription drugs, 154; qualifying for, 143, 157
medications, 150–55; alternatives to, 154; daily routine and, 14; patient rights regarding, 153; sexism and, 114
memory. *See* body memory; recall memory

Mental Health Parity Act, 217–18n.7
mental health treatment centers, 142
mental illness: childhood abuse and, 5–7; diagnosis issues, 139–41, 203n.2, 204n.7, 205n.15; expenditures for, 118–19, 215n.60; prison and, 215n.57
Methodists, 174
Michelle, 77–78
Milligan, Billy, 68–69
mind/body/spirit connection, 115–16, 166
mirrors and multiplicity, 73
Moon, Bella, 91
Morgan, Jill, 114
movement and healing, 80, 164
multiple personalities. *See* alters
multiple personality disorder. *See* dissociative identity disorder
Multiple Personality Disorder from the Inside Out (Cohen, Giller, and Lynn W.), 82, 102, 139, 192

Nancy G., 116
National Alliance to End Sexual Violence, 174
National Alliance for the Mentally Ill (NAMI), 178, 180, 195
National Association for the Advancement of Colored People (NAACP), 175
National Association of Social Workers (NASW), 180, 195
National Center for Health Statistics, 120
National Coalition to Abolish Corporal Punishment in Schools, 175, 203n.4
National Council of Churches, 178
National Institute of Mental Health (NIMH), 36, 177
National Institutes of Health (NIH), 177, 179
National Mental Health Association, 215n.60
naturopathy, healing and, 154
Nineteenth Amendment, 90
"no tolerance" policy, 129
Nora, 32–33
nutritionists, 154

Olson, Sarah: and fear, 130; and reporting child abuse, 42, 46, 97; resistance and, 73–74; and victim justifications, 37
organizations and support, 178–80
orgasm, 45
original personality. *See* host personality
orphanages, 93–94

pain: emotional suppression and, 67; post-traumatic stress disorder (PTSD) and, 64; and suicide, 78
pedophilia: Catholic Church and, 106, 107, 109, 174; and stepfathers, 207n.20; stereotyping of, 17, 22
Peggy J., 172–73
perpetrator bonds (trauma-bonding), 44, 99, 209n.46
perpetrators: control methods used by, 42–44, 46, 98–100; discipline as rationalization for, 92; gender/violence cycle and, 25–26, 39, 124; power and, 23–24; profiles of, 17–18, 22–26, 101, 124, 207nn. 17, 19, 20, 219n.19; stereotypes of, ix, 22, 115
Personal Responsibility and Work Opportunity Reconciliation Act, 95
Phillips, Jane: connecting with other multiples, 148; and creation of alters, 53; and experience of multiplicity, 13; and memory, 112, 113; multiple diagnosis and, 138, 139–40; sharing and, 122
physical abuse: and DID, 26; and female battery, 97–103, 206n.3, 213n.22; male victims of, 204n.5; overview of, 27–28
post-traumatic stress disorder (PTSD): and the body, 64; causes of, 6–7, 85; DID and, 7; flashbacks and, 60; Vietnam veterans and, 204n.8; women and, 85
Poupart, Lisa: familial abuse of, 17, 86–87; generational child abuse, 123–24; incest and, 29–30; self-blame and, 38
poverty: abuse and, ix–x, 89; child welfare and, 91–97; efforts for elimination of, 178–80, 181–83; and foster care, 93–97; race and, ix–x
power: adults and, ix, 18, 84, 91–92, 101–2, 103–9; and males, 4, 84, 88–91, 97–103, 206n.4, 209n.45; parents and caretakers, 19, 21, 28–30, 38, 42–45; political, 20, 45, 82, 83, 88–91, 108, 173–78
primary personality. *See* host personality
prison, 119, 215n.57

psychiatry: and medication, 114; sexism and, 110–14
Putnam, Frank, 26, 116

racial issues/racism: and death penalty, 212n.11; and foster care, 96–97; poverty and, ix–x; power and, 88–89, 123, 211–12n.5; and women of color, 89
Rafael, Sally Jesse, 205n.20
rage: body reactions and, 65, 67; borderline personality disorders and, 203n.2; gender conditioning and, 126; traumatic abuse and, 23–24, 36
rapid switching (rolodexing), 69–70
"The Rat's Nest" (Poupart), 86–87
Reagan, Ronald, 95
recall memory, 52–62 (*see also* body memory): and amnesia, 33–35, 51, 57, 59; co-consciousness and, 56, 68–69, 71, 150; EMDR and, 60; flashbacks and, 36, 60, 64, 169; hypnosis and, 60
religious institutions, 103–9, 173–74 (*see also* Roman Catholic Church)
reporting of abuse: by children, 42, 46; inadequacies in, 206n.3, 207n.12, 214n. 48, 214–15n. 49; medical profession and, 114–15; religious institutions and, 106–9
repressed memory. *See* recall memory
resistance. *See* bodily resistance
resources: books, 133–35, 191–92; for healing, 142–50, 180–81; for locating therapists, 144–45, 194–95; websites, 136, 193
revictimization, 122–29, 218n.9
ritual abuse, 31–35, 208nn. 32, 35; and DID, 26; HealingHopes internet support website, 193; surfing internet, 149–50
rolodexing (rapid switching), 69–70
Roman Catholic Church (*see also* religious institutions): and gender abuse statistics, 214n.37; moral principles and, 104–6; neglect by, 103–4; pedophilia and, 106–9; and policy changes, 129, 174; silence policy by, 106–9
Roosevelt, Theodore, 94
Ross, Colin, 116

Sarah F., 102, 103
satanism. *See* ritual abuse
Schnall, Maxine, 54
schools: corporal punishment and, ix, 92, 175; sexism and, 88–92, 176
Schreiber, Flora Rheta, 59, 216n.2
Seeley, Lynda, 48–49, 98–99, 209n.53
seizure disorders, 57
self-blame, victims and, 38–39
self-control, and shame, 67, 71–72, 139
self-defense training, 166–67
self-help healing techniques, 162–64
self-love, healing and, 131, 161, 162
self-mutilation, 75–78, 211n.26 (*see also* cutting)
self-numbing, 36, 79–80
seriously mentally ill (SMI), 143, 155
sexism: abuse and, xiv–xv, 25, 124–26; learned traits and, 124–26; media and, 89, 212n.7; medical establishment and, 12–13, 110–14; schools and, 90, 176; society and, 88–92, 211n.3; violence and, 204n.6, 206n.4, 213nn. 22, 27; work value and, 125
sexual abuse. *See* child sexual abuse
shame: control and, 38–39, 67, 71–72, 139; disability and, 157; incest and, 30, 42, 44; isolation and, 42, 44–45, 82, 121–22; mental illness and, 82, 121–22, 132, 139; self-mutilation and, 76; sexual arousal and, 30, 45; switching and, 71–72; women and, 209n.48
Sheppard-Pratt Hospital, 32–33, 34
Shotokan karate, 166
sibling abuse: cycle of violence and, 13, 23–24, 43; gender conditioning and, 74; traumatizing effect of, 27
Sidran Foundation, 143, 146, 178, 193, 194
silence: abuser manipulation and, 42–43; backlash and, 121–22; Catholic Church and, 106–9; dependence and, 42, 91; disbelief by others, 20, 42; loyalty/bonds to abuser, 42, 44, 100; shame of abuse, 20, 42, 45, 72, 100; shame of mental illness, 113–14, 121–22; societal indifference and, 172–74; threats/fear of repercussions, 20, 29–30
"Silent Screams" (Peggy J.), 172–73
Silverman, Sue William, 8, 30, 75
"6 Years Old" (Gayle R.), 40

Sizemore, Chris Costner ("Eve"), 59, 61
skeptics, 13–14, 143–44, 205n.21
sleep issues, 35–36, 47, 62, 66, 151, 153
Social Security Disability (SSD), 143, 155–57, 197–99 (*see also* health insurance; Medicare; welfare)
society: and costs of child abuse, 118–29; denial by, 82, 97, 101–2, 121–22, 127, 185, 205n.21; inequality and, 16, 17–18, 211n.3; and reporting of abuse, 42, 46, 97; violence and, 83–88, 92–93, 101–2
Southern Arizona Center Against Sexual Assault (SACASA), 175
Steinberg, Marlene, 54
stepfathers, 207n.20
stereotyping: language and, 131–33, 213n.22; media and, 11–12, 89, 131, 205n.20; by medical profession, 12–13, 110–14, 135, 144; of perpetrators, 22
Stout, Martha, 15
suicide: cult programming and, 34, 208n.32; DID and, xi, 10, 55, 203n.2; family loyalty and, 44; guns in homes and, ix; self-mutilation and, 78–79
support groups, 147–50
survivors, control and, 38–39, 67, 71–72, 74–75, 139
Survivors Healing Center, 180
switching: definition of, 68; experience of, xiii, 69–71; reactions by others, 121, 135, 152; and shame, 72; "stuck" while, 69–71; therapy groups and, 147
Sybil, 11, 59, 131, 210n.14, 216n.2
Sylvia (Seeley alter), 48–49, 209n.53
symptoms of abuse in children, 35–39, 46–49, 208nn. 35, 38

TANF (Temporary Assistance for Needy Families), 95, 176, 181–82, 212n.17
therapists: prejudice and, 135; resources for finding, 144–45, 194–95; selection of, 143–47
touch, benefits of, 165
toxins, bodies and, 51, 65, 80, 81, 131, 169
Trauma and Recovery (Judith Herman), 36–37, 191
trauma-bonding, 44, 99, 209n.46
traumatic abuse: and anticipation, 63–64; body memory manifestations, 62; experience by children, 35–41; memory storage of, 52; symptoms in children, 35–39, 46–49, 208nn. 35, 38; systematic nature of, 85
trust: and friends, 140; and healing, 131, 161, 169; and therapists, 145, 146; trauma survivors and, 27, 29, 35, 36, 39, 80–81
truth-telling, 121–22

United Methodist Bishops, 174
U.S. Department of Health and Human Services, 177, 179

van der Kolk, Bessel, 116
Veterans Administration, 127
Vietnam veterans, post-traumatic stress disorder (PTSD) and, 204n.8
violence: dependency and, 42, 91; federal government and, 92–103; prevention of, 186–87; sexism and, 206n.4; society and, 83–88, 92–93, 101–2; statistics and, 206n.3; systematic nature of, 85; witnessing of, 27–28, 98, 207n.14

Walters, Barbara, 205n.20
welfare (*see also* government aid; health insurance; Medicare; Social Security Disability): children and, 93–97; discrimination and, 91; state programs, 159
Welfare Reform Act, 95
West, Cameron, 64–65
When Rabbit Howls (Chase), 56, 192
White House Conference on Children, 94
wife battery. *See* female battery
Wilber, Cornelia, 216n.2
"Within and Without" (Seeley), 48–49, 209n.53
women: and, anger, 126; DID overrepresentation of, 204n.3; mental health and, 5–7; post-traumatic stress disorder (PTSD) in, 85

yoga, 80, 164